PENGUIN BOOKS

A FORTUNATE LIFE

A. B. Facey was born in 1894 and grew up on the Kalgoorlie goldfields and in the wheat-belt of Western Australia. His father died before he was two and he was deserted by his mother soon afterwards. He was looked after by his grandmother until he was eight years old, when he went out to work.

His many jobs included droving, hammering spikes on the railway line from Merredin to Wickepin and boxing in a travelling troupe. He was in the Eleventh Battalion at the Gallipoli landing; after the war, he became a farmer under the Soldier Settlement Scheme but was forced off the land during the Depression. He joined the tramways and was active in the Tramways Union.

A. B. Facey, who had no formal education, taught himself to read and write. He made the first notes on his life soon after World War I, and filled notebooks with his accounts of his experiences. Finally, on his children's urging, he submitted the hand-written manuscript to the Fremantle Arts Centre Press. He died in 1982, nine months after *A Fortunate Life* had been published to wide acclaim.

A. B. Facey, 1914, aged twenty

A. B. FACEY

A FORTUNATE LIFE

ILLUSTRATIONS BY ROBERT JUNIPER

PENGUIN BOOKS

Penguin Books Australia Ltd
487 Maroondah Highway, PO Box 257
Ringwood, Victoria 3134, Australia
Penguin Books Ltd
Harmondsworth, Middlesex, England
Penguin Putnam Inc.
375 Hudson Street, New York, New York 10014, USA
Penguin Books Canada Limited
10 Alcorn Avenue, Toronto, Ontario, Canada M4V 3B2
Penguin Books (NZ) Ltd
Cnr Rosedale and Airborne Roads, Albany, Auckland, New Zealand
Penguin Books (South Africa) (Pty) Ltd
5 Watkins Street, Denver Ext 4, 2094, South Africa
Penguin Books India (P) Ltd
11, Community Centre, Panchsheel Park, New Delhi 110 017, India

First published by Fremantle Arts Centre Press, 1981
Published by Penguin Books Australia Ltd, 1981
Reset with Afterword, 1985

27 29 30 28 26

Typeset in Century Old Style and Copperplate by Dudley E. King, Melbourne
Made and printed in Australia by Australian Print Group, Maryborough, Victoria

National Library of Australia
Cataloguing-in-Publication data:

Facey, A. B. (Albert Barnett), 1894–1982.
A fortunate life.

ISBN 0 14 008167 4.

1. Facey, A. B. (Albert Barnett), 1894–1982.
I. Title

920.71

www.penguin.com.au

I dedicate this book
to the memory of my wife, Evelyn.
It was her patience and understanding
which made it become a reality.

CONTENTS

ANOTHER LIFE
1915 – 1976

STARTING OUT

1894–1905

MANY PEOPLE HAD LITTLE FEELING
OR SYMPATHY FOR THOSE IN NEED.

1

A Prelude

I was born in the year 1894 at Maidstone in Victoria. My father left for Western Australia just after this, taking with him my two older brothers, Joseph and Vernon. The discovery of gold in the West had been booming and thousands believed that a fortune was to be made. At that time there were seven children in our family: I had four brothers – Joseph, Vernon, Eric and Roy – and two sisters – Laura and Myra. My mother stayed at Maidstone with the younger children and my father arranged to send money over to support us until he could find us a home.

In 1896 Mother got word that Father was very ill. Typhoid fever had broken out and hundreds were dying of this terrible disease. A few days later Mother received the sad news that Father had died. When Mother had got over this terrible shock, she decided to go over to the West, as Joseph and Vernon were still only teenagers. Mother left the rest of us with our grandparents at Barkers Creek. I was then nearly two years old.

Barkers Creek was situated sixty-three miles from Melbourne on the Bendigo road, three miles from the small town of Castlemaine. Grandpa and Grandma, whose surname was Carr, had a small property with a few acres of orchard and a five-roomed house. There were no aged pensions in those days, nor were there any free doctors, hospitals and medicine, nor baby bonuses or endowment payments. So my grandparents had to live, and keep us children, on their own resources. Our mother was to send money to support us, but although she wrote many letters she always made excuses for not being able to send us anything.

At the age of seventy-seven, Grandpa was a big man, over six feet tall and weighing around two hundred pounds. Grandma was a small woman in her early sixties, about five feet tall, and between seven and a half and eight stone. They were very poor. Grandpa depended on odd jobs, such as ploughing orchards and pruning, to get a few pounds to keep us all. He, with my brothers, Eric and Roy, trapped rabbits, and the boys used to go out picking fruit on Saturday mornings during the fruit season.

Early in the year of 1898 Grandpa became very ill. A doctor came from Castlemaine twice a week to give him treatment, but his condition got worse and he died in October that year. I had turned four years old in August and remember Grandpa's illness and his funeral quite well.

After this tragedy Grandma became very worried as our only bread winner had been taken. She wrote to our mother telling her of our plight and asked for financial help. Although Mother wrote, she was unable to send any money. She said that she had married the man who had employed her as a housekeeper, as she was forced to find work when she found that Father had died not leaving enough money for her to live on. Our two older brothers found it hard to get jobs, as they were too young to go down the mines on the Goldfields. The surface gold had been worked out, leaving the mines and woodcutting in the bush as the only ways of obtaining work.

Grandma was shocked at hearing all this after the terrible ordeal she had just been through. She went out working – house-cleaning, washing and ironing. She was also an expert midwife. Nearly all the babies born in and around Barkers Creek were attended and helped by Grandma Carr and very few women needed a doctor. Grandma knew as much as any doctor on the subject.

My brother Eric, who was then twelve years old, had to leave school and go to work. My eldest sister Laura went to help our uncle who had lost his wife in an accident. He was a hawker, carrying stores, drapery, medicines and anything he could sell. My sister was ten years old, and Uncle's place was about three miles from Castlemaine on the Ballarat railway line at a place called Campbells Creek. The accident had happened at a railway crossing. Our aunt was killed and Uncle's spine was hurt so badly that he lost the use of his legs and never walked again. He had three children, all very young.

Early in 1899 Grandma became very ill and was unable to work. In fact, she had to be seen by a doctor, who put her to bed. She had some internal complaint and the doctor came to see her twice a week for about three weeks. She was able to get up after that, but could only walk around for a short while. We were in terrible financial distress but at least Grandma could get around again.

My brother Eric's wages were all we had and they amounted to twelve shillings and sixpence a week – not very much to feed five of us.

Grandma overcame the financial trouble temporarily by getting a forward payment on her apple crop. The apples were a good eating variety and were easy to sell when ripe. Grandma recovered from her sickness but found that the paid work she had been doing had been given to others. Many people had little feeling or sympathy for those in need.

Things got so bad that Grandma decided to try and sell her property and take us over to the West to our mother. She put it up for sale and many people came to see it but they all said the price was too high. She wanted three hundred pounds for the property, which consisted of twelve acres of land, a five-roomed house, eight acres of orchard in full profit and a nice vegetable garden – all good loam. The agent advised Grandma to reduce the price to two hundred pounds. This she did and finally sold it for one hundred and sixty pounds. Some overdue bills had to be paid out of this.

About the second week in August 1899, we left Barkers Creek and went to Footscray, a suburb of Melbourne, where one of Grandma's daughters lived. We all stayed there until everything was arranged for our trip to Western Australia.

2

THE JOURNEY BEGINS

It was the first week in September, 1899, when we arrived at Port Melbourne to embark onto the old tramp steamer *Coolgardie*. Just before we went aboard I nearly lost my life. The wharf labourers were unloading bananas from the *Coolgardie* and this fascinated me as I hadn't seen so many bananas before – there were thousands of them scattered all about the place. They had come from Queensland. I went to pick one up and one of the men shouted, 'Hey, drop that!' I got such a shock that I jumped, and being so close to the wharf edge I over-balanced and fell between the wharf and the ship into the sea.

There were steps at intervals leading down under the wharf to the lavatory landings. People used to fish from these landings and, luckily for me, a man who happened to be trying his luck saw me fall into the water. He grabbed me and pulled me out, but not before I had swallowed plenty of dirty salt water. I couldn't swim. The man carried me up the steps to the wharf. I was sopping wet and feeling very sick. I'll never forget the look of anger on dear old Grandma's face. She lost control of herself and gave me a hiding with her umbrella, and to make things worse, she made me strip off all my clothes while she opened one of our travelling trunks and got me a change of clothes. I had only just turned five years old and Grandma had taught us to be modest so this hurt me more than the ducking and hiding I got.

Finally we boarded the *Coolgardie* and sailed for the West. I had never been to sea before and didn't know about seasickness. The trip to Port Adelaide was very calm and we all enjoyed being at sea, but after we left there, bound for Albany in Western Australia, the sea was terribly rough and we all got very seasick.

Owing to Grandma not having much money we had to travel steerage. It was the cheapest way to travel and the passengers were packed together with very little room to move, especially in the cabins. The one that Grandma, my sister Myra, my brother Roy and I were in had twelve sleeping bunks. Grandma and Myra slept together in one bunk, and Roy and I slept in another. The other ten bunks were all taken by women. (Eric, being older, was in an all-male cabin.) Everyone was terribly seasick.

We arrived at Albany but didn't get off the ship. We went on to Fremantle and disembarked there. At last we had arrived in Western Australia. When our luggage was brought off the ship we didn't have much – two travelling trunks and a large travelling bag and three travelling rugs. Between us we carried these to the Fremantle Railway Station, about two hundred yards from the wharf.

There was no one to meet us. Grandma had expected our mother or at least our Aunt Alice to be at the wharf. Aunt Alice, who was Grandma's eldest daughter, had come over from Victoria with her husband, Archie McCall, and their family at the same time as our father. She had five daughters, Alice, Ada (Daisy), Mary and May, and one son, Archie, who was called Bill, and they lived three and a half miles out of Kalgoorlie on the goldfields.

At the railway station we put our belongings near a seat and Roy, Myra and I were told to stay there until Grandma came back. She took our older brother Eric with her and went into the town of Fremantle. They came back about an hour later and we all boarded a train for Perth.

It was only a short ride to Perth – about forty minutes. We arrived at about midday, and were again left at the railway station with our luggage. This time Grandma went out alone. When she came back she brought us some sandwiches, cake and also some bottles of cool drink. We were very hungry and made short work of such luxuries.

After this Grandma had a long talk with the Station Master. There was still no one to meet us and Grandma looked very worried. We waited on the platform until about five o'clock that afternoon (the time went quickly because we were very interested watching the trains coming and going). The railway station at Perth looked very small after the Melbourne stations.

It was between five and six o'clock when we got on the Goldfields train. After a while the train moved out and we were on our way – to our mother, we thought. We were all very tired. I remember the train going through a long tunnel, and just after that darkness came and I went to sleep. I was awakened later, it was still dark, and Grandma said we had to get off the train as that was as far as her money would take us. She said the name of this place was Northam, a small country town – only a few houses, one hotel and the Post Office, which was also a store.

After getting off the train we again waited with our luggage while Grandma had a long talk with the Station Master. He came with her to us and then showed Grandma an unused railway carriage that we could sleep in for the rest of that night. We made ourselves at home in it. Grandma slept on one seat, my brothers on the other seat, and Myra and I on the floor.

Next morning Grandma and Myra went to the ladies waiting-room and changed their clothes and freshened up. We boys had a wash under a tap and changed our clothes in the railway carriage, then we joined Grandma and Myra on the platform where we had a breakfast of sandwiches and a glass of milk.

We then took all our luggage and went to the Northam Post Office. Grandma went into the building leaving us kids outside. She was in there for quite a while. When she came out she said she had sent a letter to our mother and Aunt Alice, asking for money. Then she told us that we would have to find a place somewhere out of town to make a camp until she got a reply to her letters. So we set off all carrying something.

After we had gone a little way along the road leading out of the town a man came along. He had a spring-cart, and seeing us he stopped, thinking we were going to some place out of town, and asked if we would like a lift. He told us that he was a bachelor, his place was fifteen miles out of Northam and he would be glad to help if he could. Grandma spoke to him, explaining our plight, and he told us that there was a Government Reserve about a mile further on. There was plenty of water and we could make a camp there for a few days, as there was plenty of bush and scrub that we could use. He said that they didn't get much wet weather this time of year.

We got into the spring cart with our luggage and were pleased at not having to carry the things. At the spot that the man pointed out to Grandma, we got off the cart, thanking the stranger for his help. We carried our things and put them under a beautiful shady tree, then Grandma sent Eric over to the farm-house, about half a mile away. We could see it from the spot where we intended to make camp. Eric was to try to borrow an axe and spade, and to do this Grandma said he was to tell the people why we wanted the tools.

When Eric came back a man came with him. The man told us that he had a cow and some fowls, and offered us milk and eggs, and said his wife would be glad to give us any bread we wanted. He helped Eric to cut poles out of the bushes and scrub. About an hour later we had somewhere to sleep and have our meals in.

The next day Eric cut more poles and we all carried and dragged them in and built another bush mia-mia. Grandma said the ground that we had slept on in our camp was very damp, so before we built the new mia-mia we had to carry dry twigs and leaves and small sticks to build a fire on the ground to dry it out. When the fire burnt out we scraped all the hot ash and coals off, then built the mia-mia. We used this one to sleep in and had our meals in the other one. After about three days we got used to living like this.

The people living around where we camped were very good to us. I am sure that none of us will ever forget those wonderful people. They kept us supplied with fresh meat and eggs, bread, vegetables, milk and many other things. They would not hear of any kind of payment. Grandma offered to let the boys work to pay for the goods.

Each day Eric walked into the Post Office in Northam, hoping for a letter from our mother or Aunt Alice. We had to wait nearly three weeks before a letter came. Aunt Alice wrote, and in the envelope was a money order for the Northam Post Office sufficient to pay our fares to Kalgoorlie. Our mother didn't write.

Eric arrived back with the letter near midday; Grandma explained what was in it and said we would catch the train that night. So we packed our few things, returned all the things that the people had lent us, and the man that first helped us make camp came and drove us to Northam Railway Station. Grandma thanked him and all the other good people for their kindness.

Just before midday we arrived at Kalgoorlie and Aunt Alice was there to meet us. We had been unable to see what the country was like as we had travelled during darkness for most of the way and slept during daylight. Aunt Alice had her two older daughters with her. Grandma, Aunt Alice and Myra left the two girl cousins to help the rest of us take the luggage out to Aunt Alice's place. Grandma and Aunt Alice went to see our mother. We found out later that Mother wouldn't have us at her place but was glad to keep our sister Myra. Grandma said our mother was going to have another baby.

3

ON THE GOLDFIELDS

When we arrived at Aunt Alice's place we were dog-tired and hungry. Aunt's place, which was only a hut, was built near a big hill. It consisted of bush poles for uprights with hessian pulled tight around the poles making an enclosed space of about thirty-six feet by twelve feet, sub-divided into three big rooms. The outside walls were white-washed with a solution of chalky clay mixed with water which stiffened the hessian and made the inside private. The roof was bush timber and galvanised iron. The three rooms of the hut were used as bedrooms. A few feet away from the hut was another structure, the kitchen, and this had a fireplace at one end and a large table with a long stool along one wall. The kitchen was fourteen feet by sixteen feet. We were to have all our meals in this room.

We had been there about an hour when Aunt Alice and Grandma arrived. They had left Myra with Mother. We were told that our older brothers, Joseph and Vernon, were no longer living with Mother. Joseph had left Kalgoorlie to work with a surveyor and Vernon had joined the Australian navy.

Grandma said that she had had a long talk with Mother about our situation and that Mother was very ill and would see us when she was well enough. So until then we were to make Aunt Alice's place our home. The house and furniture showed that Aunt Alice didn't enjoy a surplus of money. There were many families living in similar circum-stances.

The surface gold was just about prospected out, and the men had to find other means of employment to keep their families. Aunt Alice's husband, Archie, was away chopping wood for the mines at Boulder, and for the many condensers that were condensing the water for all the Goldfields people. In those days there was no fresh water, and it became too costly to have water carted. There was plenty of salt water underground so this was pumped up from wells and bores and converted to drinking water by the condensers. There was a large condenser about a mile from Aunt's place and the water obtained from there had to be carried home in buckets. It cost two shillings a gallon if you carted it yourself, or two shillings and six-pence a gallon if you had it delivered. The condenser people wouldn't deliver less than fifty gallons at a time and as Aunt Alice couldn't afford to buy that much at one time we had to go and get it.

Uncle Archie used to come home every two or three weeks, and we had been there for about a week when he came home. That was the first time I had seen him. He would come home on Saturday and go away again on Sunday afternoon. When he went away this time he took Eric and Roy with him. Eric was nearly fourteen years old and Roy was nearly eleven. Uncle said Eric could help with the wood stacking and Roy would be useful around the camp boiling the billy, washing-up the dishes and doing many other little jobs. So my brothers could not go to school.

Aunt's three older girls – Alice, Daisy and Mary – went to school in Kalgoorlie and they had to walk nearly eight miles each school day.

We lived there with Aunt Alice until 1902. Uncle and my brothers came home for a weekend once a month and two Christmases came and went.

We used to have a lot of fun when a heavy shower of rain came and made the ground very wet. We would all go out into the diggings looking for gold that had had the earth washed off it, and between us we found quite a few pieces. It was worth twenty shillings an ounce.

Aunt Alice found another way to make a few shillings – she took in washing and ironing. She made us kids – May, Bill and myself (she now had another child, Jim, but he was still a baby) – go to the camps and get the washing, and after it was washed and ironed, take it back to the owners and collect the money.

Also, Grandma and Aunt Alice used to take all us kids, who were too young to walk the long distance to school, to hunt miles around for places where prospectors had camped. The prospectors lived on tinned foods. When the tins were emptied they were just thrown into heaps near the camps.

Aunt and Grandma gathered the tins, then we would gather bushes, scrub and sticks, spread them onto the ground, and pile the tins on top. A pile would be left for a few days until the bushes and scrub, which were mostly green, dried enough to burn. Then we would come back and set it alight. The heat from the fire would melt the solder that was in the tins, and it would fall down into the ashes and onto the ground.

Then, when the fire finished burning and cooled off we used to sieve the ashes and the ground under the ashes, to get the solder that had melted into small lumps. We put these into a bag and took them home. When we had enough Aunt Alice would melt them in an iron pot. Then she would wet a small piece of level ground, make impressions in the damp soil to the size of a stick of solder, and pour the melted solder into them. When the solder cooled she used to wash it and take it into Kalgoorlie where she got five shillings a pound for it. A fairly large heap of tins would be worth about thirty shillings. All this used to help, and, as Aunt Alice said, it gave us something to do.

In August 1901, just before my seventh birthday, Uncle came home one weekend and didn't go back on the Sunday afternoon. He sent my two brothers back, to carry on with the wood-chopping as usual, and then, on Monday, dressed himself up in his best suit. I heard him tell Grandma that he was going to Perth to see about the land the State Government was offering to encourage people to settle as farmers.

Uncle was away for over two weeks and when he returned he had selected one thousand acres of first class land under the Government's conditional purchase scheme, and a homestead block for himself, Aunt Alice and Grandma. The Government was giving a homestead block to any approved person over the age of twenty-one for twenty shillings, and that land, one hundred and sixty acres, became the freehold property of the person concerned. The conditional purchase land could be obtained at twenty shillings per acre for the first class land, and second class and other land was priced according to its classification. Some of the poor land could be purchased for as low as two shillings and sixpence per acre.

Uncle's one thousand acres were classified first class. The conditions of purchase were that the settler paid nothing for the first five years, then paid so much a half year for the next twenty years to complete the purchase. The Government wouldn't sell land straight out as a cash sale.

Uncle went out to my brothers and brought them and all the tools home. He had got a new job working as a plate-layer on the railway the Government was building from Kalgoorlie to another gold find. Uncle had worked on a railway construction job in South Australia before coming to Western Australia. Eric got a job on the same gang as Uncle. His job was one of messenger, and bringing tools to the men and so on – they called him a 'nipper'. Uncle's wages were good on this new job and so were Eric's. Roy got a job in Kalgoorlie with a grocer, helping to deliver groceries and doing odd jobs around the shop. This was the first job that Roy would be earning wages at, as he had never been paid by Uncle Archie.

The new jobs meant we were all home together at night, and we had Christmas 1901 together. After Christmas, Uncle and Eric had to camp out, as their work was getting too far away to travel to and from each day. So Uncle arranged for Aunt Alice and Grandma to take all the kids and leave Kalgoorlie and go to York. Uncle's land was twenty-six miles east of a town named Narrogin (a native name) and York was about one hundred miles north from Narrogin.

So we packed all our goods and chattels. A man with a horse and four-wheeled trolley came and took them to the Kalgoorlie Railway Station. My brother Roy stayed with the grocer and was paid six shillings a week and keep. Our uncle got his groceries from this store, and Roy's wages helped to pay for them.

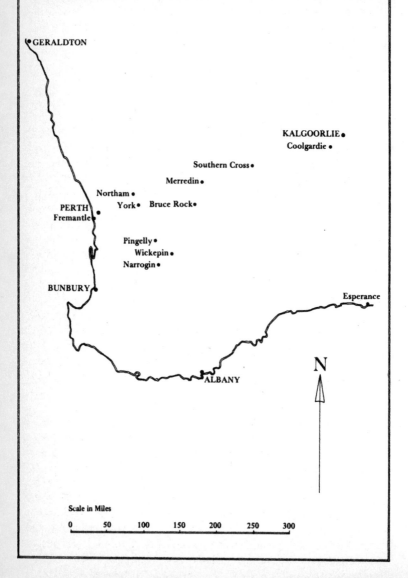

SOUTH-WEST OF WESTERN AUSTRALIA

GERALDTON

KALGOORLIE •
Coolgardie •

Southern Cross •

Merredin •

Northam •
PERTH   York •   Bruce Rock •
Fremantle

Pingelly •
Wickepin •
Narrogin •

BUNBURY

Esperance

N

ALBANY

Scale in Miles

0   50   100   150   200   250   300

4

A Long Walk

We left Kalgoorlie in February, late in the evening, and arrived at York the afternoon of the next day. We kids had to wait at the railway station while Aunt and Grandma found a place for us to stay. We waited for about two hours before they came back with a carrier. He had two horses hitched to a four-wheeled lorry. We all helped the man to pack our household goods and luggage onto the lorry (the heavy beds, and so forth, had come on a special train), then we all piled on and away we went.

Aunt had rented an old mud house about four miles out of York on the banks of the Avon River. This was too far out for us young ones to go to school. I was then seven years old and had had no schooling, but eight miles was a little too far, so Grandma said.

This old mud house, which cost five shillings a week to rent, was all Aunt could afford. It had one big living-room with a large fireplace, and three bedrooms. I'll never forget the first night we spent there. There hadn't been anyone living there for some years. We got settled for the night, beds fixed and made, and a nice fire going in the big fireplace. Aunt Alice got out the lamps, filled them with kerosene and lit them, and we all seemed pleased although very tired.

Then Aunt and Grandma fixed a meal, mostly bread and jam. We were all sitting at the table, the women and girls were talking about the trip, when suddenly there was a terrible scream. Two of the girls jumped onto the table pointing to the floor where there was a big black snake, over six feet long, with its head raised about eight inches from the ground. The screams of the girls seemed to make the snake stop. He was staring at us. Grandma said, 'Don't move! Stay still!' She took off her apron and put it on the floor a few feet away from the snake, then walked backwards towards the door, then through the door and all the time she kept saying, 'Don't move. Leave it to me.' Then she appeared again through the door with a long-handled shovel in her hands. She walked across the floor as if she was going to pass the snake, then suddenly turned quickly, and hit the snake with the blade of the shovel cutting its head off. Oh! what a relief that was to us all.

Just before this happened we were all sleepy and tired, but I don't think any of us had any sleep that night because of the snake, and a possum that kept running over the roof. Two days later Aunt killed another snake, a much smaller one, at the back of the house. The floor of this old house was dirt, and there were little holes going under the walls to the outside, but after the killing of the first snake we blocked up all the holes we could find. Grandma said that the snakes would be looking for somewhere to stay for the winter, as it was nearly the end of February. It wasn't until near the end of April that the rains came and the snakes were forgotten.

We kids were very happy living there. It was so different to Kalgoorlie. There was plenty of water and wood; we only had to fetch the wood out of the bush. The nearest neighbour was a mile away. We lived there until the end of August, and one day, just after my eighth birthday, Uncle and my brothers came. They had finished the railway work, and Uncle had come to make arrangements to go onto his land and start farming.

The McCalls were one of the first families to settle in the wheat-belt of Western Australia under the Government land settlement schemes.

We kids thought we would be going by train to Narrogin, but we got a surprise when Uncle said he didn't have enough money to pay all our fares because he would have to buy a horse and cart and harness. We would need these to be able to get our stores from time to time, as we would be twenty-six miles away from the nearest town of Narrogin.

So Uncle bought the horse and cart and we set off by road. Uncle said we could take our time; the land was about one hundred and forty miles by road from York, so we could do it in short stages. There would be plenty of water along the road, and at night we could pitch tents to sleep in. So about a week later, having purchased the horse, cart and harness, early one morning in the first week of September 1902, we packed all our belongings onto the cart and left the old mud house for Uncle's 'dream land'.

Uncle Archie was born on a farm in South Australia, and when he was old enough to work and understand, his father, who had skills as a veterinary surgeon, taught him all about animals. Now Uncle had his chance to fulfil the ambition of his life, and, as he would be one of the first settlers in the great wheat-belt, with the knowledge of animals he could be of great help to other settlers. When Uncle's father died, the farm in South Australia hadn't been big enough for the four sons, who had all married, so Uncle went to Victoria just after he and Aunt Alice married. He worked the mines at Bendigo, and on the building of some of Victoria's railways, and also on many farms. Now Uncle was returning to the land and he and the women were very excited about the venture.

Uncle didn't have much money but he said there were many ways of making some until we got the farm going. He explained that there were thousands of possums in the bush up where we were heading, and that their skins were worth a shilling each. He said he had bought the necessary string and fine wire to make the snares to catch them. Also, he told us, there were hundreds of kangaroos and their meat was good to eat. He intended to buy a kangaroo dog so that we would be okay for meat. All these possibilities we discussed at meal times before we left, and all the way to the wonderful land.

The trip was hard. Only one person was allowed to ride up on the cart and that was the driver. Uncle, Aunt and Grandma did all the driving while the rest of us walked. We averaged about ten miles a day while travelling, but there were about five days when it rained and we camped on those days. The trip took us nearly three weeks, but we made it. We kids went without boots on the trip – it was Grandma's idea, as we couldn't afford to buy new ones when the ones we had were worn out.

5

Uncle's Settlement

The night before we expected to arrive at Uncle's land, Uncle, Aunt, Grandma and Eric got to making possum snares under Uncle's directions. They made about two hundred between them. Uncle said we were camped at a place called Gillimanning – an Aboriginal name – but no one lived near, and his land was about eight miles away. We had spent the rest of the money we had in the last town, a place called Pingelly, by purchasing stores such as flour, baking powder, golden syrup and jam. We had followed the road along the railway line until we reached Pingelly, then we had gone in an easterly direction along an old bush track.

We were all up early the next morning, very excited. We were soon to see this wonderful land that Uncle Archie spoke about so much. We had our breakfast and were soon on our way. About two hours later we arrived, and Uncle took a map out of his pocket and checked the survey pegs. He stood up and said, 'That's it, that's my land,' pointing to a big belt of tall trees and undergrowth, and I thought, 'A chicken would find it hard to get through.'

Aunt Alice, Uncle and Grandma left us sitting under a nice shady tree while they walked over Uncle's land to find a suitable place to camp. About an hour later they came back, explaining that they had found the spot where they would camp and later hoped to build a house. We moved to the place they had picked out and Uncle and my brothers set about putting up the tents. They also made a fireplace for the women to do the cooking. Towards evening Uncle and my brothers set some snares for possum. We were all very tired and went to bed early that night. We didn't expect anything to trouble us, as Uncle said that the blacks around this place were friendly.

When everyone had turned in and everything seemed quiet, there was a terrible frightening howl; long, sharp and very clear. Then a few minutes later another one further away, and another one closer. These howls frightened the wits out of me. In another tent Grandma and Aunt's three older daughters were in bed, and the girls all ran out to Uncle and started to cry. The howling made by the dingoes went on all night, and when a howl sounded close to our camp I could feel a shiver go up my spine.

We spent the next few days looking around, and towards the evenings, setting snares for possum. The first morning Uncle and the boys caught twenty-two possums. They skinned them and pegged the skins out on big trees. Uncle called the trees 'white gums'. The skins were nailed on with small nails. These skins, when dry, were about nine inches wide and about one foot long, although some would stretch to bigger than this, and some smaller. When dry they were worth a shilling each. They had to be nailed at least six feet off the ground to stop the dingoes pulling them off and destroying them. Aunt, Grandma and we kids used to stand on a box to nail them out.

Uncle had bought a kangaroo dog for three pounds while we were in Pingelly. The man that sold it to him said it was a good dog and would kill a kangaroo, then come back to whoever took it out hunting. It would then trot back slowly to where it had killed the 'roo. They used to call this 'kill show'. Uncle and Eric went out hunting with the dog early the second morning and sure enough, the dog caught two 'roos – one fairly big, the other about three parts grown. The smaller ones, we found out, were the best for eating. The meat looked like steak but tasted a little different, but very nice. Up to this part of my life I hadn't been given much meat because Grandma couldn't afford to buy it.

The main work from then on for the women, girls and us kids was setting snares for possums. (They called Aunt's youngest daughter, her son Bill and me 'the kids'.) We always stuck together, we were all scared stiff of the dingoes. They came around a lot for the first few weeks.

Uncle Archie and my brothers were busy building a house. I suppose it would be called a humpy. They cut the poles about twelve feet long, and six inches thick at one end and about three to four inches thick at the other. They cut hundreds of them and carted them to where they intended to build the humpy. They then cut the smallest ends off the poles with a handsaw to make them all the same length and level. Then they dug two trenches three feet deep and twelve feet apart, both fifty feet long. They put the poles side by side in the trenches on their ends, the thickest ends in the trenches, then shovelled the earth back in, tramping it tight around and on each side of the pole. When the poles were put the full length of the trenches they formed two walls fifty feet long. Then

Uncle and the boys dug a trench at each end and put poles in them in the same way, joining the two fifty foot walls together. Then they put up two dividing walls, also in the same way, making a twelve by twelve room at each end of the structure and leaving a living and dining-room in the centre, twenty-six feet by twelve. They then put a timbered roof over the three rooms and thatched it with blackboy spines.

The blackboy is a native grass-tree that grows in the West Australian bush. It has spine-like leaves that grow out of the top, and as they become older they dry out and go light brown. Uncle had a plentiful supply of this tree on and around his property.

After making the house, Uncle and my brothers carted home some large granite rocks (there were plenty of stones on the surrounding hills). They built a big fireplace in the main room, then they built a large table out of bush timber, and made two long stools for us to sit on to have our meals. So, that was our home.

Uncle Archie and Aunt Alice had one of the twelve-foot rooms for their bedroom and Grandma and the girls the other. We boys slept in tents outside. Uncle made a door frame for the big room out of bush timber, and sewed kangaroo skins on to it to keep out the cold weather and water. The doorways leading into the bedrooms had only curtains over them. When the building and thatching were finished, Uncle and the boys dug out clay from the creek which ran through the property, and after making it very wet and soft, they pushed it into the cracks of the poles that made the walls. When it was dry it made the place nice and weather-proof.

While this was going on, the rest of us were getting on with our work of setting snares, skinning possums and pegging out the skins. It took about eight hours to dry them, then they were ready for market. All of us put the skins we had done together for Uncle, and he would go into town every month and sell them to buy food. This was our only way of existing. There wasn't any other income.

When the humpy was finished Uncle and my brothers started to work on the land. They were chopping small trees down and ring-barking the big ones, ready for burning down the next year. We found out that bushfires were a menace and we had to take great care as there were laws that made it an offence to light fires in the open from the fifteenth of November to the fifteenth of February each year. No clearing could be done until after this time.

Day by day our life was much the same. 1902 went and 1903 came but we had no Christmas. One day was the same as the other so far as we kids were concerned.

Our boots were worn out and we got used to going without them. Uncle, Aunt, Grandma and Eric managed to get boots. We kids had a lot of trouble with our feet when the burning season opened. On the first of March that year, Uncle put a fire through the areas that they had chopped down and we all had to pitch in and help with the clearing whenever we could. We got our feet burnt badly at times.

Everything was hot and dry and hard during the summer months but not so bad in the winter. During the summer months we had to carry water for drinking and general household purposes. The women used to carry all their washing down to the Government well a mile from our home, and do it there. The well was sixty feet deep and we had to haul the water up with a rope attached to a bucket and a winder. The bucket held six gallons and it was beautiful water.

Uncle's trips to town took three days. One day to go twenty-six miles to town, then he would always give the horse a day's rest and come home on the third day. When Uncle was away on one of these trips he was approached by a man who wanted a small boy to stay with his mother while he was away from home. He explained to Uncle that he and his three brothers were away for long periods. He said they were contractors and did all sorts of contract work, such as clearing and fencing and horse-breaking, and often went into the bush kangaroo hunting and catching wild horses. His mother was getting very old and was nearly blind. He said that the boy wouldn't have much to do in the way of work, just be a companion for the old lady.

Uncle told us all about this when he returned home from his trip. Grandma came to me later and told me that Uncle would like me to go. He had said that the man would give me five shillings a month and keep, including clothes and boots and socks. I told Grandma I didn't want to go. She said that the man would be coming in a few days to see if Uncle had managed to talk her into letting me take the job.

About a week later the man came. He was a big man, about thirty-five years old, with a big black bush beard. He was riding a horse and leading a very pretty pony. It had a saddle on ready for me. I didn't like the look of the man and I told Grandma so, but she explained that I would be helping Uncle if I went as it would mean one less to feed, and I would get plenty of good food, and clothes and boots, and also five shillings a month.

The man camped at our place that night. He came to tell me about his mother and said that she kept cows, pigs and fowls, so she had plenty of good fresh cow's milk, fresh eggs and bacon. And there was plenty of fresh meat from a cousin who lived about five miles away.

Then he said that if I went with him and didn't like the job, I just had to say so and he would bring me back to my uncle. He asked me if I would like the pony he brought for me to ride. I was very fond of animals and this pony was lovely, such a pretty little thing. I asked him how far away from Uncle's his place was, and he said thirty miles. Then he said, 'You can have the pony to do what you want with if you will take the job.' But I said that I couldn't ride it. I had never ridden a horse. He said, 'Don't worry, I'll learn you in a few minutes.' After tea we all went to bed. I hadn't agreed to go but my brothers said they wished they had the chance.

Early next morning Grandma came to me and said, 'You go, and if you don't like it you can come back home again.' Grandma had been the only mother I had known and I loved her, and I believed in her judgement. She had taken us in and worked hard to feed and look after us when our mother had deserted us. So, on this darling old lady's advice, I agreed to take the job. Grandma told the man. He had just returned with his horse and my pony from where they had been grazing tethered out for the night.

I had a problem now. I had to ride the pony and this troubled me. I was frightened, being so young – although I was big for my age I was still under nine years old. (I would turn nine in August but still had three months to go.) The man's name was Bob – 'Short for Robert,' he said. 'They all call me Bob.' He put the saddle on the pony, then he helped me into it and led the pony around by the reins with me on its back. I grabbed the front of the saddle and held on. The pony didn't mind a bit, and it didn't seem too bad. Then Bob put the saddle on his horse and got on its back and trotted it around in a circle to show me how to rise to a trot. I got the idea of this, but not before I had fallen off several times, to the amusement of Uncle, Aunt, Grandma and the other kids.

So about ten o'clock that morning we set off. Grandma gave me a single red blanket. She put all my clothes and things in the blanket, wrapping it up like a swag. Then the man strapped it on to the front of the saddle. This made it safer for me to ride, at least I thought it did.

It was hard leaving Grandma and the rest of the kids. After we had been travelling for a while Bob suddenly wanted to go faster. He explained to me that when you made a horse go faster than trotting it was called cantering. He set his horse into a canter, and my pony responded at once, but I didn't. I started to lose my balance and let go of the reins and held on like blazes to the saddle. The pony was off, going as fast as it could. We were on a bush-track which wasn't straight, and the pony didn't bother to keep to it. A limb of a tree caught me, lifted me clean out of the saddle and dumped me on the ground. The pony didn't bother to stop. I felt sure that it was glad to get rid of me.

The fall shook me up badly, but I wasn't hurt. Bob told me to wait while he went after the pony. I waited a long time before Bob came back with the pony, and it took a long time before I plucked up enough courage to get back into the saddle. Finally I did and we were on our way, but we didn't try to canter again.

It was past midday when Bob said we had better rest the horses. He picked a place where there was plenty of good grass for the horses and tethered them, and we had a rest ourselves and ate some food that Bob had with him. When we got going again I found that riding horseback wasn't all fun. My bottom and legs were getting very sore, in fact so sore that I had to hold all of my weight up out of the saddle by standing up in the stirrups.

The sun was going down and it was near dark when we rested the horses again. Bob undid my blanket and spread it over my saddle. This was soft and would make it better for me. How sore I was. My legs were red raw. After awhile we got going again and arrived at Bob's mother's place about nine o'clock that night.

The old lady was waiting for us. I was too tired to notice much about the place, and after having some supper, I was asleep almost as soon as my head hit the pillow. I never even knew the old lady had rubbed some kind of ointment on my sore legs and bottom until next morning.

6

CAVE ROCK

Next morning when I woke up I found that the house was a big mud brick humpy with a roof of corrugated iron. There was no ceiling and no floor boards, just a dirt floor. The place had a lovely setting: in a flat, surrounded by huge granite hills. The area was called Cave Rock and got its name from the many caves in the hills. These caves were a breeding ground for dingoes. The dingoes would go hundreds of feet into the caves to have their litters undisturbed, away from man. On these hills there were big granite boulders hundreds of feet high. You could climb up on top of some of them and see for miles.

The old lady was over seventy years old, and as Bob said, she could not see very well. She told me she had four sons and one daughter. The sons' names were Alfred (usually called Alf), Alec, Bob, and the youngest was Jack. She said Alf and Jack were married and that they all went away for long periods, sometimes as long as four months. The boys, as she called them, worked together trapping brumbies in the bush, and breaking them in for riding and pulling a cart or plough. The old lady said that sometimes when they came home they drove a herd of horses, as many as sixty, and they did the breaking-in there.

I soon found that my job wasn't going to be light. In fact, I had to keep going from daylight to dark. The old lady had some fourteen head of cattle, thirty sheep, four breeding sows and a boar pig, and a lot of fowls. She made me rub ointment on my sore legs and bottom three to four times each day, then on the third day I had to commence my duties.

I had to get up at daybreak and go and bring the cows in. Seven had to be milked. They were always turned into a hundred-acre paddock at night and brought in early in the morning. When the milking was over I had to turn them out to graze where they liked in the open country. Now I had never learnt to milk a cow and didn't know how to go about it. When I had put the cows into their yard the old lady was waiting with the milk pails. She said that I must learn to milk, and the thought frightened me. The cows all had big, ugly, long horns and they looked at me like they would use them if I came near. The old lady called out, 'Bail up, bail up,' and the cows seemed to understand. The ones that had to be milked walked into their stalls and put their heads into a railing that the old lady called a bail. She then walked alongside the cow in each stall and pushed a vertical rail, that was bolted at the bottom but loose at the top, towards the cow's neck until it was fairly firm, and then secured it at the top with a bolt that was hanging on a piece of string for the purpose.

I was told to stand close while the old lady was milking and take notice of the way that it was done. She milked two cows, then made me sit on the milking-stool with the milk-pail on the ground under the next cow to be milked. This frightened the wits out of me as I was afraid of cows. The old lady showed me how to squeeze the teats to make the milk come out. But try as I may, I couldn't squeeze hard enough, being under nine years old, and a little too young for milking. So the old lady sent me up to the house to get Bob to help finish the milking. After milking we had breakfast.

I then had to let the sheep out of their small yard near the house. The old lady came with me. She told me the sheep had to be protected and someone had to be with them while they were grazing away from the home paddocks during the day on account of the dingoes. She had about thirty sheep, all sorts and sizes. She said that when they had had enough feed they would return to the house paddock so we just had to follow them until they came back themselves. She said that they were well trained. We were away for about two hours. I was told that I would have to do this every morning, and again in the afternoon from about three thirty until five o'clock. (After she was satisfied that I knew how to look after the sheep, the old lady used to have a rest each afternoon for about two hours.)

I was shown how to feed the pigs and the fowls, and told that I had to bring in the cows at night to be milked. When the boys were home they all used to help with the milking. I also had to get wood for the house. The old lady had a two-wheeled hand-cart and I had to take this out and pick up wood anywhere I could find it.

So I found that my light job, 'just keeping the old lady company', turned out to be a daylight to dark job that made me dog-tired, and many times I wished that I was back with Uncle, the kids and dear old Grandma.

The old lady used to put the milk into flat tin trays, each one holding about two gallons. She would then put these into a large bag cooler and let them stand like that for about twelve hours. By that time the cream would have come to the top of the milk and she would skim it off and make it into butter. Her daughter's children used to come and take it away and sell it, and the money from this and the eggs that she sold were her only cash income.

The daughter's children were teenagers and I didn't like any of them. They used to bully me, and there were always two or three of them so there wasn't much I could do about it. They were nearly twice my size. They called me names such as 'dopey' and 'kid', and they used to pull my shirt out of my pants. I often wished I was older and bigger.

After I had been there about two weeks, Bob and his brothers went away on one of their trips and an old man called Albert came to stay with us. He was a nice old man and he used to help me with the milking, and sometimes he would help me get wood and feed the pigs. The old lady asked me how I liked the job after I had been there about a month. I told her I didn't like it and wanted to go back to Uncle's place. I said that was the arrangement that Bob had made with my Uncle and Grandma. She said, 'You had better like staying here because you'll not be leaving and don't think you can run away because the blacks will get you before you get outside the paddock.' That frightened me because I didn't know that there were any Aboriginals around.

A few weeks later the boys came home and they brought a lot of horses with them. The old lady told Bob about me wanting to go home and he came to me and said, 'Get that out of your mind, you're here to stay whether you like it or not.' So for a few days I waited, and then I asked Albert if he could write a letter for me. I couldn't read or write, as I hadn't had any schooling. He asked me who I wanted to write to. I told him Grandma, and he said, 'Son, if I could I would, but like you I never had any schooling and can't even write my name.' He advised me not to say anything to anyone about writing home because 'this mob' (meaning the old lady and her sons) were a bad lot. He said that if I got the chance to get away from there to take it, but to be careful because if Bob caught me he would horse-whip me. He said, 'I'm only staying here because I have nowhere else to go.' He was too old to do hard work, and he got his food there, and was able to snare possums and sell their skins to buy tobacco and clothes.

I could see no hope of getting away for the time being so I carried on. My clothes were getting very ragged and my feet got frozen every morning because I didn't have any boots. I had no overcoat either, and sometimes, on wet days, I would be soaking wet-through all day.

I had my ninth birthday while I was there. I don't think the old lady or her family knew, but I knew that dear old Grandma would remember, and didn't I wish I was with her. I didn't get any letters. This puzzled me as Grandma never missed wishing me a happy birthday and had always given me some small present to remember it by. But this ninth birthday, nothing.

As the weeks and months passed by, I got to know the cows more, and the sheep all seemed to know me and we all became very close friends, I got to like all the animals. The pony that Bob gave me had been taken away and sold. Old Albert told me about that.

The weather became warmer and the grass began to dry off. This meant more work for me as the stock had to be watered out of a soak with a small bucket tied on to the end of a rope. It was nearing Christmas 1903.

One day the boys came home with another mob of horses, and about twenty head of cattle of all ages and sizes. They had with them two blacks and two other men. The whites were cousins, old Albert told me. The day after they arrived they started roping the horses and getting them used to being handled.

First they would put a rope around a horse's neck and tie it to a post. The rope was made into a slip-knot, so that when the horse pulled back it would pull the rope tight and choke itself and fall flat on the ground. When this happened one of the men would run over and pull the rope loose so that the horse could breathe again. In a few seconds it would recover enough to get up. Sometimes a horse would try it again, but generally once was enough to teach them that they had no hope of getting away, and from then on they could be led easily on a rope.

After a horse had completed this first lesson it would have a saddle put on it, then one of the men would get onto its back while it was still tied to a post. The men got a horse used to this by getting off and on a few times. Then they would put a bridle on the horse, force the bit into its mouth, and fasten a long, thin, strong rope to the bridle on one side. With this in place they would make the horse run around in circles, first to the right and then to the left. This is what they called mouthing, and was to make the horse know that when the rein was pulled tight on one side of the bit leaving the other side slack, it was to go that way.

These men were experts at roping and breaking-in horses. When the animals were all broken-in they were branded with a branding iron. (The brand was registered in the old lady's name. The cattle that they handled were also branded.) When this was finished the men drove the horses to the nearest market to be sold.

About two days before Christmas the boys came home, and on Christmas Eve the old lady's daughter, and two granddaughters came, along with several other women and girls who were strangers to me. They were soon busy preparing a Christmas feast. Old Albert told me that they did this every Christmas time. He said that on Christmas Day there would be hell to pay as they would all get drunk and they usually ended up in an all round brawl. Late Christmas Eve, cases of beer, rum, wine and whisky arrived.

It was very hot at this time of the year and that night all the men and boys slept in the shed on the floor or on a haystack, and the women and girls had the house. The next morning everyone was up early and they all helped me with my work. After breakfast I took the sheep out to graze, arriving back near midday. The spree was in full swing and the men were all getting too much to drink.

Then dinner was ready and we all sat down to eat. They had arranged a long table to seat about twenty. Dinner had only been going about ten minutes when one of the men, who was unsteady on his feet, fell and knocked one end of the table over, breaking crockery, glasses and bottles of beer and spilling drinks. One of the other men called him a 'so and so', then an argument started and the others joined in. As old Albert had said, a brawl started, and the women all took sides. I grabbed a plate with plenty of good food on it and as many of the cakes as I could carry, and got out. I went down behind the shed under a nice shady tree and finished my dinner.

The yelling and swearing up at the house was awful. The men were fighting, knocking each other down, women and all. I had never seen people carry on like this before. And then some of the visitors commenced to get their things and leave. Some were too drunk to harness up their horses, some went and lay under a shady tree and went to sleep. I looked after the watering and did my jobs and kept out of the way as much as possible. Old Albert was drunk also.

One of the Aboriginals came to see me and said he would help me. He was the first black man I had talked to. At first I was not too happy but he seemed to be nice and he said he didn't touch any grog. So we became good friends. He was about twenty years old and he told me he hadn't had any schooling. He told me to call him Charlie. He could do almost anything with horses and he milked the cows for the old lady. He said that she had locked herself in her bedroom when the brawling had started and wouldn't come out until it was over. He said he had been working with the boys on and off for about three years. I asked him what wages he got and he told me that they gave him a few pounds every time they sold a large mob of horses.

We went together to the house after Charlie had done the milking and things had quietened down, and we found men and some women lying around, some inside and some outside, all hopelessly drunk. We got some food and Charlie filled a half-gallon dipper with milk. We took the food and milk down to the stable and had our meal. Then we lay on some hay and slept the night there. It was very hot weather so we didn't need any covering. We slept in our clothes.

Next day was a day of sore heads. All the visitors had gone and things were very quiet. Charlie helped me all day and I felt for the first time since I left Uncle's place that I had a friend. We had breakfast with the old lady and the midday meal also. She never mentioned anything about the brawl. Alec was the first of the boys to appear. He had two badly blackened eyes and bruises all over his face, with bits of skin knocked off his knuckles. Jack could not be found and Jack's wife was missing too. Then Bob came out and he was as bad as Alec. The other black man had cleared off and Alf and his wife were also missing.

For the next few days the men did nothing, only lay around until all their bruises and scars were better. As the New Year came, all those that were missing came back, a few at a time, and by the third day in 1904 everyone seemed to have forgotten Christmas Day. They were planning another trip away to get some more horses and cattle.

Charlie was a real pal to me. He helped me with the watering and with the cows and feeding the pigs, and I began to think that what I had been told about the blacks wasn't true. You couldn't have had a better mate. I hadn't met anyone, apart from Grandma, Uncle, Aunt and my brothers, who helped me and showed me so much. Charlie told me he didn't know who his father was and that his mother had died when he was born, and he had been brought up in the bush with the wild blacks.

A few days later the boys all went away again. They always said they were going kangaroo shooting – they all had Winchester 44 rifles – but I had never seen any skins brought home, only horses and cattle. So the old lady, Albert and I were the only ones left.

The weeks went by slowly and I was now in rags. I still hadn't been given any wages and had no boots. I patched my trousers with bag whenever a hole wore in them or they were torn. Then one day a few weeks later, Old Albert had been to town, and he brought home for me two pairs of trousers to fit a boy of about ten. I was only nine and they were too big for me although I was big for my age. Old Albert bought them out of his possum skin money. He said it pained him to see me so neglected, with no clothing. He said he would have bought me some boots but he didn't have enough money. I felt grateful to the old man. When he was sober he was very good to me.

My work was much the same: looking after the sheep, bringing the cows in and turning them out when milked, feeding the pigs, hauling water for the stock and getting wood for the house.

The old lady did her cooking on an open fire. She made what was called damper and that was our bread. She used to put so much flour in a large dish, then so much baking powder, then salt, then mix it well. Then she would add so much milk when there was plenty, and water when the milk wasn't plentiful, and mix the lot to a soft dough. Before she added the liquid she always built a big fire and waited until it burnt down to a hot ash. Then she would scoop out a large hole in the middle and when the dough was ready, place it in the hole and cover it completely with hot ashes, leave it about forty-five minutes, then scrape off the ashes, and the bread, or damper, would be pulled out with a shovel. The damper was always round and about four inches thick and usually eighteen inches across. A damper this size would last for about three days for the three of us. This kind of bread was beautiful to eat.

The boys had been gone about twelve weeks and the nights were getting very cold. The old lady hadn't heard from them and old Albert said that they hadn't been away that long before. I heard him say to the old lady that something must have gone wrong. I asked what he meant by 'something going wrong', and he said they may have had an accident or something, or perhaps they were sick. I never took much notice as my work was much lighter when we had only two or three horses to water, but I would have liked Charlie to come back.

Then one day, about three weeks later, a man came on horseback. At the time I was handling water at the soak. He rode up to the house and the old lady came out with old Albert. The man got off his horse and Albert led it over to the water-trough for a drink. The man stayed talking to the old lady. Old Albert said to me, 'That man is a policeman. If he asks you about horses or cattle tell him you don't know anything about them.' He said, 'The boys are in trouble. The policeman says those horses and cattle they have been bringing home, well some of them have been stolen and he is here to find out as much as possible about them.' Well I didn't know where the animals had come from or where they went, so there wasn't much I could say.

The policeman stayed with us that night but he never mentioned anything to me until next morning. When I was putting the cows into the yard he was there, and he asked me my name and where I had come from and how long I had been there. I told him. Then he asked how many cows they had when I came and did I see, at any time, many horses and cattle. I told him about the horse-breaking and branding. He asked me if any of the men had told me not to say anything if I was questioned and I told him no. I never said anything about the warning that old Albert had given me. He then asked me how they treated me, and I told him rotten. I said the old man Albert was nice and treated me fine and I told him about the new pants he bought me. The policeman then asked what they would do to me if they thought or knew what I had told him. I said that they would half kill me, that they and Bob were very cruel. He said, 'Don't worry, they will never know and thanks, you have given me a clue.'

I asked the policeman if he ever went near Uncle's place and he said that his district didn't go that far. I said that I would like to get word to my Grandma to come and get me, as they were not paying me my wages or giving me any clothing or boots and the work was too hard. He promised to try and get word to Grandma.

After breakfast the policeman got on his horse and rode off. I went to the house for something and the old lady was crying. Old Albert told me that Alec and Jack were in gaol and Bob and two of their relations had gone bush until things cooled down. He said that Charlie had also cleared out with the other black man called Ben. They had gone back to their tribe.

Weeks, then months went by and winter came. It was a very wet winter and very cold. It was late in September, about three weeks after my tenth birthday when Alec and Jack came home. They never talked about where they had been. The old lady told me that Bob and two of her daughter's sons were doing a big clearing contract for some new settlers and that Alec and Jack were going to work with them. They were only home for a week.

After they had gone I heard the old lady and Albert arguing about the boys. Old Albert said they would do it again, and the old lady said they had a bad time in gaol and she didn't think they wanted any more of that. But Albert said, 'That's what you said last time.' So by what I had heard I knew they had been in trouble before.

The old lady (which was what she was called by the family in her absence, and Mother in her presence), must have been short of money, because two weeks after Alec and Jack had left to join Bob, three men came. Two were on horseback and the other was driving a wagon with four horses attached. They came late in the afternoon. One of them spoke to Albert and they then unhitched the horses from the wagon and turned them out into the paddock with the two saddle horses, and stayed the night.

Next morning there was good news for me. The old lady had offered some sheep, cattle and pigs for sale and the three strangers were new settlers who had come to see the stock with a view to purchase. Albert and the old lady showed the men the stock and after a lot of bargaining they purchased all the cows except four, all the sheep except fifteen, and the only pigs that were left were three sows with litters only a few days old. This made my work much lighter. The pigs were loaded into the wagon, to which the men had attached railings so they couldn't get out. Then one man on horseback drove the cattle away and the other man drove the sheep away. I asked old Albert why the stock was sold and he said that the boys hadn't sent any money home, so the stock had to be sold so we could live.

I had an easy time for the next few weeks compared to what I had been doing.

About three weeks before Christmas, Bob, Alec, Jack, two of the old lady's grandsons and four other men came home for hay-cutting. Cutting hay was a slow and painstaking job. It had to be done by hand with scythes, and we had eight men each with a scythe, and six or seven men, women and kids tying the cut hay into sheaves and putting the sheaves into stooks.

There was a severe thunderstorm just before we started cutting the hay. A flash of lightning struck the ground at the bottom end of the paddock of oats and travelled through the whole forty acres leaving a track some ten yards wide, the shape of a huge snake travelling. This was a most unusual thing. The track went black in two days and a lot of people came to see the freak, huge winding black track like the letter S.

7

A Christmas Celebration

The grandsons who had come with the men were George, who was eighteen, and Bill, who was sixteen. Bill and I got on well but George was a bully, always ordering me around. I didn't like him. Bill used to help me, and one day I asked him if he knew about Alec and Jack being in gaol. He said he did. Then he said, 'Serves them right. They have been stealing horses and cattle for years.' Bill said that the old lady was no good and he didn't like her. He told me that she had never been married but had lived with a man called Alf, and he was his (Bill's) mother's father. When Alf left her old Albert came and lived with her and he was Bob's father and he was the only one who stopped with her.

When he had told me this Bill said, 'Now you know the truth about them all don't tell anyone that I told you. My mother told me all about them. She said that none of them had ever been to school.' He continued, 'As soon as I'm old enough I'll get away from here, and you should get away too if you can, they are a lot of drunken robbers.'

Bob and Alec took two horses in a spring-cart and Bill said they were going to town for supplies. Town was thirty miles away. That night I couldn't sleep, thinking about what Bill had said, and I made up my mind to get out of that place as soon as I could. Bill and I often talked of getting out. He told me I would have to be very careful because the boys were all good trackers. They had learnt from the blacks who they had lived with at times. Alec got speared through the leg for interfering with a woman once and the blacks had been after Bob several times for the same thing.

When Bob and Alec returned from town they had the cart loaded with stores and cases of grog. Bill remarked that there would be another brawl on Christmas Day, as it happened every Christmas.

He was right. A day or so before Christmas Day the relations and friends came and the women set to work cooking and getting everything ready. Then on Christmas Eve Bob called them all together and told them that this Christmas there wasn't to be any trouble. He said, 'Let's forget the past and show that we can have a good Merry Christmas without any brawling.'

When there was a crowd stopping the night I had to sleep in the back of the stables on bags of chaff and corn, or a pile of empty bags. This time Bill came and slept there with me. On Christmas Eve we talked for a long time after we had made our beds. Bill suggested that we hide some of the grog. He pointed out that by doing this there would be less to drink and it would help to stop any brawling. He said, 'It is only when they get very drunk that they brawl.'

After we had talked about this we decided that we would hide some of the grog. Bill said he knew where it was because he had seen Alec and Bob putting it in the large hessian cooler used for the milk.

The cooler stood out on the back verandah. It was very large and had a container on top that would hold about eight gallons of water. There were strips of bag running from the water down the hessian sides and the water soaked up into these, then onto the sides of the cooler making the inside very cold. Being outside on the verandah in the fresh air made it cooler still. The bottom shelf was packed with the drinks for Christmas Day.

Bill and I agreed that when the lights up at the house went out, and we were sure that everyone was asleep, we would carry out our plan. Bill said, 'If they find out some is missing they will never expect us to be the ones who took it.' I asked, 'Where do you think we should hide it?' Bill suggested that the top of the stable roof would be the ideal place because it was covered with about twelve inches of straw.

It was a very dark night and we carried out our plan in the early hours of the morning. We took three bottles of whisky, three bottles of rum and four bottles of wine. They were all quart bottles. We weren't seen by anyone. Bill climbed up onto the roof of the stable and I handed the bottles up to him. Bill put them in holes that he made in the straw, then covered them over.

Next morning, Christmas Day, everyone was asleep when I went up to light the fire. Bill went with me to get the cows, then we filled up the water-troughs at the soak. That took nearly and hour, but there was still no movement over at the house. They were still asleep. We fed and watered the pigs and Bill milked the two cows that had to be milked. We took the milk up to the cooler and then the old lady came out and told us to get our own breakfast. After we had our breakfast we took the sheep out to graze and arrived back near midday. The women were busy preparing Christmas dinner. The men were all under the weather, some couldn't walk.

When Bill and I went in to dinner everyone was drinking. Some were so drunk they couldn't sit in their chairs properly. We had our dinner and then went and refilled the water-trough. After that we had a sleep in the stable until it was time to bring the cows in. I went for the cows and Bill filled the water-trough again. Besides the cattle and horses, the sheep had to have extra water in the summertime. This Christmas Day it was really hot – a hundred and one degrees fahrenheit in the shade.

When I got back with the cows it was nearly sundown. Bill came to meet me and said that there was a big row on at the house. The grog had run out and Bob was blaming everyone for getting away with it, or stealing it, even the old lady. This made Bill and me very scared. Bill had heard Bob say that last Christmas he had found some bottles planted in the stable and he would search it this time from end to end. Bill suggested that we take the grog that we had planted and put it somewhere else.

We got the bottles off the stable roof (it was getting dark), and put them into two bags. We put these on top of the pig shed roof. A little while later Bob and three others commenced looking for the missing bottles. They were still pretty drunk, so we felt sure they wouldn't find them.

About half an hour later Bill's brother George came and told us that Bob wanted Bill up at the house. Bill went up to Bob and I stayed in the stable. Later I heard Bill yelling and I knew then that he was copping a belting. They were trying to make him tell them where the grog was. This made me frightened so I thought I would shift the bottles from the roof of the pig house in case Bill gave in and told.

It was very dark by then so I went to the pig house and brought the bottles down to the ground. I intended to put them in a bag and hide them. The pigs were all asleep, so I knocked the heads off the bottles and emptied them into the trough with the pig feed. This would save me two trips to get rid of the grog, as I couldn't have carried all the full bottles but the empties were easy to manage in a bag. I put the bag, full of broken bottles, over the fence and took it down into the gully close to the soak.

When I was clear I heard loud voices going towards the pig house. I couldn't see who it was, but one of the voices was Bob's and I could also hear Alec. I was safe as it was very dark, and as long as I didn't make a noise I would be all right. All at once it came to me to let the bag and broken bottles down into the water. There was always about eight feet of water in the soak and the weight of the bottles would hold the bag down, and no one would be able to find it. Having done this I sneaked back to the pig house and could hear that Bill was copping it again. They were belting him and calling him a liar, then Bob's voice came above the others and said, 'Find Berty. Then we will get to the bottom of this.'

They all started looking for me. I had no boots on so I quietly got away into the bush and stayed hidden. They never came near where I was. Then a terrible din came from the pig shed. Two or three pigs started to squeal, then a few more, then finally all the pigs were squealing. Oh, what a noise. This brought all the half-drunk men and the women to the pig house. I sneaked up as close as I dared, wondering what was wrong. Then I heard. Bob yelled out, 'The young sod has poured the grog into the pig trough and they're all drunk. Wait until I get hold of him, he'll be sorry for this. I'll skin him alive.'

This made me go back into hiding in the bush. About two hours later things became quieter. The pigs were not so noisy and everyone seemed to be settled down for the night.

It was in the early hours of the morning when I ventured into the stables to get my blanket. Bill was not there. Everything was quiet. My idea was to wait until daylight came, then clear out and try to get to Uncle's place. I was very tired and fell asleep and when I woke it wasn't only daylight but the sun was well up, and standing over me was Bob with a stock-whip in his hand. I had not undressed for bed. I still had on my pants and a shirt, and an old rag hat. These, along with my red blanket, were all my belongings.

Bob said, 'Well, how much grog did you and Bill put into the pig trough last night? Now there's no use denying it, we thrashed it out of Bill last night and you've still got yours coming. Come on get up, where's the rest of the grog?' I didn't speak, just stood looking up at him. He gave me a cut around the legs, then he lashed me three or four times around the shoulders and body. I jumped up and tried to run out of the stable. As I got out of the doors he caught me around the legs again and I fell to the ground. He continued to whip me. The whip was one he used to tame the horses with and he was an expert. He knew how to use that whip. I don't know how many times he cut me because I must have fainted.

The next thing I knew I was up at the house on a sofa in the living-room. The old lady and some other women were washing my back, legs, arms and shoulders, and applying some kind of ointment to my cuts. Some of the cuts were an inch wide, and up to twelve inches long, and went into my flesh half an inch in places. I was so ill, I kept fainting.

They seemed to be terribly worried about me and one woman said, 'I think he will die, this is shocking. What were the other men doing to let Bob flog the boy like this?' Old Albert said that Alec had stopped Bob and knocked him down. They had fought and Alec and Alf had given Bob a hiding. After that Bob had got on his horse and cleared out. The old lady asked where Alf was. Albert said that he had gone to get a woman to attend my wounds. She was a new settler's wife and had been a nurse before she married, so she would know how serious my condition was. Albert said that Alf should be back soon because it was only seven miles to the settler's place. The old lady was very worried.

It was a long while before Alf came back, but the nurse was with him. She came straight to me. I was terribly sore but I could understand what she was saying. She washed my wounds clean of the ointment and dabbed some sort of white powder onto the whip marks. This eased the pain just a little. I felt very bad. The old lady gave me a drink of milk and she used an old teapot because I couldn't sit up; in fact, I couldn't move my arms or legs – they were stiff.

Then I started to vomit. The nurse looked very worried. Alf came in and asked me how I was but I couldn't talk. The nurse asked Alf how far it was to the nearest doctor. I heard Alf tell her it was about thirty miles when the doctor was at the nearest town, but he served several towns and could be a hundred miles away. It could take a week or more to get to him. The nurse said, 'That would be too late. We will have to do the best we can.'

It was dark by this time and they had the lights burning. Everyone was too worried to leave the place. The nurse was an angel. She stayed up with me all that night and kept putting the powder onto the cuts and this slowly eased the pain. Near daylight the next morning, I dozed off.

It was nearly midday when I awoke and I thought I felt a little better. Albert was the first to notice that I was awake and he asked how I was. I tried to talk but was unable to make any sound. My neck was very sore and swollen, as the whip had caught me around the neck and throat. Albert went out and the nurse came in to see me. She said, 'Can you hear me?' I couldn't reply. Then she said, 'If you can hear me just close your eyes and open them again.' I did this and she smiled and said, 'I think that you will come through this all right, you must be made of leather.' Then she told me that she would put some hot packs on my neck and try and get the swelling down. She said that if that worked I would be able to talk, and then maybe keep some food down. My legs and arms were still swollen, and I couldn't move them.

For the next few days the nurse kept hot packs around my neck and arms and legs. This was hard to stand at first, but it did reduce the swelling, though for a while I could only whisper. Then my voice came back and I was able to move my arms and legs. Two days later the nurse left, leaving instructions as to what was to be done. She said goodbye and told us that she would come back again in about a week's time to see how I was getting along. I had to do exercises with my arms and legs.

8

JOURNEY AT NIGHT

So now we were in 1905. Bob hadn't returned, and a lad of sixteen came to help the old lady while I was unable to walk. His name was Jimmy. He was a part-blood Aboriginal and he did all my work and made friends with me.

When the nurse came to see how I was getting along, about eight days later, I was much better. I could sit up, and I could eat anything without fear of vomiting, and although I was still very sore, the swelling had gone down to almost normal in places. I could use my hands and turn my neck about without much pain. The nurse was very pleased with my recovery and only stayed for about two hours.

I made up my mind to clear out from Cave Rock as soon as I was well enough and could find a way that would not attract too much attention. Jimmy had travelled around a lot and he told me that the gully where Uncle's land was was called Connigin Creek by the blacks. I asked him how far it was from Cave Rock. He replied that it was about thirty miles.

A few days later a man came looking for strayed horses. He stayed the night because his place was near Gillimanning, about fifteen miles away. My bed had been moved to the living-room when I was ill, so I could hear all that the man said. He left next morning and I asked Jimmy where this Gillimanning was, and he told me that it was on the road leading to my uncle's place. I knew this road because Bob had pointed it out to me once.

It was about the middle of January before I could walk properly. One day Alec came home to see how I was. He had been away working and he told me that he had sent Jimmy to help until I was well again. One night I was lying awake – I couldn't sleep because of the heat – and thinking about how I could get back home again, when a scheme came to me. I had a lot of time to myself since Jimmy was away a lot with the sheep and busy doing my other chores, so I worked out a plan to escape.

I had no boots. This meant that I would have a rough time walking at night, so I went down to the stable when no one was around and cut bags into pieces to make coverings for my feet. I could walk very well again and move around without my arms or legs hurting so much. My skin felt very tight, and any quick movement brought pain. I was getting better but I didn't let anyone know just how well I was. I knew that I would have to get away before Jimmy left. The old lady kept asking me how soon I would be well enough to do my work, and so did Albert, but I made out that my arms and legs were not working properly and it would be a few more weeks yet.

I made four pairs of bag boots and hid them under a rail in the stable. I had to wait then until there was no moon, or until the moon set at about eleven o'clock in the evening, so that I would have at least six hours to travel in before daylight. I had to work out a way to make them believe I had taken a different direction to the one that I intended to take. I made up a story to tell Jimmy. I was going to tell him that he was not to let anyone know, but the nurse's husband had offered me a job that would give me five shillings a week and keep but I was too frightened to ask the old lady to let me go. I hoped this would throw them off my trail, because the nurse lived in the opposite direction to what I would be taking when I ran away. I didn't intend to tell Jimmy until the evening I was to make the break.

Bob came home near the end of January. He was very nice to me, asking a lot of questions about how I was and what the nurse had said. I told him I didn't have much to say to the nurse because I had been too ill to bother about anything. He said to me, 'You shouldn't have taken those bottles. I lost my head and am very sorry for what I did and I will make it up to you later on.' I never answered him, and after a few minutes he left. I could hear him asking the old lady if she thought that my people would do anything about it if they found out what had happened. The old lady suggested that Bob go away and not let anyone know where he was for at least six months. She said, 'You could get years in gaol for what you did.' She told him that when everything was safe she would let him know through Charlie's tribe. So Bob left early next morning. I never saw him again.

Near the end of February I judged the moon was about right for my break, so I got my things ready. All I had was a single red blanket and the bag boots I had made. I managed to put some home-made bread and a small jar filled with butter together, and I rolled them up with my boots in my red rug. I also found a small knife to take with me, and had put aside a clean jar to fill with milk. Now I was ready to ask the old lady if I could go and work for the nurse's husband. So that day I told Jimmy about the job, and the next morning I asked the old lady. She thought for awhile, then she said, 'No. Not on any account can you go there. What have you and that nurse woman been hatching up between you? Now don't let me hear you mention this again, and don't think you can run away because Bob will soon get you back again and you know what he will do to you, so just you forget it.'

The night came and everyone went to bed early. The moon was very bright and I guessed it would set at about ten thirty or eleven, so I went to bed the same time as the others. Jimmy came in and talked with me before he went to sleep. He slept on a small verandah on the north side of the house.

That evening I had filled the bottle with milk and planted it along with my other things in the stable. I was all set. Jimmy asked me if I had asked the old lady. I told him what she had said and that I'd have to forget about the job because I didn't want any more trouble with them. Jimmy said that he would like to work for the nurse and that he thought that they would be nice. I started to yawn on purpose and made out I was sleepy, so Jimmy went to bed. It was now about nine thirty and the moon was getting low. I was all alone in the living-room, where I still had my bed. I waited and could hear old Albert breathing heavily and the old lady was very quiet. I stayed awake waiting for the moon to set. Three or four times I started to doze off and had to sit up to keep myself awake. I had gone to bed that night with my clothes on, or I should say rags, because that's just what they were. The moon went down and it became very dark. I got out of bed very quietly and slowly edged my way to the door. It was always left open during the summer nights. I got away without anyone knowing. I got my swag and set off towards Uncle's place and freedom.

When I got clear of the Cave Rock homestead I sat down and put on my first pair of bag boots and tied them to my feet with string. This enabled me to walk off the track a few yards and not leave any footprints that could be followed. I walked all that night and when daylight came I was very tired. It had been a tiring and frightening night. I wasn't used to the weird noises made by the wild animals: the sharp, piercing howl of the wild dog or dingo. The dingoes were close to me and no doubt watching me all night. One of them would howl and then a few minutes later its mates would answer. Each time one howled close to me, a funny, frightened feeling went up and down my spine.

I knew that Jimmy would be the first to notice that I had gone. He would no doubt look around to be sure before he told the old lady. Then it was possible that they would send Jimmy over to the nurse's place before they searched anywhere else, so I felt safe. I continued on my way until well after the sun had come up, then I turned into some very thick scrub and prepared a place to sleep. I would set off again when it was dark. I had used two pairs of my boots and my feet were starting to get very sore. After making a place to sleep, I had some bread and drank the remains of the milk. I lay down on the rug and fell asleep.

I must have slept for hours, because when I woke the sun was set low in the west. I felt rested but very frightened. I was thirsty and had nothing to drink. I ate some bread and butter and then got up and had a look outside the patch of thick scrub and bush. Everything was very quiet. The birds were flitting about and the noise that they made was lovely. I lay down again and watched and listened to the many species of birds. I wasn't game to move until darkness came. The spot I chose to hide in was nice and shady, and cool. I could see that it was a hot day because some of the birds had their wings hanging when they sat on a limb. I had seen fowls do this with their wings on very hot days.

The sun went down and darkness approached. I got my rug and rolled it up into a swag, putting the remains of the bread and butter inside. I had worn out two pairs of bag boots so on went the third pair to start the second night's walk.

Night came, it was a bright moon, and I came out of hiding. I walked on the track because there weren't any fresh hoof marks, and I felt that if a man on horseback came I would hear him long before he saw me. Walking on the track was much better for my feet.

So I went on. Oh! was I thirsty. My mouth was very dry so I picked some leaves from a tree and chewed on them while I was walking along. I hadn't gone very far when my friends the dingoes started to howl. They frightened the very devil out of me. The bush seemed to come alive at night. The possums calling to one another sounded like a flat, loud whisper, and occasionally there was a distressed noise, some possum or kangaroo rat fighting for its life. The kangaroo rats only came out at night. They are a small animal, about the size of a house cat, with a body and legs and tail like a kangaroo, and a head like a rat's. When the native cat catches one of these small animals it puts up a real fight. The native cat is the most savage of all the small animals in Western Australia. It is a little bigger than the average house cat and has a longish head with little ears and powerful jaws, and teeth like a dog's. It is like the dingo in that it won't harm you unless it is cornered. Then it will put up a real fight for its life. A domestic dog usually won't attack a dingo or native cat on account of their viciousness.

As I walked along the winding bush track, I kept listening for the sound of horses approaching, ready to move off the track if I did. My listening for the horses so keenly made the bush noises seem extra loud – I heard more bush noises that night than the previous night.

After walking for about three hours or more, I judged the time to be about ten or a little later. (I was judging the time by the moon as I knew it would set at eleven thirty.) Then, while walking over a small hill, I noticed a faint light. It was a long way ahead of me and looked to be in the right direction. This lifted my feelings and I started to walk faster; I even forgot how thirsty I was. It might be Gillimanning. There was an old settler there, so Jimmy had told me. Each time the track went over a rise I could see the light, and it seemed to be brighter each time, so I knew that I was getting closer. I forgot about the weird noises and the chance of horsemen coming. My ambition was to get to that light.

I must have travelled two or three more miles before I came close to the light. I could see now that it was a fire; it looked like a fire that someone had left. I remembered that we were all taught how dangerous it was to leave a fire burning, as the bush was a fire hazard. All new settlers were warned. Then, as I got closer I could see people, some were standing and some were sitting around the fire. Then all at once my feet felt sore. I had left the track walking towards the fire, and in my excitement I had forgotten about my bag boots. The pair I had on had worn through and I had been walking on the rough ground. So, I sat on the ground and put on the last pair of boots and then I approached the fire.

When I got within one hundred yards, I could see the faces of the people who were around the fire. Then all at once two big dogs came towards me, barking savagely. A large man came after them, calling to the dogs. Then he called out, 'Who's that there?' I kept walking towards the fire and yelled, 'It's me, a boy.' As I approached the fire the man said, 'Where in the blazes did you come from?' I said, 'I'm on my way to my uncle's place. It's near Snows Well.' The man seemed surprised to see a boy at this time of night. He was a short man, but very broad shouldered, and he looked big to me in the fire light.

As we walked back to the fire he noticed my bag boots and asked me why I was wearing moccasins. I didn't know what he meant and he told me that 'moccasins' was the name of the type of boots I was wearing. A lady, his wife, then spoke to me and asked me had I had anything to eat. I told her I was very thirsty, and one of the children got me a pannikin of water which I drank and then asked for more. I told the lady that I hadn't had any food since early that morning and that I had walked many miles. She got me some food at once, she was a nice person.

The couple had four children; two boys and two girls. After I had eaten the food the man told me to come and sit on the box near the fire and tell them all about my troubles. 'You look like you have had a bad time', he said. So I told them all that had happened to me since I went from Uncle's with big Bob, including the flogging. To prove it I pulled my rag shirt off and showed them the whip marks. The man said he wouldn't have believed that anyone could be so cruel and that if anyone did that to one of his kids he would kill them. He went on to say that they were new settlers and that they had only been here about three months. They were from Scotland. He said he knew about Snows Well and he had been told about Uncle and, as luck had it, he wanted to have a talk with Uncle about buying some horses and a cow. He said that he believed Uncle was an expert with stock, and continued on to say, 'In the morning I will drive you over to your uncle's place in my spring-cart. It is about nine miles or so. Now we must go to bed.' He called his eldest son, Jack, and told him that I was to doss in with him for the night. I felt very shy as the boys changed into their night clothes and I had to sleep in the clothes that I was wearing; all I took off was my rag hat and bag boots. I had no sooner laid my head on the pillow than I was asleep.

The next thing I knew it was daylight. The lady was up and the man had gone to get the horse that was in a paddock they had made by running barbed wire from tree to tree around a few acres. During the day they hobbled the horse and let him feed near the camp with a bell on so they could hear where he was. After breakfast the man and the second son, about my age, got into the cart with me and we set out for Uncle's place.

The road was just a winding track – there were no made roads in those days. We arrived at Uncle's place, as I could guess by looking at the sun, at about eleven o'clock in the forenoon. Judging the time by how far or near the sun was to overhead was the only way I had of knowing the time. I never had a clock or watch.

Arriving at Uncle's place I could see the many changes that had been made. They had about one hundred acres cleared and a lot of the land had been fenced. They were all out working, clearing more land for cropping in the winter. This was to be the first crop that Uncle planted. He had bought a milking cow and the women were making their own butter.

One of Uncle's daughters saw us and ran to tell the others, and they all came to see me. Dear old Grandma threw her arms around me and cried with joy. The Scotsman made himself known to them and told them how he came to be there and also about the scars all over my body. Uncle made me take off my shirt and Grandma, Aunt Alice and Uncle Archie stood and looked at me. Uncle went white with rage and he made me tell them what the flogging was for. Then he said he would go to Narrogin the next day and see what the police had to say about it. Grandma and Aunt got me some of my cousin Bill's clothes. He was about the same age as I, but I was much bigger. His clothes fitted me all right though, because Aunt always bought them a little big for him, as he was growing.

After we had had our midday meal, Uncle had a long talk with the Scotsman before he and his son set off back home. I thanked him for his kindness and for bringing me home. Grandma, Uncle and Aunt also thanked him and Uncle said he would give the Scotsman all the help and advice he could. When he left, Grandma made me have a bath and washed my feet in salt water, then made me go to bed.

The next day Uncle went to town to see what could be done about having Bob punished. I was kept in bed the three days he was away. When Uncle Archie returned he was not very hopeful of bringing Bob to justice. The police knew of him and the whole Cave Rock mob, but had said that it would be hard to prove anything against them because everyone living near was scared of them. But the police said they would send a man to make enquiries and see what could be done. They told Uncle that the Cave Rock mob were a bad lot and had been gaoled for horse and cattle stealing, and that anyone giving information against them put themselves in great danger as they would stop at nothing to get even. There were many ways that a new settler could be attacked so that it was hard to prove who had done it.

Grandma looked after me like a baby and would come and talk with me for hours. She made me tell her all about my stay at Cave Rock and she shed many tears for letting me go. Uncle bought me a pair of boots, two shirts, two pairs of shorts, some socks, and also a cap and coat while he was in Narrogin. I was now over my sore feet and able to go and help with the clearing and possum snaring. They were still dependent on the possum skin money to make ends meet.

Bush Schooling

1905-1908

'I DIDN'T KNOW YOU. YOUR SWAG IS BIGGER THAN YOU ARE.'

9

A SNAKE BITE

I turned eleven years old on August thirty-first 1905. My birthday went unnoticed, a common thing those days. I stayed with Uncle until October 1905 and by then he had one hundred acres of wheat growing and would be ready to harvest in about twelve weeks. It was a lovely crop, the first wheat grown with an artificial fertiliser which the farmers called Thomas's manure. It was a bluish black colour and very heavy. The Government helped the settlers with the purchase and delivery of this fertiliser.

Grandma told me about a new scheme the Government had brought in to help the settlers become established so that they could grow enough wheat, and stock their properties. The scheme was that the Government would pay twenty shillings for every acre the settler cleared ready for cropping. Also, they paid so much for fencing and any other improvements that were made. This money was by way of a loan, and a mortgage of the full amount at the end of the year was taken out against the property. This money was free of interest and the settlers were to pay it back over twenty-five years. No repayments were to be made, or interest charged, for five years, to give the settler a chance to have his property producing before the repayments started. There was also provision made for loans for stock and machinery. That was how a settler could take up land and settle on it without much or any money. By this time all the land around Uncle Archie's had been taken up so that now he had neighbours on all sides.

A new settler took up land adjoining Uncle's. He was a short, stout man about fifty years old, with a wife in her twenties. Uncle said that the man was hard to get along with, and Roy and the other kids were all scared of him.

The new settler built a mud and stone house of two rooms, with a roof of iron and a dirt floor. He had to cart water from the soak near Uncle's place, so the first thing he wanted to do was to put down a well. He came and asked Uncle to give him some advice as to where he might find water. Uncle was always happy to give advice and went with the man to have a good look over his property. He finally pointed out a spot where there might be water, about forty to fifty feet down. The neighbour said he would sink the well at the place Uncle had pointed out.

One morning, about two weeks later, Roy, Aunt Alice, Grandma, and us kids were working in a paddock not far from the house, when we heard a man's voice calling loudly, 'Nell, Nell, this way Nell.' Roy said, 'I think that's the man from next door.' As the man got closer, still calling, 'Nell, Nell, this way Nell,' at the top of his voice, Aunt said, 'Something must have happened to their child.' Roy told me and the other kids to get under a big log that lay on the ground near us, and he got an axe and said, 'If he comes near you kids I'll whack him with this axe.'

The man was now only about one hundred yards away, and still yelling out. Aunt Alice went to meet him calling out, 'What is the matter? What has happened?' He was only a few yards away from Aunt and he was panting and gasping for breath. Finally he said, 'I've been bitten by a snake, a big black bugger,' pointing to his right arm just below the shoulder. His wife, Nell, had put a tight cord around the arm just above where he had been bitten. He had stopped now and was looking back for Nell.

He told Aunt that Nell had cut the snake bite and sucked out the blood, and they had decided he should run to the nearest neighbour for help to get a doctor. His nearest neighbour was three miles away, and as Nell had to carry their two-year-old daughter, he had run ahead and yelled all the way, so that she would know where he was. When he got close to the neighbour's place he remembered that he had quarrelled with him the day before, so he wouldn't go there, but continued running on to Uncle's place, two miles further on.

Aunt Alice sent Roy to get Uncle who was doing some fencing not far away. When Roy told Uncle what had happened Uncle hurried home. He harnessed the horse to the cart and handed the man a drink of brandy. The man wouldn't drink it as he said he was a teetotaller.

Uncle put him in the cart and drove him over to a neighbour who had a smart horse and sulky. With this neighbour, who insisted on going with them, they set out for the doctor at Narrogin.

Uncle was away three days and when he came home he told us about the terrible time they had with the man, trying to keep him awake. They had had to leave their horse on a farm about twelve miles from Narrogin as it was exhausted, and the farmer lent them another horse to complete the trip. When they arrived at Narrogin the sick man wouldn't go to the doctor until he had seen an agent named Watts who represented a firm, Elder Shenton and Company, which had sent him a letter about an account he hadn't paid. He wanted to tell Watts what he thought of him and the firm, in case he died. That convinced Uncle that the man was mad.

The doctor kept the man in hospital for about five days. He completely recovered and got a ride back with another settler. A few weeks later his wife became very sick. She went to see the doctor who found that she was suffering from blood poisoning. She had several decayed teeth, so that when she had sucked out the poison from the snake bite wound, some had entered into her bloodstream. She was very ill and had to stay in hospital.

Aunt Alice and Grandma minded her two-year-old baby girl while she was away; she was such a lovely, pretty little girl. The father was very grateful to Aunt and Grandma for taking care of her. He was terrified of snakes and every time he came to see his daughter he would give Aunt a lecture about snakes. As the weeks went by, then the months, the mother got worse and finally she passed away. After she was buried her husband took the little girl to his sister who was living in Perth.

10

Taken Again

By now my brothers, Eric and Roy, were becoming unsettled because Uncle couldn't afford to pay them wages. They took a contract job to clear land for one of Uncle's neighbours and left in early October. Then one day another of Uncle's neighbours offered me a job at five shillings per week and keep. He knew Uncle and Grandma and asked them before approaching me, saying that I was free to work for him if I liked. He was a big Irishman named Moran, and was single and wanted a boy for company and to look after his poultry. He had about two hundred fowls.

So with Grandma's blessing, I went. At first I liked the job and my new boss was good to me and took me with him every time he went to a dance or picnic. Also the food was good and I was given new clothes.

The first two or three months the boss used to go away on Monday morning and arrive back the following Saturday evening. He was building stockyards for a man who ran cattle. The job was eight miles away and it was too much travelling for him to come home each day as his only way of getting around was on horseback. He finished the job early in the New Year and then, like Uncle, he started to get some land cleared for cropping that year.

From then on things changed for me. My boss expected me to work all day in the paddock and do the other chores around the house as well. This went on until near the end of April and by then we had cleared, ready for the plough, sixty acres of land. Knowing that he was getting twenty shillings from the Government for each acre cleared, and as I had never asked him for any wages (although he used to tell me how much he made building stockyards), I quietly asked him one evening for five pounds. I had more than this amount coming to me. I said to him, 'Tom,' (he always insisted that I call him Tom), 'could you let me have five pounds?' He looked at me and said, 'Who said that I was going to pay you wages?' I said, 'You told me, Uncle and Grandma that you would pay me five shillings a week and keep.' He replied, 'So I did, but not also buy your clothes, your keep in food and a place to sleep.' 'But,' I said, 'you haven't bought me any clothes. Up to now all I've got is what you gave me when I came here.' With this he replied, 'If you're not satisfied you know what to do. There's no money for you.' That was all that was said.

The boss went over to a neighbour's, about four miles away, to see if the neighbour would sell him some wheat. When he had been gone about an hour, I packed my few things together and cleared out. I was frightened of this big Irishman and felt sure that he would have belted me for leaving, and have bullied me into staying.

My experience up to now made me doubt the word of everyone. I went to Tom's neighbours, two Germans named Otto and Herman Meikle, who lived five miles away in a north-west direction. About a month before, Otto had been over at Tom's place. I was working clearing not far from the house and Otto had had a talk with me about my job with Tom and what wages I was getting. I told him the set up and he said that I was not being paid enough, and that if I ever wanted a job he would give me ten shillings a week and keep and that I wouldn't have to work as hard for him as I did at Tom's. When Tom refused my wages I remembered what Otto had said.

The Meikles welcomed me and when I told them that I had left Tom they both agreed I could have the job on the terms Otto had offered me. It was late in the evening when I arrived and they showed me where I would sleep. They only had a two-roomed bag hut with a small lean-to verandah built on the north side. I was to sleep in the lean-to. They had two kangaroo dogs that slept under the lean-to, near me.

One of the Meikles was preparing the evening meal when I arrived. We sat down at a home-made table which consisted of four forked posts put into the ground, two bush rails put across from fork to fork, and boards nailed across these, which were about six feet long and about two feet across. The floors were earth, like in all new settlers' huts. The meal consisted of two boiled eggs (they kept fowls), a cup of black tea and dry damper. That night I was nearly eaten alive by dog fleas – there were thousands of them. In fact, while I was sitting at the table I was pestered by hundreds crawling up my legs.

The next morning we had fried eggs for breakfast with dry damper, then fried eggs for the midday meal, again with dry damper; and with all meals, black tea without sugar or milk. This went on for six days and my stomach couldn't take any more. As fast as I tried to swallow the eggs I would have to run outside and vomit them up again. This suited the dogs as they didn't mind them. They were waiting for me to vomit each meal time; they were half-starved.

At the end of the sixth day I couldn't stand it any longer so I packed and left. When I asked about wages I got a reply that made me even less confident about Man's word. The Meikles told me that they had no money and couldn't afford to pay me. I asked them why they had said they would pay me ten shillings a week, and they replied that I wouldn't have come if they hadn't.

So off I went back to Uncle's place. Grandma was disgusted with Moran and his promise to pay me five shillings a week and keep and clothes. Uncle supported Grandma and they decided that there was nothing that could be done as there was nothing in writing. Uncle said to forget about the Meikles.

I stayed at Uncle's place for a few days and then I was offered a job with a married settler. He was a small Frenchman married to a big Irish woman. They had no children.

I asked Uncle and Grandma what they thought about the job. Uncle said that the name of the people was Phillips and that they used to be big condenser contractors on the Goldfields. They had plenty of money so Uncle thought that I should get paid if I worked for them. He promised to speak to them about my wages first, if I went with them. Grandma said that it was no good that you couldn't take the word of most of these people. Uncle suggested that I take the job on trial for awhile; then if it wasn't any good, leave, as no one could go on working for no wages. He said it was pretty low to take a kid down.

11

A New Home

The Phillips' place was about six miles north-west of Uncle's and about three miles from the Scotsman who befriended me when I cleared out from Cave Rock. Uncle and Grandma drove me over in the spring cart. When we arrived we found that the land was much more improved than Uncle's place. The Phillips had a two-roomed iron house, several out buildings, and about three hundred acres of cleared land. Most of their property was fenced. They also had two cows, six horses and some pigs.

The place gave me a feeling of security as we drove from the front gate to the house, a distance of about a mile. Uncle said that the Phillips had been there only two years and had their clearing and fencing done by contractors. They didn't have to worry about Government grants and possum skins to make a living.

The Phillips were home when we arrived and they made us feel very welcome. Uncle told them the purpose of our visit and they said that they badly wanted a boy and would be pleased to give me a job. Uncle asked about my wages and if they intended to keep me as well. He told them how unlucky I had been at Cave Rock and Moran's. He also told them I could ride a horse and about the different kinds of work I had done. Mr Phillips said he would pay me five shillings a week and full keep; also that I could draw my wages once a month and that they would treat me as their own. He said, 'Everywhere that we go he will go. Mrs Phillips has been going to town alone, now she can take him with her for company.' Then Grandma suggested that I take the job on trial for a month and if I liked it I could stay; if not I could come back to Uncle's. This was agreed. We had some lunch, then Grandma and Uncle went home.

Mr Phillips was about fifty years old and Mrs Phillips was about forty-five. Mrs Phillips showed me where I would sleep and she also explained what they expected of me. She asked me about Cave Rock and about Moran, who she said she knew. He was the district's M.C. at all the dances and she was surprised at him not being a man of his word.

So I settled into another job and wondered how this one would go. I was a quiet boy and never spoke unless spoken to. I had never been to school and it took me a long time to write my name. I didn't have much confidence in myself and the previous two and a half years hadn't helped.

Mrs Phillips showed me around the place. She showed me the pigs, and the layout of the paddocks, and also where the cows were and how to bring them home at night and put them back into the paddock in the morning. She told me that I would be called in the morning and my first job would be to light the fire in the kitchen and put the kettle on, then feed the pigs. (There were a lot of pigs of all different sizes. They had a five acre pig paddock, fenced with posts about eight feet apart. One end of each post was put about two feet into the ground, then eight barbed wires were run between the posts, covering four feet from the ground. This was considered a good pig-proof fence. There were six or seven pig houses, and small post and rail fences inside the pig paddock.)

Mr Phillips was getting ready to put his crop in. (The sowing season for wheat was May and June.) He would get out of bed when I was called, and attend to the feeding and the harnessing of the horses. He usually did this before breakfast. My job, after I had fed the pigs and fowls and put the cows out, was to go to where Mr Phillips was ploughing and pick up all the roots that had been pulled out by the plough. I put them into small heaps so they could be carted to the house for firewood or sometimes, when time was short, burnt. This was hard work and made me very tired. Walking on ground that had just been ploughed made my legs ache, as the earth used to stick to my boots and become heavy.

Mrs Phillips asked me to call her Mum. She said that she would like that, if I agreed, and Mr Phillips told me to call him Frank. They called me Bert, short for my first name, Albert. I agreed to this. I got along fine with these people and they treated me as if I was their own son. Plenty of good food, best I had since I came to the West. Mrs Phillips, or Mum, was a good cook. She was very clean and had a heart of gold. Frank was moody, and he had a vile temper, but was fair.

I had to work hard for a boy not yet twelve years old. I didn't mind this, and I did as much work as I could, as I wanted to please and stay with these people.

When Frank was busy, every fortnight or three weeks Mum used to go to town for stores. They had a smart pony and a light sulky, which they used for these trips, and a heavy spring-cart for carting heavy loads.

Narrogin, twenty-nine miles away, was our nearest shopping centre. I went with Mum on her shopping trips to keep her company. It took us one day to get there, then we would rest the horse the next day and do the shopping. On the third we would set off early for home.

I used to look forward to these trips; they were fun and a break away from the farm. We always stayed at a boarding-house or Coffee Palace, as some were called. The Coffee Palace was like home – nothing flash. At meal times the girl waiting on you would ask you what you would like, and the beds were just like my own. All my meals and bed were paid for. The lady running the Coffee Palace was a close friend of Mrs Phillips. I don't remember one single trip that Mum didn't buy me some new clothes; sometimes a coat or a pair of pants, or shirts, socks and also boots. I was looked after fine. She would give me a couple of shillings to spend as well and none of these things were ever taken out of my wages. (I was paid twenty shillings every four weeks.) The prices at the places where we stopped were very cheap. A good meal cost one shilling and a bed for the night, one shilling and sixpence. A feed for a horse, with the use of a stall in the stable, cost one shilling.

After the seeding was over, Frank used to plough the land that he was going to sow the next year – this was commonly known as fallowing. The farmers used to say that land ploughed for cropping the next year held the moisture better. Should the next season be dry, the farmer stood a better chance of a good crop. If rain came during the summer the ground so ploughed could be scarified and harrowed, which destroyed any weeds and made seeding easier and quicker.

12

THE BOAR

In September, just after my twelfth birthday, Frank wanted a boar pig for his six breeding sows. He had bought the sows and they all had little ones which were now being weaned. Some had already been weaned and were getting into the porker stage. Frank borrowed a large black boar from his brother-in-law. This boar was very savage and every time I went to feed the pigs he tried to attack me. I had to be very careful; he had large tusks and he used to froth at the mouth. I had to jump from pig pen to pig pen to dodge him when feeding them. I was scared stiff of this boar and he seemed to know it. As soon as I went near the pig pen he would have his eye on me.

One morning early in October, when the weather was getting much warmer, I was passing the pig pen to get the horses in. The boar seemed worse than ever. He never usually bothered me when I was just passing, but for some reason this morning he left the sows and ran down to the fence near where I was walking. He was frothing at the mouth and making a kind of roaring sound.

At first it didn't worry me, but then he tried twice to get through the fence. The pig fence joined the race where I had to bring the horses, and if the pig did get through my chances against him were nil. I reached the corner of the piggery; beyond that point there was bush and trees. The boar followed the fence along to the corner. I felt gamer now – I had the trees and scrub to run to if he got out.

Being a boy, I couldn't resist heaving a rock at the boar. When I did this he made one terrific charge at the fence and came straight through and after me. I ran for a large tree leaning at about a forty-five degree angle. It was a sheoak tree with a lot of small limbs attached to its trunk and, with the boar right on my heels, I bounded up it. I had never known my luck. I was just in time – another two yards and he would have had me.

The boar tried to climb the tree but without success. So there I was, up in this tree. It was the nicest tree I had known, and I was pretty safe as long as I could stay where I was. But what about the horses? The sun had begun to rise. The boar at first sat on his haunches looking up at me. Then he rooted a furrow under the tree big enough for his body and laid down.

I was trying to think of a way out of this pickle that I was in. The sun was getting well up into the sky, and guessing by the way my bottom and legs were aching, I had been there about an hour or so. I broke off some small branches and used them as spears. Each time I speared the boar he would get up, walk around the tree, let out a roar, then go back to his furrow and lie down again.

Then, looking down to the house, I saw Frank walking towards us. This horrified me and I wondered how I could warn him about the boar. I made up my mind to call out to him when he got within hearing distance. But Frank had other ideas. He took no notice of me, although I was yelling at the top of my voice. I paused to hear what he was calling out to me and I heard him saying, 'I'll give you bird-nesting when I send you to get the horses.' I called out to him that the boar was loose and that he was here under the tree, but Frank was too riled up and kept coming. Then all at once the boar got up and bounded towards him. As soon as Frank knew the danger he turned and ran for the house.

It was downhill and if anyone had told me that Frank could run as fast as he did I wouldn't have believed him. He had a little luck because at one stage the boar almost grabbed him. Frank was running along the side of the track and there was a heap of stones about two feet high. Frank jumped this but the boar, being so intent on getting Frank, didn't see the stones and struck them with his front legs. He fell heavily and that saved Frank.

Frank got inside the house and slammed the door shut. I got down out of the tree and set off for the horses. Then I heard two loud gun shots almost together and I wondered if he had shot the boar. When I returned to the house I saw the boar lying dead about ten feet from the door of the house. Mum had told me several times about Frank's temper but this was the first time I had seen him properly raged.

My feelings had changed several times during the few minutes of the race between the pig and old Frank. At first I felt amused, then my feelings turned to fear as the boar was catching him, then relief when the boar fell. The fear again gripped me until Frank dashed through the door and shut it. When this happened I felt complete relief.

Frank never said a word when I returned to the house for my breakfast. He looked terribly upset. When Mum gave me my breakfast she asked me what had made the boar get through the pig paddock. I said that I didn't know but that he had seemed extra savage that morning.

Old Frank usually never took the team out until after the midday meal. That morning he went over and told Jack Connor, Mum's brother, what had happened. When he returned he was very upset and I heard him say to Mum that her brother was a dirty scoundrel. She didn't like this and they had a real go-in. At first I thought he was going to hit her but he didn't. He went over to the stable and harnessed the horses and took them out ploughing – he wouldn't stop to have his dinner.

When I went into dinner Mum remarked, 'Now Bert, you have seen Frank in a temper. What do you think of it?' I said that he goes pretty mad and she said that if he ever got that way to keep away from him. She said that he soon cooled down and that he would be all right again that night. I asked what her brother said about the shooting of his boar. She told me that he had made Frank pay ten pounds. He thought that the boar was worth that but they knew it had only cost him two pounds. Mum said, 'Jack is like that. He would take his own mother down if he could.'

When Frank came in that night he had gotten over the whole upset and was quite jolly. He said to me, 'What went through your mind Bert, when the boar was chasing me down the hill?' I told him about my changed feelings. He laughed and said that he had never got to the house quicker and that the boar nearly had him once, but fell behind. He could almost feel the boar's teeth. He didn't know what had happened because he didn't have time to look behind. I told him about the rocks and said that I felt sure they had saved his life. He said, 'Oh well, it's over now. Did Mum tell you what that miserable sod valued that boar at? To think that I nearly lost my life.'

The next morning he sent me over to the plough to get a swingle bar and set of chains. He brought a harnessed horse up to the house and fixed a chain around the pig's head and dragged it into a timbered paddock where we piled up logs and bushes over it and burnt it.

13

KILLING THE PIG

Frank finished his fallowing about the end of October 1906, and things went fine until Christmas time. Three days before Christmas Frank suggested that we kill a large porker. Mum said that it was a grand idea. They had about forty pigs at the large porker size. Then Mum asked who would kill it. She said, 'You can't very well ask Jack on account of what has happened to his boar.' (Jack was a butcher by trade before he settled on the land.) Old Frank said, 'Not to worry. I've seen him kill hundreds so I'll kill it. Anyway, it is only a porker and it's different from killing a big pig.'

So two days before Christmas, I was told to light a fire near the shed close to the house. I had to pile large stones on each side of where the fire was to be lit, and put two iron bars from one wall of stones to the other. These iron bars had to be far enough apart to stand three kerosene tins full of water side by side on them, so that when I put the fire under them, the water would come to the boil. We needed boiling water to scald and clean the pig.

Frank told me to have the water boiling so we could clean the pig at about four o'clock in the afternoon. A few minutes before four, he turned up with a knife and we went to the pig-sties. I had some grain in a bucket to put into a small sty to coax some of the pigs in. When Frank picked out the one he wanted to kill, I was to shut the gate to keep it in. He said that when he grabbed the pig I was to let the others out and shut the gate again.

When he grabbed the pig by its back leg it started to struggle and squeal. I opened the gate and all the small pigs bolted out, but the two sows that were in there didn't waste any time in coming to the aid of the one Frank was struggling with. It was squealing blue murder and one of the sows grabbed Frank by the leg. I grabbed a stick and hit her over the snout. She let go of Frank and ran out, but then the other sow attacked him. He yelled to me to shut the gate. This I did and jumped over the fence out of the way. Frank was holding the pig he wanted by one of its hind legs, and using the knife in his other hand on the sow as she rushed him. He sliced her snout with the knife. I opened the gate again and the sow, with her snout pouring blood, bolted out.

Frank let go of the pig he was holding and went after the sow, waving the knife at her. I managed to slam the gate shut, stopping the pig he wanted to kill from getting out. Frank chased the sow for a while, but soon gave up and came back to where I was. He was white with rage, his trousers were badly torn, and so was his leg. When I said that he should go and get his leg attended to, he said, 'If it's the last thing I do, I'll kill that bastard of a pig!' I drew his attention to the pig that he wanted. 'Oh!' he said, 'you managed to keep it from getting away. Good boy.'

I suggested that if we lifted the pig over the side of the sty we would have no interference from the other pigs. So Frank got over the sty first and I dragged the pig to where he could reach it. He took hold of the pig's back legs and I grabbed it by the ears and we lifted it over the fence. Then I got over and all was ready for the killing.

Frank said that he had seen Jack kill many pigs this size and that he always sat them up on their bottoms, holding them between his legs, clasping one hand over the snout and bottom jaw. If this is done, the pig cannot bite, and you have one hand free to stick it with the knife.

So Frank sat the pig on its bottom and grabbed the snout with one hand, like a professional slaughterman. I handed him the knife. He looked at me and said, 'I've seen Jack kill dozens of pigs this size, but I'm not sure whether he stuck the knife straight in and down or a little to the left. What do you think Bert?' I replied that I thought it was straight in and then straight down. Frank said that he thought pigs were similar to us inside and so the heart would be a little to the left.

While he was deciding what he was going to do, the pig was trying to get away. Frank let one of his fingers slip into the side of the pig's mouth and the pig closed its jaw on it. That started something. Frank let out a yell and plunged the knife into the pig's neck, a little to the left. Then he let go of the pig, expecting it to die. What a surprise he got when the pig got up and ran away. It was bleeding, running on three legs and squealing for its life. Frank took off after it, waving the bloody knife.

We were in the paddock where Frank had had hay a week or so before. It had been a beautiful crop of oats and was all in stooks. So there was the wounded pig and Frank, dodging around these hay stooks. Frank ran after that pig until he was completely knocked out. Finally the pig ran into a large stook to try to hide, and Frank caught it.

However, while Frank was chasing the pig he had lost the knife. So there he was, holding the pig by one of its back legs, so tired that he sat down on the ground, still holding the squealing pig, and yelling at me to find the knife.

All this time Mum was waiting, with the water boiling, for us to bring the pig for scalding. We were at this time about half a mile from the house. I found the knife and brought it back to Frank, who was so mad he had been kicking the pig and belting it over the ears with his fists. Mum came to see what was going on and asked him what was wrong. He yelled what went wrong and what didn't go wrong, and she said, 'There's no sense in knocking the pig about, it will be so badly bruised it will go bad.' Frank replied, 'Go away woman and look after your own work.' With that he sat the pig on his back again and stuck it. Again it ran away. Mum called him a cruel madman, and with that he threw the knife as far away as he could and went home, leaving us to manage the best way we could.

We gave chase to the poor devil of a pig and luckily it ran back to the pig-sty where we cornered it. I held it while Mum went and found the knife. Then we sat it up and she held its front legs while I stuck it as I had seen Jack do. The pig staggered a few yards, then fell over and bled to death in a few minutes. I went home and got the wheelbarrow and we lifted the pig in and wheeled it back to the house. Mum had left the fire stoked up and we found that the water was still boiling.

Now to scald and clean the pig was a two-man job. Mum had a large tub near the fire and she had arranged a large board to put the pig on after this. The pig had to be placed bodily into the tub, with enough hot water at a temperature right for scalding (two buckets of boiling water to half a bucket of cold). The pig then had to be turned in this water until the outside skin and hair came off easily. Finally it had to be put onto the board and rubbed all over until the hair and outside skin came off. The body and legs of a pig are very white and clean when it's washed down.

Mum and I set about to try and clean this pig on our own, as Frank was nowhere to be found. Mum made the water right for scalding, and as the pig was nearly cold and getting stiff, she only put in a small part of cold water. She said it would be okay because the body heat had mostly left the pig.

Just then Frank came to see what was happening. He was quite over his temper and he said that he and Mum would lift the pig into the water. Mum got hold of the back legs and Frank the front, and they lifted it up over the tub to let it down gently. But Frank suddenly let go of the front legs and the front part fell with a flop and splash, spilling hot water all over his legs and into his boots, badly scalding both his feet. He let out a yell and ran over to the house. Mum let go of her end of the pig and went to see how badly Frank was burnt.

The pig was half in and half out of the water, a lot of which had been spilt. There was still one more tin of water boiling on the fire so I got a dipper and ladled the right proportions of hot and cold water into a bucket and poured this over the parts of the pig that weren't already scalded. I kept rubbing the pig with a stick until the hair came off clean. I wasn't strong enough to lift the pig out of the tub, and I knew that if it was left in the hot water too long the hair wouldn't come off. So I turned the tub onto its side and let the hot water drain off and cleaned the hair and outer skin off the best I could.

Mum fixed Frank and put him to bed, then joined me and helped finish cleaning the pig. We carried it to the shed nearby and fixed a small bar to its back legs. Then we tied a rope to the bar and put it over a rafter in the roof, and between the two of us we got the pig hung up, head downwards. Then Mum washed it all over and it looked good. She put the tub under the pig and cut the insides out, keeping the liver and the heart as they are good to eat. By the time we had finished (my first active part in killing a pig, and I hoped it would be the last), it was nearly eight o'clock.

Frank's feet were badly burnt and he wouldn't be able to walk for a few days. He was laid up all that Christmas and into the New Year.

14

MUM'S SNAKE

When Frank was well enough to work again he started to harvest his crop. The only method for harvesting was to strip the crop with a machine called a stripper. This had a comb arrangement that could be lowered or raised according to the height of the crop and it had to be kept just below the grain heads. The grain was carried up a broad elevator or chute. It was then beaten and threshed and ended up in a big box-like holder. When the box was full the driver would pull the machine out of the crop, and by opening a door at the back of the holder, he could rake the contents of the box out onto a large tarpaulin spread on level ground.

Each time the box on the machine was emptied it was my job to shovel the grain up into as small a heap as possible and keep it heaped up. This went on until the whole of that patch or paddock was stripped.

The reason for putting the strippings into one heap was to have the wheat ready for the winnower. This was a machine for cleaning grain and was operated by a group of men who travelled around from farm to farm. It usually took three or four men to operate it. One man turned a handle that worked the machine and another ladled the threshed wheat into it.

The winnower had sieves and a fan; the sieves were on rockers that worked from side to side like a dryblower, and the fan blew the chaff and straw away as the wheat fell through the sieves. There were generally three sieves – the two top ones cleaned the wheat enough for market, and the bottom one, which was shorter than the others, caught the small grain and cracked wheat, which ran down a chute to be bagged for stock feed. The good wheat was also bagged by the machine. The man turning the handle worked the blowers and sieves and the elevator all at once. It was hard work and the farmer paid the men so much per bag of clean wheat.

The wheat bags held four bushels in those days. Frank and I had to sew the tops of the wheat bags up when they were taken off the winnower. They were then ready to take to the nearest siding. In this case the nearest railway station was twenty miles away. A man with a team of eight horses hitched to a large boxed wagon carted the wheat for Frank at so much per bag. It took all the strength I could muster to up-end one of those bags of wheat.

Growing wheat in those days was a gamble. The only fertilizer they had was Thomas's cereal fertilizer ('Thomas's manure'). This came in one hundredweight bags and had to be used very sparingly because it was so costly.

Frank's wheat crop turned out to be extra good. It covered five bags to the acre, and that was a good crop in those days.

After harvest, with the hay and wheat all carted, the burning season was getting near. Frank and I had about eight acres left to clear; the big timber had been burnt down the previous winter and all the small timber and scrub had been chopped to ground level. While waiting for the burning season to open, we were busy clearing a firebreak around the land we intended to burn and clear. This was about half a mile from the house.

Mum had an arrangement to give us an idea when it was lunch-time. She would peg a white tea towel on the clothes line near the house at ten minutes to midday. By the time we got home and had a clean up, lunch would be ready.

One day, at the signal, we started walking towards the house. We were about fifty yards away when we heard Mum let out a terrible scream. She came running out of the lavatory holding up her dress with one hand and clutching her bottom with the other. She was yelling out loudly, 'I've been bitten by a snake!' Frank and I ran to her and helped her inside the house. Frank took her into the bedroom and told me to run over to the Connors' place and get Jack to bring his horse and sulky to take Mum to the doctor. It was a little over two miles to Jack's and I ran all the way. It was a very hot day and I was done in when I got there. It took me a few minutes before I could explain what had happened.

Jack wasn't long putting the horse in the sulky and we drove back. Mum was crying when we got there. Frank told Jack that the snake bite was very distinct and he had cut it with a razor and sucked out as much blood as he could.

Mum looked very pale and was badly shocked. After giving me some quick instructions as to what to do while they were away, they set out to get Mum to the doctor in Narrogin as soon as possible. Jack's sulky horse was a beauty, one of the best in the district, and although Frank and Jack were at loggerheads over the boar, they had forgotten about it with the crisis in hand. The trip to Narrogin would take them all afternoon and well into the night.

After they had gone I got a nice handy stick, about four feet long, and went into the lavatory after the snake. This lavatory was mainly used by Mum; I never used it and Frank only sometimes. It was made of galvanised iron and had a small hole cut out at the back to allow Mum to slide the pan in. (The pan was an old kerosene tin cut off to fit.) A bag was hung onto the back wall to cover the hole. With the stick I approached the lavatory, carefully looking in and around, but I couldn't see any sign of the snake. I lifted the bag up very slowly (I was scared stiff), then I heard something move. Quickly I dropped the bag and jumped back. Then all was quiet again. I lifted the bag once more. This time I noticed some feathers, and as I lifted the bag further, more feathers came into view. All at once I knew what had bitten Mum. It wasn't a snake and all my fears turned to mirth. In fact, I almost lost control of myself with laughing.

Mum's snake was a hen. The hen had made a nest close to the pan to lay her eggs and Mum hadn't noticed her. She didn't mind Mum sitting on the lavatory at first, but when she went broody – a hen can be placid while laying and vicious when broody – she had decided to peck Mum on the bottom.

Mum was very frightened of snakes and also terribly frightened of dingoes. She wouldn't venture outside on her own, except in special circumstances.

They were away for nearly four days. When they came home Mum seemed jolly and didn't show any ill effects from the shock she'd had. I asked her how she was and she said that the doctor had said that he didn't think it was a snake that had bitten her and if it was it wasn't poisonous. She asked if I'd looked around the lavatory for the snake and I said that I had and that I had found the thing that had bitten her. I said that it was still in the lavatory and I offered to show it to her.

We went to the lavatory and I lifted up the bag. She looked under and exclaimed, 'Good God. No!' She said that the doctor had said it looked like beak marks but it never occurred to her that a hen might have done it. She stood for a while and seemed to be thinking, or working something out in her mind. Then suddenly she said, 'Did you have any visitors while we were away or see anyone?' I said, 'No.' 'Well,' she said, 'don't you say anything, not even to Frank or anybody, about this. If you do I'll be the laughing stock of the district.' She said, 'Bert, I love you, but if you tell anyone about this I'll kill you.' I promised not to tell anyone. Nothing more was said about the 'snake bite'.

15

A PROPOSITION

Frank and I finished the fire-breaks, and Frank ploughed around the fallen timber that we were going to burn up as soon as the fire season opened and the first still day came. We would set it alight all around the outside of the eighty acres, and let it burn quietly inwards. That was the correct way to burn off in the wheat-belt in those days. If a fire got away into virgin bush it could do untold damage to neighbouring properties.

Some of the neighbours, and Jack Connor, who was friendly with Frank again, came and helped put the fire through. One very hot day, at about eleven in the morning, they set it alight. We kept walking around the burning patch all day, throwing lighted pieces of wood back from the edge into the burnt part so a spark wouldn't set alight the outside dry grass. This went on until evening. When the danger of a spark had gone, the neighbours and Jack went home.

This helping was the usual neighbourly co-operation between new and old settlers in the early days of the great wheat-belt of Western Australia. Nobody expected payment or gave any payment for any help no matter what the problem.

We commenced the clearing the day after the fire went through. I liked this work – it was very dirty. My job was picking up all the small pieces of wood that hadn't completely burnt, packing them into heaps around stumps, and keeping the heaps stacked and burning until the stumps were burnt down to ground level.

When the clearing was finished we had to go back over the cleared ground and fill in all the stump holes. Some of the stumps were from highly inflammable trees and burnt down into the ground and into the large roots under ground for several feet.

Mum used to come and help with the clearing nearly every afternoon. She always put on a bag apron when doing things that were dirty to handle. Clearing was dirty work as all the wood was blackened from the fire.

In the paddock we were clearing, Frank had found a damp patch of ground on the surface a year before. He dug a hole there and it filled with good fresh water. This was what they called a soak. Water would sometimes seep up like this through a crack or thin spot in the layer of clay and make the surface damp. By digging down through the clay to let the water come up, a soak was formed.

Frank had made a large hole about five feet deep and eight feet across and laid large stones inside the hole for a wall. This hole filled up to the surface with beautiful fresh water. We watered all the horses and cows at this soak, and carted water for the house, and all the other uses. Many settlers had trouble getting permanent water on their properties and had to cart water from Government wells miles away, so a soak like that one was a blessing to a farmer.

One windy day we were working near the soak. Mum and I were packing wood onto stumps and lighting it, and Frank was about one hundred yards away rolling some heavy logs together to burn into smaller pieces for handling. The wind was blowing at about thirty miles an hour, away from Frank towards us.

Suddenly I heard Mum scream. I looked up and saw that she was almost enveloped in flames. She was about fifteen yards away from the soak and I was about twenty yards away from her. I ran to her and pushed her bodily into the soak. She fell from my push, almost head first, and went under water. Then she stood up and called to me, 'Look out!' And in almost the same breath, 'No Frank no! No, he saved my life. I was on fire.' Frank had seen me push her into the soak but hadn't seen why. He had picked up a stick about four feet long and one and a half inches thick, and intended to wooden me out. He would have too if Mum hadn't called out. He apologised to me and said that when he heard the scream and looked up, he thought I was attacking Mum.

My hands were badly burnt because I had pushed Mum in front of me for about ten yards, and the back portion of her clothing had been blazing. Poor Mum was sopping wet to the skin but wasn't burnt. They hadn't noticed my burnt hands in the excitement. Frank took Mum home to change her clothes and came back a little while later. He had a cup of tea with Mum, then brought me a jug of tea and sat on a large stone while I had it. It wasn't until then that he noticed my burnt hands. They had several large blisters. Frank had a look at them and straight away took me to the house, and Mum washed them and put some ointment on them and bandaged them up. I was unable to use my hands for over a week.

This incident made both Frank and Mum take a greater liking to me, and the next day Frank said he was raising my wage to ten shillings a week and full keep. This thrilled me and made me very pleased with myself. He also told me that they were going to put a proposition to me, and if I liked it they would go ahead and make it a reality. He said Mum would tell me about it later.

The next day Mum was talking to me in the kitchen. She suddenly looked at me and said, 'You will be thirteen years old next August, Bert, and you haven't had any schooling have you?' I said, 'That's true.' Then she said, 'How would you like to be our son? We haven't any children of our own and Frank and I would like to adopt you. Would you like that?' She continued, 'You don't have to answer me straight away. We are very sincere about this and of course we would have to see your grandma and uncle, and your mother would have to consent. We feel sure that the authorities will agree. If you would like to be our son and the adoption can be arranged, we will send you away to a boarding-school and have you properly educated so you will be able to read and write and get to know all about what is going on in the world. You think it over and let us know later.'

It didn't take me long to decide. Here were two lovely people who had treated me better than anyone, except Grandma, so of course I agreed. I told them my decision that evening. They were delighted and Mum went crazy and kissed me and Frank hugged me. A few days later we drove over to Uncle's to talk it over with Grandma, as she was the only one that mattered as far as I was concerned.

We arrived at Uncle's place at about ten o'clock in the morning. Grandma, Aunt Alice and the girls were home but Uncle Archie and cousin Bill were out working in one of the paddocks, and we had to wait until they came home for lunch. While waiting, Frank and Mum had a long talk with Grandma and Aunt Alice, and the girls asked me all sorts of questions about the farm, what work I had to do, the wages I was getting and all about Mum and Frank.

When Uncle came home he insisted that we all stay and have lunch with them. Bill and I unharnessed the horse and put him in Uncle's stable and gave him a feed. I had my lunch with the girls and Bill in the kitchen. Uncle Archie, Aunt Alice, Grandma, Mum and Frank had theirs in another room so they could discuss the adoption without us kids hearing what was going on. I never told the girls or Bill anything.

After lunch I was called into the room where Uncle and the others were. Uncle told me that they had talked the adoption over from all its angles and he, Grandma and Aunt were all in agreement. He said they had agreed to all meet in Narrogin where they would talk the matter

70

over with the authorities. So, on the set date, we all met in Narrogin, and Mum and Frank, Grandma and Uncle Archie went to see someone at the Police Station.

While I waited I walked around the town. Narrogin was one of the largest towns of the fringe of the wheat-belt. It had two hotels, two boarding-houses, two shops, a doctor, a chemist and a small hospital on a hill away from the railway station. It was on the Great Southern railway line and a train went through once a day each way from Perth to Albany.

When I returned to the Police Station I waited until Frank came out and called me inside. Uncle, Grandma and Mum were all sitting around a large table and an official-looking man was sitting at the far end. There was a policeman there also, with three stripes on his sleeve.

The official-looking man said to me, 'Is your name Albert Barnett Facey?' and I said, 'Yes, sir.' He then said, 'Mr and Mrs Phillips want to adopt you. Do you agree to this adoption?' I said, 'Yes, sir, very much.' He then said, 'So you know what this would mean to you?' I said that I believed that I would be their son and would be bound to them for the rest of my life. He then said that if I did anything wrong against their wishes they could punish me or give me a whipping. This stunned me for a few seconds. I knew what a whipping was like. My hesitation made the official look up and then Grandma said, 'Excuse me, sir. I think you should understand that when he was ten years old, he was flogged with a horse-whip by a coward of a man.' She told him about what had happened to me at Cave Rock and said that I still carried the scars. With that I was told by the official to take off my coat and shirt. I did this and Grandma pointed out the still visible scars. The official said, 'Not that kind of whipping son, that is shocking.'

The policeman then told the official that an officer had been sent out to find someone willing to testify in court about the flogging, but although there was plenty of evidence, it was impossible to get anyone to come forward because of fear of revenge. He said that the old woman, her sons and their friends were a bad lot, and that some of the sons had done time for horse and cattle stealing. The official then said to me, 'We'll cut out the word whipping. Do you still want these people to adopt you?' I replied, 'Yes sir.'

A few minutes later we left the Police Station. Uncle had a large blue paper which was something to do with the adoption because he said, 'We will have to get an envelope to put this in and post it.' The next day we went home.

Frank had arranged for his brother-in-law, Jack Connor, to look after things while we were away. We found everything okay when we arrived home. My hands were better now and we continued with the clearing. We had a lot of heavy rain the day after we finished clearing, so Frank started ploughing and would soon be getting ready for seeding.

The Government had started a mail delivery once a week. It came from Narrogin along a bush track through the lower part of the wheat-belt to a place called Gillimanning. The mail coach stayed at Gillimanning overnight and returned to Narrogin the next day, a distance, overall, of about sixty-five miles. The coach was a light buggy and had two beautiful horses. The mailman delivered mail to all letter-boxes placed in a suitable positon close to the track, and the farmer had to have his full name painted on the box. The mailman would also pick up any letters for posting, but they had to be properly stamped. Our letter-box was about three miles from our home and I had to go and get the mail, if any, on mail days. Frank arranged to get papers by mail also.

It was early in May that a large letter came with O.H.M.S. on the top. I always got the mail about four o'clock in the afternoon on a Thursday. Frank was busy seeding and Mum always opened the mail after dinner when Frank was home. This large letter had something to do with the adoption, because Mum and Frank were both quiet after reading it. They filled in a large white form, and the next day, sent me over to a spot on the road about four miles away where the mailman passed. It was early in the morning and I had to wait until the mailman came to give him two letters. One was large and the other was ordinary. Having done this I returned home to finish doing my usual chores.

Mum called me in and told me that there was some hitch about the adoption and that the letters that I had posted were to my mother and to the Government. She said that they wouldn't know the outcome until they got a reply from my mother, who had refused to sign the adoption paper. Mum said, 'We wrote her a letter explaining what we were prepared to do for you and asking her to give you a chance, and to ask why she didn't give her consent.'

It was in June that a letter from my mother came in reply to the one that they had written. When this letter was opened, Mum looked at Frank and said nothing. We had been so happy up to this point. They never read the letter to me but they said that the adoption was off. My mother wouldn't give her consent.

16

A BITTER END

From then on the Phillips' attitude to me changed. I did not know why. I was still doing my work; I worked hard and tried to please them all I could, but they wouldn't let me join in when they were talking and never took me with them anymore when they went to a dance or out visiting. I asked Frank one day if he would agree to me buying myself a push-bike so I could ride over and see Grandma occasionally and be able to go places. He refused, telling me that my place was there and not running around the country.

About the middle of March, Frank accused me of taking apples from some delicious variety apple trees in his garden. He told me to leave the apples alone, but being a boy and having little or no fruit, the temptation was too great.

Each tree had twenty or thirty apples. I think Frank must have counted them, because one morning I heard him say to Mum that there were two more apples missing. He came to me a little later and told me to get a spade and dig around each apple tree till I was at least twelve feet away from the trunk. He also said, 'Don't go taking any of the apples.'

I thought that this was mean. Anyway, I did as he required and never touched the apples. With doing my usual chores each day, it took me two days to finish digging around the four trees. Then Frank made me get the garden rake and smooth the ground where I had dug, so that anyone who wanted the apples couldn't get them without leaving tracks. So my apple supply was cut off.

Or was it? At first I worked out that if I got my two apples (that's all I ever took at once), then raked over the ground, he wouldn't be any the wiser. But his cunning ways stopped this – he locked the rake in the tool shed.

Now I had become as determined as he was that I was to have my two apples each day. I found a way around the problem, and next morning, two more apples were missing. Frank told Mum and they pondered over it, Mum making all kinds of suggestions. She said, 'Set a trap.' They did this, but every morning two more apples were gone. They were really baffled.

I thought then that they might guard the trees. A neighbour suggested that possums may be taking the apples, so Frank set snares. He never caught a possum but still the two apples were missing each morning. This went on until all the apples were gone. I often wondered if they had found out how I got those apples.

This is how I did it. One day down at the stable, I noticed two six foot lengths of guttering soldered together, and tied up over the part of the roof where the horses went in and out in the winter time. The guttering was tied very loosely and I found it was easily removed and put back. So after Frank and Mum had gone to bed and their light had gone out, I would wait until I could hear Frank snoring – he snored loudly and a lot (Mum was always complaining about it) – and then I would sneak out and get the guttering. I would take it to the apple tree that I had selected during the day and lift one end up to a nice red apple. Then I would move the end up and down until the apple stem gave away, and the apple would simply run down the guttering to me. I suppose it could be called stealing, but nobody was hurt and the apples were very nice. If they had given me an apple now and then I wouldn't have dreamed of taking them.

I made up my mind to go out occasionally for a day, usually Sunday. I would get up early and do my chores and cut enough fire wood to do for the day. Sometimes I would go over to a neighbour's place. Some neighbours who always made me welcome were the Bibbys. They were middle-aged and had no children, but were very fond of them. Their place was four miles away and I had to walk. I had been there several times with the Phillips. The Bibbys wouldn't hear of me walking back home when I visited them and would drive me back to our gate. They told me to come as often as I liked.

Mr Bibby was a medium-sized man and very jolly. He was very fond of telling funny stories, and Mrs Bibby was very nice, but she wasn't enjoying good health. They had a boy working for them who was two years older than me but he didn't know much about farming. He was from the city and didn't like the country. He was lazy too. I didn't like him. He always called the country boys 'country bumpkins'.

On one of my visits Mr Bibby asked me how I was getting along with my job, and I told him not too good since my mother had refused to sign the adoption papers. He said that this had hurt the Phillips very much, but he didn't think they should take it out on me. He went on to say that he didn't want me to think he was trying to take me away from the Phillips, but should anything happen so that I was looking for another job, they would be glad to give me one on the same terms as the Phillips. I said that I wouldn't like to be the cause of the boy losing his job. He said, 'Don't worry about that. We're sending him back to his people in the city. He is no good to us.' Now with the knowledge that I would be welcomed, I liked the idea.

About two weeks later Frank made me drive four horses pulling a three-furrow stump jump-plough. He told me I was big enough to learn to do all kinds of farm work. I had seen this ploughing done and knew how to do it, but what I didn't like was that I had to do all the chores around the place as well as get the horses in early in the morning, harness them and take them to do the fallowing. I was working from five in the morning until seven at night while Frank was the gentleman of the place.

After a week of this I said to Frank, 'Do I get a raise in my wages while I am doing a man's work or do you expect me to do all this for ten shillings a week and keep?' That started something. He told me that if I wasn't satisfied to get out. I never answered him but went about my work.

Three days later, a nasty boil formed on the back of my neck. It was very painful and driving the plough didn't help. There was a seat on the plough and the bumping of the plough going over the uneven ground and stones made the pain worse. After the boil came to a head and burst I was much relieved, but a few days later two more boils came up in the same place. They were twice as large as the first one and more painful.

One morning I complained and said I couldn't stand the jolting of the plough. I asked Frank to relieve me of the ploughing until the boils were better. He looked at them a few seconds, then grabbed me around the neck and started squeezing the boils. The pain from this was terrible. I swung my hand towards him and struck him in the stomach, knocking him down. Mum ran out demanding to know what had happened and I told her.

I didn't take any chances with Frank. I knew what a vile temper he had, so I went into the shed near the house and locked myself in. I expected him to come looking for me as soon as he had recovered enough. But to my surprise, he sent Mum out to tell me he wanted to talk to me inside. I went inside. I wasn't very brave about it though and went in behind Mum, so that if it was a trap I had a clear get-a-way.

Frank said, 'Why did you hit me?' I told him that I didn't know where I had hit him because I was in so much pain. I had to do something to make him let go, so I struck out in his direction and hit him in the stomach. 'All right,' he said, 'I shouldn't have done what I did, but I will not employ you any longer.' With that he paid me what was coming to me. I packed my bags, or roll, slung it over my shoulder and walked off.

As I was leaving Mrs Phillips called to me, 'You had better come and have some breakfast before you go.' I called back, 'No, thank you,' and continued on my way. All of my hopes of a permanent home were dashed because of the actions of an unworthy mother. I never found out what actually happened, but I think that she probably asked for money in exchange for me.

17

THE BIBBYS

I set out along the track leading to Bibby's house. My swag was heavy so I rested several times. The first time I rested was after I got out the back gate of Phillips' property. I suddenly became very depressed and I couldn't help it, I cried and cried. I felt alone in the world again. Why was it, I asked myself, that my mother had deserted me when I was two years old and didn't care if I lived or died, but was still allowed to prevent me from being adopted by someone decent who wanted to send me to school and give me something that most other kids had, a home and comfort? After awhile I pulled myself together and again started off, towards another job I hoped.

I arrived at Bibby's place before lunchtime. The dogs came out barking when I neared the gate leading to the house. (They had a six foot fence around the house and orchard, enclosing about two acres of land.) Mrs Bibby came out to see what the dogs were barking at. She stared at me, then all of a sudden she commenced to laugh. She said, 'I didn't know you. Your swag is bigger than you are. Surely you never carried it all the way from Phillips' place.' 'I did,' I said. She continued, 'Why didn't you leave it there? We could have fetched it for you in the sulky.' I said, 'I wasn't sure of getting a job here, and I'd want my swag if I had to move on.'

Mrs Bibby noticed how careful I was when I moved my head and she asked me what was wrong. I told her that I had two boils on the back of my neck. She asked me to show her. I did, and she took me inside and washed the boils in a fluid – Condy's Crystals, I think. Then she put a bandage around my neck covering the boils. This treatment eased the pain.

A few minutes later Mr Bibby arrived home for lunch. He greeted me, and Mrs Bibby told him about me leaving the Phillips and how it came about. He laughed and said, 'I'd give a tenner to have seen you drop him. It must have knocked the wind out of him or else he would have tried to knock you down. I always reckoned he had no guts.' Mr

Bibby then said, 'Do you want to work for us?' I said, 'I would like to if you'll have me.' He replied, 'Of course we will. We are not as well off as the Phillips are but we have plenty of work. We are doing our clearing on the Government grant of one pound an acre and we don't get paid until it's cleared. They won't pay till we have twenty-five acres or more cleared, because they have to send an inspector to measure up. He gives us a cheque on the spot. I'm telling you this because we may not be able to pay your wages until we receive the cheques. We will pay you the same as you were getting at the Phillips' place. I believe that was ten shillings a week and full keep. Will you be satisfied with that?' I said that that would be fine. 'Then you will not have to work as hard,' he said, 'that I will promise you. We don't work long hours, but we work hard while we are working.'

The Bibbys were very nice people. They had only been there about two and a half years and had come from the Goldfields. They'd taken up one thousand acres on conditional purchase and they both had a homestead block of one hundred and sixty acres. They had one hundred and fifty acres cleared and in crop – one hundred acres of wheat and fifty of oats for hay. They had most of their land fenced, and owned cows, a very nice team of six horses, about twenty pigs, some fowls and geese, and also about thirty sheep and twenty lambs. It was lovely land, as good as the Phillips' but not so rocky. It was more level and easier to cultivate and clear.

The Bibbys had a four-roomed house. They gave me a room all to myself and a lovely single bed with sheets and blankets and a bedspread. It was the first time that I had sheets to sleep between since we left Victoria. It seemed too good to be true. They wouldn't let me work until my boils got better. Mr Bibby insisted that I call him Charlie.

I settled in with these nice people who were struggling, like many. For a start, my work was chopping the small trees and scrub off level with the ground. All trees six inches to a foot thick, Charlie and I chopped down at waist height, then we knocked the bark off the stump and put the pieces around the base. By doing this the stump and bark would dry off, and when the burning season came in February, a lot of the stumps would burn down to ground level. Those that didn't would get scorched and would easily burn when we came to them when clearing. The very big trees, from one foot upwards, were burnt down. I liked chopping and burning down. It was hard work and I got big water blisters on my hands for the first week or so, but then my hands got used to it and became tough.

I had my thirteenth birthday the first week I was at the Bibby's. Nobody knew; I hadn't told them as birthdays were nothing to me. They came and went. I used to hear a lot about birthday parties from time to time, but who was going to bother about me.

We got on fine, the Bibbys and me. Charlie said that I was real good with an axe. I was big for my age, and although I never had any schooling, I could learn things, such as farm work, very quickly. I could ride a horse, harness a horse to a cart or wagon and drive a four-horse team.

Charlie worked hard on the chopping and burning down for two and a half months, and in that time the two of us had one hundred and thirty acres ready for firing in February. We had cleared a strip around it, and Charlie ploughed a fire-break so that when the fire was put through, it could be controlled. Charlie was so pleased with the work that we had done, he would skite about it to the neighbours when they came to visit.

Besides the chopping and burning down, we had to look after the stock morning and night. When I got out of bed in the morning at six o'clock, I would light the kitchen fire and put the kettle on, then call Mrs Bibby. Then I would feed the fowls and the pigs and let the sheep out. All the fowls had to be locked up and the sheep yarded at night, on account of the dingoes and native cats. We had to put the sheep where they could be seen during the day. Mrs Bibby spent a lot of time with the sheep when Charlie and I were working where we couldn't see them. The dingoes were very bad and the Bibbys had lost quite a few fowls and sheep during the daylight, so if we went away for the day, they had to be locked away.

I bought a 44 Winchester rifle from a travelling man. Charlie gave me permission to buy the rifle and some cartridges for twenty-five shillings. The man showed me how to use it. At first I was nervous, but it didn't take long to be able to hit a small jam tin at a one hundred yard distance.

One day Charlie and I took the two kangaroo dogs out for a run. There were plenty of kangaroos around so I took my rifle. We hadn't been gone for long when the dogs startled some kangaroos on the run and scattered them in all directions. One big boomer came towards us when the dogs were after the others. It was about a hundred yards away when I had my first shot, the first time I had shot at anything other than a target. Charlie said, 'You missed him.' Then the boomer slackened his pace and crouched as he was hopping, and finally fell. Charlie called, 'You got him, Bert.' And that was so. My first shot had killed the boomer.

Charlie's dogs never caught many 'roos. The undergrowth was thick and the 'roos could beat the dogs unless they got them out in the open. Charlie was very excited. The boomer had been hit through the chest and was dead when we ran to him. It was as much as Charlie and I could do to carry the body, even after Charlie had taken its insides out. Mrs Bibby was also delighted. It meant that they would have plenty of meat for their dogs and domestic cats. They had four cats; one was a lovely black-and-white, and he followed me all around when I was near the house.

It was now near the end of November 1907. In the slack two or three weeks until hay-cutting time, Charlie and I went out kangarooing many times and got quite a few. I shot several; some I only wounded but the dogs caught them and killed them. Charlie insisted that I keep the skins of all I shot or wounded. Mrs Bibby would take the skins into town when she went for stores and sell them for me (she always gave me the exact amount she received for them). Sometimes this would amount to several pounds. A large boomer skin was worth about three shillings, so I did quite well out of kangaroo skins. Nearly every evening, near dark, I used to take up a position in some scrub near the edge of a crop and wait for the 'roos to come to the crop for feed. I got a lot this way.

One day, in the second week of December, Charlie and I were putting down a foundation for a haystack big enough to hold about fifty tons of hay. (The foundation was made with logs laid one against the other on the ground creating a space large enough for the estimated stack). Suddenly we heard Mrs Bibby's geese making a loud terrified noise some two hundred yards away from us. Charlie said, 'Sounds like something is after them.' I grabbed my rifle and ran towards the geese. A dingo had killed one and was in the act of dragging it away. The dingo kept stopping as the goose was heavy and it had to keep spelling itself.

I waited my chance and when I got a clear view, I fired and shot the dingo dead. As I was about to run to the spot where it lay, I spotted another one in some scrub looking at me. It appeared to think I was unable to see it because it never moved, although I shifted my position. I moved over a few yards, then fired. The dingo sprang into the air, and for a second or two, I thought my shot had missed. Then, to my surprise, the dingo was bounding towards me. At first it was covering some six to seven yards with each bound. I was scared and unable to move for a few moments, then my fear turned to joy. After the dingo had covered some forty or fifty yards it fell into a heap, dead.

Charlie saw this and ran to me. He threw his arms around me and yelled, 'You're wonderful, Bert. Two shots, two dingoes. How about that!' After the excitement, he ran to Mrs Bibby who had heard the shots and had come out to see what was happening. Charlie called out, 'The dingoes got one of your geese but what do you think of our boy, he shot two of them.' By this time I had gone to make sure the dingoes were dead, and I noticed that the goose was still alive, though badly bitten. Charlie and Mrs Bibby examined it and said we would kill it and it would be all right to eat.

Charlie was a terrific skite and he told everyone about the incident, and I got many words of praise about my shooting. Charlie used to say to his neighbours and friends, 'The kid's only thirteen years old.'

Dingo scalps were worth twenty shillings each from the Government. This was paid as a bounty to encourage people to destroy the pests. It cost farmers a lot of money protecting their stock, especially sheep. It was a horrible sight to see what a dingo could do to a sheep in a few minutes.

Charlie had three paddocks fenced in for the sheep, but as these were not dog-proof, he set man traps outside the fencelines. The man traps were wide apart – six to seven traps were set around at intervals. Charlie put a notice close to the fence to warn people that man traps were set at or near that spot. An old trapper had shown him and told him all about the dingoes' cunning.

Charlie caught many kangaroos but only part of a dingo's leg. The traps worked though because, although Charlie didn't catch any, the dingoes were scared of them and stayed away.

Soon after this we started hay-cutting. A neighbour purchased a reaping binder and he and Charlie came to an understanding that Charlie could use the binder if he later lent the neighbour the harvester he had on order. The reaping binder was a machine that would cut the hay, pack it into sheaves, tie it with twine and drop the sheaves in rows. This made the hay much easier to stook, ready for carting. The harvester was a new invention that took the place of the stripper and the winnower. It stripped the wheat, then threshed it and cleaned it in one operation as it travelled through the crop. The clean wheat was elevated up into a large container where it could be fed into bags ready for market. We finished the hay-cutting Christmas Eve.

18

AN EVENTFUL CHRISTMAS

The Bibbys were very good Christmas caterers and put on a lovely Christmas dinner. Charlie invited Mrs Bibby's sister and her family down from the Goldfields for Christmas. The sister's name was Mrs Mutton and she was a very nice lady. She had two children – a boy four years old and a six-month-old baby girl.

After Christmas dinner, I asked Charlie if I could go over to Uncle's place in the afternoon to see Grandma. The Bibbys often gave me this pleasure and always lent me the sulky and horse for the trip. Their place was only seven miles from the McCalls. Charlie asked Mrs Bibby and they agreed that I should stay the night and come back the next day. This suited me fine, as it gave me lots of time to see and talk with the grand old lady. It was good of the Bibbys because it meant that they would have to look after the stock and do my chores while I was away.

I got away about two o'clock in the afternoon and arrived at Uncle's two hours later. They were all pleased to see me. Grandma's face always told me that she was pleased to see me, and she always wanted to know how I was being treated. Uncle Archie said, 'You have quite a name for shooting dingoes and 'roos.' Aunt Alice and my cousins wanted to know all about the shooting.

We all had a cup of tea, then I helped with the evening chores. Cousin Bill was anxious to get me alone to ask all about the rifle and how I came by it, and why I didn't bring it with me. He said to me, 'Do you think my dad would buy me one? There are plenty of 'roos and dingoes around here.' I said, 'Why don't you ask him. You're only two months younger than I am.' I told him that, with a little instruction, he should be able to shoot as good as anyone.

Bill's father didn't like firearms much and didn't like them being about, that's why I didn't bring my rifle with me on that day. Bill said, 'I'll ask Mum to ask him. I'm not game. You are lucky in a way, Bert. You haven't any father or mother to boss you around and you can do as you like.' I replied, 'Don't you worry about that, Bill. You have a home and loved ones, a father and mother to care for you. I wish I was like you many times.' I told him that the people I had been working for were not like my own – 'Most of them have no feeling for you and some can be very cruel – remember the flogging I got.' I said that the Phillips were all right and that the Bibbys were lovely people. 'They treat me just like I was their own son. It's just like my own home only it isn't. That's the difference, Bill. Sometimes I feel very lonely.'

And that's the way it was. On Sundays, when we didn't work much, I would often go into the bush and watch the birds and they were lovely. In some ways they were like me – they had to fend for themselves as soon as the mother bird thought that they were old enough. And there were always other birds and animals trying to catch them to eat them. That's how the bird and animal life goes, one cannot live without the other, from the largest bird right down to the smallest – the animals are the same.

We had our evening meal that night, all very happy, and later in the evening Grandma and I had a long talk. She told me that my mother had written to her saying that she may be going to Subiaco to live (Subiaco is a suburb of Perth), and when she did she would like the boys (meaning my brothers and I) to go and see her. Grandma said, 'Be careful Albert. She may only want your money, so don't tell her how much you have.' I told Grandma that I had promised the Bibbys that I would stay with them through the harvest and burning season and next year's cropping period, so I wouldn't be able to leave until next September. Grandma and I talked together until well after the others had gone to sleep. As we retired, I asked Grandma to call me early the next morning as I wanted to leave early.

At about five o'clock the next morning Grandma woke me. She had cooked me breakfast. She was always an early riser no matter what the weather was and had been down to the stable and watered and fed my horse. The rest were still in bed when I left. Grandma gave me a loving hug and kiss and made me promise to come to see her as often as I could. So after a short but pleasant visit, I left Uncle's at six in the morning.

It's strange, but although I have been earning my living since I was nine years old, I get a kind of knowing when something is wrong, and after I left Uncle's that morning that feeling came over me. It had come over me so many times before and had been true. I just couldn't think what could go wrong, or what had gone wrong, but there it was – something wasn't as it should be. I went along thinking along these lines. The pony knew she was going home and trotted along accordingly.

I arrived back at about eight o'clock and everybody seemed to be still in bed; the pigs hadn't been fed, the cows were waiting to be milked. Then I noticed that the sheep-yard gate was knocked down and I realised that something was wrong. I put the pony in the stable and ran to the house. The back door was open. I knocked and called out, but the only reply was the Muttons' baby crying. Then Mrs Mutton came out and told me that the men had taken more drink than they should and were very drunk and that Mrs Bibby had also had too much. Then she said, 'What is wrong Bert?' I said, 'The sheep have broken out of their yard. I'll have to try and find them.' So I got my rifle and set out to find the sheep.

It wasn't long before I found out what was wrong. I could see that something had frightened the sheep so that they crowded up against the gate and caused it to collapse. Then I noticed dog tracks following the sheep tracks and could see that dingoes had made them. (The dingo makes a track very different from a tame dog. The claws of the feet of the dingo dig deep into the ground and an ordinary dog's are more of a smoothing nature. It's as if a dingo runs on his claws.)

Within one hundred yards of the sheep-yard I found two dead sheep – they had been killed by dingoes. Their insides were ripped out and pieces of flesh were ripped out all over their bodies. A few yards further on were four more, one dead, and the other three so badly savaged I had to finish them. I followed the other sheep tracks and found more dead and many badly bitten. Then I found about sixteen, huddled in a heap in the corner of a twenty-five acre paddock. I drove all the sheep that could walk back to the yard and did the gate up, then went to the house to see if I could get help. Mrs Mutton didn't understand much about stock, and the others were too drunk and wouldn't wake up, so I had to do the best I could.

The dingoes had killed eleven sheep and twelve lambs, and eight more were badly bitten. I had to kill four that were too badly injured to save, and then doctor some of the others. Charlie had a mixture of castor oil, kerosene and whale oil that he put on the sheep to keep away the blow-flies. Blow-flies were bad on the sheep in the hot summer. I used some of this mixture on the injured sheep and lambs. As well as keeping blow-flies off, the kerosene in the mixture stopped infection and the castor oil stopped any chill. I wasn't strong enough to lift the big sheep up into the cart so I treated them where they lay. I managed to get the lambs home into the shed near the house.

By now it was midday. I milked the cows and turned them out. Mrs Bibby had sobered up enough to know what was wrong, and she managed to get Charlie awake although he seemed to be in a daze. At first he didn't seem to understand. I wanted him to come with me to help get the injured sheep home. I said, 'I can't shift them up into the cart,' and drove him down to where several of them lay. All of a sudden Charlie exclaimed, 'What in the hell went wrong!' I told him and that made him sober up quickly.

Later Mr Mutton joined us and we got all the injured sheep home. Then we carted the dead ones and put them in a heap near the inside of the house fence. The three of us set about skinning the sheep as the skins not too badly torn would be worth a few shillings when dried out ready for market. All the carcases were put into a copper to be cooked for the pigs.

So, taking count of the damage the dingoes had done that night, it was an expensive Christmas for the Bibbys, and the whole cause was booze. It wasn't until the next day that Charlie realised the full effect of the dingo attack. He estimated his loss at fifty pounds.

19

My Wild Life

Two days later, Charlie got a letter advising him that his Sunshine harvester had been forwarded to Cuballing, the nearest railway siding. This siding, on the Great Southern railway running from Perth to Albany, was twenty-four miles away.

The following day Charlie and I started on our way to bring the harvester home. We put a horse in the sulky, and loaded on all the harness and gear we would require to haul the harvester. It took four horses to pull it while it was working stripping the crop, but two could pull it easily at other times. We took all of one day to get to Cuballing, then rested the horses for a day before setting off for home. Charlie drove the harvester and I drove the sulky, keeping just a few yards behind.

New Year came and went; the Muttons returned home to the Goldfields and Charlie and I were busy carting hay. Charlie was the stack builder. He said he hadn't learnt how they built stacks in Australia, but when he was a boy in England he worked on a farm and knew how the stacks were built there. He said the only difference was that the hay over there was loose and had to be packed in rows whereas here it was in sheaves and should be easier to handle. He built a beautiful haystack.

Carting hay was very hard work for me. I had to pitch the hay sheaves up to Charlie, one at a time, while he stacked them on the cart. When we got the cart loaded and into the haystack yard, I had to pitch the sheaves from the cart down to Charlie who put them into position on the stack. This knocked me out and on hot days it was worse. It took us two weeks to cart the hay.

Then Charlie started harvesting. He had one hundred acres to strip, and as his harvester was one of the first to come to the district, there were many farmers coming to see how it worked. Some of the farmers were amazed at the results of this method, which was wonderful compared with the older way of harvesting. Charlie drove the harvester and it took him a little over two weeks, working Sundays as well, to harvest the hundred acres of wheat. He was delayed a lot having to stop and show the many interested farmers how it worked. Charlie got just over four hundred bags from the one hundred acres, which was a good return because a lot of the wheat had been eaten by parrots, jays, kangaroos and other bush animals.

I had to sew the wheat bags up when they were filled by the harvester. A man with eight horses and a large box-wagon carted the wheat to Cuballing. He charged one and sixpence a bag and he used to cart sixty bags each load. This was the first year that wheat bag sizes had been reduced from four bushells to three bushells, so sixty bags would be near enough to five tons.

The contractor would bring back a load of superphosphate after delivering each load of wheat. He could bring sixty bags back each time and charged one shilling a bag. The superphosphate ('super' it was commonly called) was a new kind of artificial fertiliser subsidised by the Government and delivered to the settler's nearest railway siding. The freight was only five shillings per ton. It was a boon to the settlers, in some instances improving the crop by forty percent.

In the evenings, after dinner, I usually helped Mrs Bibby to wash the dishes, then went to my room. One night as I was saying goodnight, Charlie said, 'Wait Bert, I want to tell you something. Sit down. I've been thinking about you and how you have worked and looked after the stock, and we haven't forgotten Boxing Day. We look like getting a good price for our wheat, so we have decided to raise your wages to fifteen shillings a week and full keep, starting one week before Christmas.' This thrilled me and I felt so pleased I didn't know what to say.

I thanked Charlie and Mrs Bibby for the raise in my wages and told them how pleased I was and how happy I felt. Charlie said how sorry he was about getting drunk and that it wouldn't happen again. He said that they hadn't seen Mr Mutton for about four years and made the mistake of drinking wine and whisky with beer. He finished by saying, 'It cost us dearly.'

Burning-off season opened and several neighbours came to help put the fire through the chopped and burnt down timber like they had helped Frank the year before. When one of our neighbours wanted help with putting a fire through, we always helped them. This co-operation went on with all the new settlers, and they used to meet at each other's places from time to time to discuss and exchange ideas on farming, clearing, fencing and stock. My Uncle was the one who gave advice on all kinds of stock and stock sickness.

That burning season, Charlie had what was known as a 'good burn'. This term was used when the undergrowth, scrub and timber burnt freely and left only the large logs and stumps. We then started on the clearing. Charlie and I worked hard and long hours six days a week from the middle of February through to the end of the first week in April. During that period we cleared the one hundred and thirty acres that we had chopped and burnt down during the previous August, September and October.

Just after the clearing was finished we had a storm with heavy rains. This softened the ground and Charlie started ploughing the new land. He had bought a disc plough which was better for working new land and was much quicker than a stump-jump plough. A disc plough could also be used for working up land that had long grass or straw on it. It was driven with six horses and covered a strip four feet eight inches wide, which was more than twice as much as a three-furrow stump-jump plough.

During ploughing and putting in the crop, my job was looking after the stock and picking up any roots pulled up by the plough. I would cart these to the house as they made good firewood.

The only time we worked on Sundays was harvest time. I had Sundays off at other times, except I had to look after the stock, and fill up the wood-box in the kitchen for Mrs Bibby. I never had any young people to play with apart from an occasional trip over to Uncle's to see Grandma. On these visits I would always join in games with my cousins. Otherwise I had no young company, so I used to take my rifle and walk in the bush. Sometimes I got a shot at a 'roo and many times I would find a quiet spot and sit down and keep quiet and watch the birds and the small animals.

The birds used to fascinate me. There were so many different kinds and most of them were friends of the farmer. The bush in those days was alive with them, their beautiful noises were something you had to hear to believe.

The martin sparrow went in packs of hundreds; it lived on small insects and made its nest in hollow limbs of large trees. It was very pretty, about the size of a canary, and had a black head, brown feathers along the sides and back, light grey underneath its body and around the neck, and bright brown under its wings. When flying, its tail-feathers were spread like a small hawk.

Then there was the willy wagtail, which had a black head and back and a white underbody – a very lively little bird with a long wedged tail. The blue wren was a small bird with a beautiful blue body. And there was the little brown and grey tom tit. There were hundreds of these, flitting in and out of the scrub and bushes. The woodpecker was bigger than the wagtail and would run up any tree by digging its sharp claws into the wood.

There were hundreds of the common magpie, and also the ground-lark, a small grey and light brown bird that wouldn't sit on a tree, but flew from ground to ground. The brown bush quail was also a ground to ground bird. The bronze-winged pigeon lived on seeds and such like and was good to eat – it was half the size of a chicken. The robin red breast was a very pretty little bird with a scarlet red marking on its breast. The peewit was a light brown bird with some black streakings on its back and wings, and a white breast marked with a U-shaped black half circle.

The plover was the same size as the peewit and had much the same markings but it was a ground to ground bird. It had a cunning way of concealing its nest out in an open patch of cleared ground. The nest and eggs looked the same colour as the ground – you could walk on the nest without knowing. The blue bird was about the size of the peewit too, but had a black head and a very light blue body. This bird was sometimes called a storm bird on account of it appearing more frequently just before the weather turned stormy. It had a very beautiful whistle-like call. There was also the parakeet which always flew in large mobs. It had pretty colouring – green, brown and red – and resembled a parrot but was very small like a canary.

There were also the night birds such as the curlew – a ground bird with extra long legs – and the owl, which lived on bush mice and rats. Also the mo-poke, which had much the same habits as the owl. There were also large flocks of black cockatoos, always making a terrible noise. They were a very large bird and the noise they made was deafening, particularly when in flight.

There were many other birds which were the enemy of the farmer. These included the ring neck parrot, which was also known as the 'twenty-eight', and was one of the most beautiful birds to look at. The name twenty-eight came from the noise it made when frightened and flying from danger. It was most destructive on cereal crops and fruit. Another parrot, smaller and of different markings, was the rosella. This bird was also destructive on cereal crops and fruit, as was the jay bird.

There were also two small species of birds that were destructive.

One was the silver eye, a small bird about the size of a tom tit, grey with silver coloured rings around its eyes. It lived on flowers, sucking the honey or nectar out, and also on fruit. It was very damaging to grapes or any fruit near ripe. The other small bird was the greeneye. This was dusty green in colour and had the same habits as the silver eye.

There were, and are, many other varieties that are hard to describe. They made the bush a beautiful place and helped one forget about loneliness.

The wild animals were also quite a study for anyone who had to live with them, and sat quietly to watch their habits. They lived in a world of fear and danger, always watching, listening and smelling for some scent of trouble.

The birds and animals of the bush were all great company and very nice to see and hear. I loved the bush.

Charlie finished ploughing the new land and then started on ploughing the land that had been cropped the year before. He then did the seeding, finishing at the end of the third week in June.

After seeding, Charlie and Mrs Bibby went away for a fortnight's holiday, leaving me in charge of the farm and stock. They drove to Narrogin by horse and sulky, and took a train to Perth.

Charlie told me before he went that he had some business to attend to in Perth, and Mrs Bibby wanted to do some shopping. He said, 'All you have to do while we are away is look after everything. Never mind anything else. You are the general manager while we are away.' Mrs Bibby cooked me plenty of food before they went and she told me to have lots of eggs. When the meat she had left was finished I was to go over to the neighbour's place about four miles away. She had arranged for the woman there to supply me with whatever I wanted in the way of bread and meat. She said I could ride over on Prince. He was a very quiet horse and I used to ride him around the farm sometimes.

So, with these instructions, they set off on their much-needed holiday. I felt very proud of myself – my fourteenth birthday wasn't until the next month but they had enough confidence in me to leave me to look after their possessions. I was a little scared at first, but soon settled to doing the daily chores. At night I used to roam around with my rifle and make sure everything was safe. I even put an extra wire around the sheep gate in case the dingoes troubled them.

20

The Cattle Thief

The weather became very wet about four days after the Bibbys left, and it rained every day for over a week. We had had some beautiful sunshine; the crops had all come up and were looking lovely.

I felt very lonely at times, although when the Bibbys were at home, I only spoke to them at meal times or at work. I could not read or write and there wasn't any music, not even a gramophone. This made the nights seem extra long.

On the morning of the twelfth day I got up at daylight, and looking over towards the new land that had a nice crop growing, I saw about sixty head of cattle grazing. This puzzled me, as we hadn't seen any cattle around other than our own. I chased them away, but I had no sooner got back to the house than they were back again. So after feeding the pigs and fowls, I got Prince in and saddled him, then rode across again to chase the cattle off. This time I took my rifle with me. I thought if I fired a few shots into the air, it would frighten them into not coming back again.

I put Prince into a canter heading straight towards the cattle, and when I considered I was close enough, I fired two quick shots into the air. Wow! I didn't expect what I got. The cattle bolted towards the bush where they had come from, and Prince jumped sideways throwing me heavily onto the ground. Then he bolted back to the stable. My rifle was thrown to the ground and was covered with thick, red, wet earth.

I picked myself up. I wasn't hurt but felt a little shaken. The cattle had all cleared out – the shots had done the job. I picked up my rifle and I was about to walk back to the house, when I heard a man on horseback coming towards me. He rode up to me and said, 'What in the hell do you think you're doing?' I said that I was chasing the cattle off the crop. He replied, 'Who gave you permission to shoot my cattle?' I replied, 'I fired the shots into the air to frighten them off.' He yelled,

'Like hell you did. There's two lying dead over the hill.' I said, 'I couldn't have fired the shots that killed them. I fired into the air, then my horse threw me off.' He came towards me saying, 'You shot them, you little stinker. I'll learn you a lesson.' He started to unwind a large stock-whip. Seeing this, I quickly brought my rifle up to my shoulder and called out, 'Don't come any closer if you want to live.' I must have looked like I meant it because he stopped, turned his horse around and said, 'You will be hearing more of this.' He rode off towards where the cattle had gone.

I walked back to the stable where Prince was waiting for me. He was frightened and went to run away, so I put the rifle down and went over to him, catching hold of the bridle. He smelt me and became his old, quiet self again.

I looked after the sheep and cows and went inside to get some breakfast. While eating my breakfast I wondered how this man could blame me for killing two of his cattle. It was only a few minutes from when I fired the shots until he appeared, and he said that his cattle were dead over the hill. This puzzled me. I felt scared but I was sure that I had fired the shots into the air and away from the cattle. I got the rifle and looked into the magazine – there were still four cartridges left and I remembered that there had been six in it. I hadn't put any more in the rifle.

After awhile I was even surer that I hadn't killed the cattle. The only thing I had done wrong was point the rifle at the man and threaten him to warn him. It was the sight of the whip that made me point the rifle at him.

The cattle never came back and late that evening I went to see if there were any dead cattle as the man had said. I walked around the crop to where the cattle had rushed off and it was easy to follow their tracks. I followed them for about a mile but there was no sign of any dead animals. I came home satisfied that the man was not telling the truth. I felt so much better. The man hadn't wanted to see my boss or asked for any payment for the cattle, so I thought that perhaps they didn't belong to him but had been stolen. What had gone on at Cave Rock came back to me. They must have been stolen cattle and the man was herding them until he got a chance to sell them.

The next few days were free from trouble – the cattle didn't come back and the Bibbys returned home. They had been away sixteen days altogether. When they found that everything was okay, they made a fuss of me, and they both had bought me a present while in Perth. Mrs Bibby gave me a lovely tweed suit. When I tried it on it fitted me fine, but was a little too big. This was all right because, as Mrs Bibby said, 'You are growing, Bert, and it is better to be able to grow into it than out of it.' Charlie bought me a mouth organ. I couldn't play it but he said I could try and it would probably help to break the monotony at nights.

I told them about the cattle and about firing the shots to scare them – I didn't leave out a thing – and they seemed amazed at the man's attitude and at his threat about me 'hearing more about it'. Charlie said I had done just as he would have done. He said, 'I can just see you when he came at you with the whip. Don't worry any more about it. The little time that the cattle were in the crop won't do it much harm.' The Bibbys told me all about Perth and how they had enjoyed their holidays.

About two days later, Charlie and I set about fencing in the new land to prevent any more cattle grazing on the crop. The land that had been cropped the year before was fully fenced, so we only had the mile or so of the new land to enclose.

It was while we were doing this fencing that we discovered the dead cows the man had spoken of. The wind was blowing from some thick scrub about half a mile away from where we were working and we were overpowered by a terrible stink. We decided to investigate and found the two dead cows. Charlie said he thought they had been dead for about three weeks. We examined them for any brands but were unable to find any. Then Charlie and I looked for bullet marks or wounds. Charlie suggested that we leave the cows there and say nothing about it for awhile and see if anyone had been troubled with stray stock. Most of the new settlers hadn't fenced their crops.

One evening, a week later, we had a visitor. The dogs barked and ran to the gate leading into the house yard. I went to see who or what was making the dogs bark so viciously, and as I neared the gate a voice said, 'Good evening, sir. May I come in?' I opened the gate and saw that the visitor was a policeman. He asked, 'Is Mr Bibby home?' I said, 'Yes, sir. Tie your horse to the fence and come in. He is inside.' We both went inside and as soon as Charlie saw the policeman he called, 'Hello, what has brought you here?' They shook hands and Mrs Bibby also shook hands and asked him if he would like something to eat. The policeman said that he would, and if it wasn't asking too much, he would like to stay the night to rest his horse. Charlie told the policeman he was most welcome and they would be pleased for him to stay the night.

When I came inside again after tending to the policeman's horse, Charlie said to me, 'This is Constable West from Narrogin. He is making enquiries about the cattle you chased off the crop. He would like you to tell him what the man looked like and describe the cattle and how many you think there were.' 'Well,' I said, 'the man was sitting on a fairly heavy, dark-bay horse with a white blaze running down from near the top of its head to its nose, about two inches wide. It also had one white leg from the hoof to the knee on the right side. I noticed this because the man was riding towards me and he was holding the whip in his right hand – the same side as the white leg of the horse. The man was wearing a rather wide-brimmed felt hat and he had a dark rain-coat on with a kind of cape. He had rather a long moustache but the bottom part of his face was shaved, and he also had sharp features and rather a long nose. He wore riding boots and spurs. The cattle would be between fifty and sixty head. They were red and white, bay, and some were black-and-white. There was a lot of young cattle about one year old, some calves. I noticed that four or five of the older cows had no horns – I think they're called polled cattle.' The policeman asked me what time it had happened. I replied, 'About seven thirty in the morning.' He then said, 'Could you describe his voice?' I said, 'Yes, it was a fairly loud voice, clear and sharp.' He thanked me and said that I was very observant and helpful to him.

I noticed that he was writing down everything I said on a sheet of paper while I was talking. He read it over to himself and said that that would do fine. Then, turning to Charlie, he said, 'Could you get the boy into Narrogin tomorrow? We would like to get a positive identification and this lad can do it for us, I'm sure.' Mrs Bibby said she could drive me to Wickepin in the morning and I could go from there to Narrogin in the afternoon with the mailman. The Constable said that he would see that I got home safely.

Charlie asked him how he found out about the cattle as none of us had mentioned it to anyone. 'Well,' the policeman said, 'it's strange how things get around. A new settler living near by had much the same trouble with cattle. A man came to the scene and made threats and said that a cocky (meaning settler) kid a few miles south-west of there had taken two shots at him with a rifle and shot two of his cattle. He also said that as soon as he could get in to the police he would make it bad for that cocky. This settler came in to Narrogin the next day and asked us what action the man could take, if any, against him for using a shot-gun on his cattle. When we questioned the settler he told us about this lad of yours who had a reputation with a rifle, so that brought me here to you. We caught up with the cattle herder and all the cattle had been stolen from settlers over a wide area north of here. He's been working south hoping to get near enough to a town with a sale-yard to sell them. Acting on the settler's report, we picked him up about twenty miles south-east of Narrogin, day before yesterday. This settler will also be in Narrogin tomorrow to identify the man. The description your lad and the settler gave are very much the same.'

Charlie told the policeman about the two dead cows we had found. He said that he would have a look at them tomorrow and see what he could make of it. Charlie told him that we couldn't find any wounds on them and he thought they might have got some poison. There was a poison bush called York Road Poison east of Bibbys and two or three mouthfuls would be sufficient to kill a cow. The policeman said, 'You show me in the morning and I'll take a sample from each of their stomachs and send it to be analysed. Then we will know for sure.' With that everyone went to bed.

The next morning everyone was up early. Mrs Bibby and I left for Wickepin in the sulky at about nine o'clock. Charlie and the policeman went to have a look at the cows.

It was eleven miles from Bibbys to Wickepin and the trip took about two and a half hours. When we arrived we went straight to the Post Office to arrange my fare to Narrogin. The postman had arrived and would be leaving on his return trip to Narrogin at one o'clock. I took the pony for a drink, tied him up and gave him a nose-bag. We always carried a nose-bag with the pony's dinner in it when we went on trips that took a few hours each way. Mrs Bibby and I had some lunch, and at one o'clock I got on board the mail coach and away I went to Narrogin.

21

POLICE WITNESS

At Narrogin the coach was met by Constable West and he took me to Bushallas Hotel where he introduced me to a Mr Jack Lander. He was the settler who had had trouble with the cattle herder. Constable West said, 'Now, I have arranged for you both to stay here at police expense. You will both share the same room. Will that be all right?' We both agreed, then the Constable said that they wanted us at the Police Station at nine o'clock the next morning. He said, 'Goodnight, sweet dreams, and see you tomorrow.' Mr Lander said, 'I think we better have our dinner. The gong went just before you arrived.'

So we went to have our meal, the first ever in a hotel for me. I was nervous, especially when we sat at the table. I'd never seen so many spoons, forks or knives for one person and didn't have any idea which one to use first. Then a waitress came with a list of what we could have to eat. I was stumped – I couldn't read or write. Then I had a brainwave and decided to have what Mr Lander ordered. The waitress luckily showed him the list first and so I got through that ordeal. The food was lovely, and I copied Jack (he told me to call him Jack, he didn't like 'Mr') in using the knives and forks.

After the meal we went for a walk around Narrogin, returning at about nine o'clock, when we went to bed. This was another strange experience. That bed was something. I couldn't remember ever having such a lovely bed. Now I didn't have any night-shirt or pyjamas – on the farm I always slept in my undershirt. Jack had pyjamas. When he undressed and put them on I told him about me not having any and that I didn't remember ever having slept in them. When I was a little boy over in Victoria all we slept in was long nightgowns. Jack said, 'Never mind. Hop into bed in your undershirt, if that's what you are used to. You'll sleep all right.' So I did. In fact I no sooner put my head on the pillow than I was asleep.

In the morning Jack was up when I woke and had already been to the bathroom and had a bath. He handed me his dressing-gown and said,

'Here put this on and go and have a bath. It's nice.' I hadn't used one of these either. I also wasn't used to having taps over the bath. On the farm, having a bath was an ordeal. You had to put the water in an empty kerosene tin and warm it over the fireplace, then you poured it into a bath tub.

After breakfast we walked around Narrogin for a while, then a few minutes before nine o'clock we went to the Police Station. Constable West was there and took us into a room and told us to wait. He said he would come and get us when the line-up was ready. Jack said that what he thought would happen would be that they would line-up six or eight men of the same size, and we would have to pick out the one that was responsible for the cattle stealing trouble. He continued, 'We have to be sure that it is the man. No use saying 'I think', you must be sure. The police will line them up where we can see them clearly but the men won't be able to see us.'

After a few minutes more, Constable West appeared at the door of the waiting-room and said that they were ready and for me to come first. He took me into another room along a passage. From there I could see seven men all dressed alike, standing side by side on a platform about two feet from the ground. Constable West said, 'Have a good look at these men. Have a good look and don't say anything until I ask you.' He made a signal to the Sergeant in charge of the men and the Sergeant called out an order. The seven men turned right and stood like that for a few seconds, then another command was given and they all turned right again, this time with their backs towards me. Then another command was given and they turned right again so that their right sides were towards me, and finally they turned right once more and were facing me again. 'Now,' said the Constable, 'now can you see the man who came to you, just after you fired the two shots to frighten the cattle off Mr Bibby's crop?' I said, 'Yes,' at once, 'the third man from the end on my left is the man that I saw that day on horseback.' The Constable said, 'All right, come with me.'

We went back to the waiting-room and I was told to stay there until Jack returned. A few minutes later Jack and the Constable came back and we were both taken to the Inspector's office. The Constable told the Inspector that we had made our positive identification and had both picked the same man. We then had to sign a statement to that effect.

Now I was in more trouble. I couldn't read or write and the police were surprised at this. I told them that I had been trying to write my name, but up to now I hadn't been able to do it well enough for an important statement like this. The Inspector said, 'You make a try at it. Take your time.' I did. He said, 'It's not the best. Now make a cross there.' He pointed to a special place on the paper. I did this too and he wrote my full name under the cross, then signed his name under mine and said, 'That is just as good.' Then he added that I should keep on trying to sign my name and that if I kept at it I'd get it in time.

Now our trouble was to get home. Constable West said, 'We have to get this lad back to his place of employment somehow.' He asked the Inspector if we would be required at the Court that day and the Inspector said, 'No, we will charge the prisoner with cattle stealing, then outline the evidence against him to the Justice of Peace. If he pleads not guilty and I think he will, we have sufficient evidence to have him sent to trial straight away. He will be committed to the next sitting of the Criminal Court at Perth.'

Jack had his horse and light spring-cart at Narrogin, and he said he could take me back to Bibby's on his way home if that was all right by the police. They agreed and paid Jack the fare that would have been paid if I had gone by coach to Wickepin – one pound. Jack was happy with this. So we agreed to have an early lunch and leave about eleven thirty. Jack arranged with the Tea Rooms to prepare some sandwiches to take on the road with us.

We started on our way home. Jack's horse was a beauty. He was only young and full of life, and when we started he wanted to go. Jack had to hold him back because we had a long way to go. It was roughly thirty-three miles to Bibby's place by road from Narrogin. As we travelled along, Jack asked me why I hadn't been to school at any time, since I was school age. When I told him he said, 'Didn't anyone try to help you? I was surprised when you tried to sign your name at the Police Station.'

Jack was quiet for the next few miles, then I broke the silence by saying, 'I think I could write my name better than I did only I was very nervous. The Inspector couldn't believe his eyes. I don't think he was too happy.' Jack said, 'No, he wasn't. That's why he made you make a cross and then he witnessed both to make sure it was a legal document. He wrote under your terrible writing that you were unlearned and a junior and uneducated.' Then Jack said, 'I'll tell you what I'll do. If you would like me to, I'll send you a couple of books that I have. They will help you to read and write. They're what I had when I was going to school. I'll send them to you by mail. You should get them by next week and when you do ask Mrs Bibby to show you how to understand and copy the letters in all the forms as they appear in the books.' I said that this would be wonderful and thanked him.

The horse was still jogging along at a good bat. Jack let him walk up all hills and then sent him trotting along the down sides and on the flats.

We had covered nearly half of the journey home but hadn't noticed on account of being so interested about my schooling.

When we arrived at the twenty-five mile mark we stopped near a creek, took the horse out of the sulky, gave him a drink and then put the nose-bag on him for his meal. Jack and I sat on a log and ate our sandwiches. This man was one of the nicest and most understanding I had ever met. He told me he was from Scotland and that his father was financing him to become a farmer. He was twenty-four years old and hoped that when he got properly settled on the land he would build a house and get married. He told me that he was engaged to a lovely girl. She was willing to come over from Scotland to marry him as soon as he could make her a home. He also told me that his mother and father were living in Perth and that his father was a businessman. Jack had put two years in at the School of Agriculture to learn how to grow wheat, and also learn all he could about stock and generally equip himself with as much knowledge as possible to be a successful farmer. He told me that the hardest thing was the loneliness. He said, 'The only time I see anyone is when I go to town for provisions or over to another settler's place. Sometimes I make up an excuse so I can call on another settler just to have a friendly chat.' He asked me how I managed. 'You haven't had much of a life, always being with middle-aged people and no other children to play with and be with. Don't you get lonely?' I told him that I had at first, when I had to go out to work so young, but I was used to it now and I didn't feel lonely. There were always the birds and the animals in the bush. 'They are like music to me.'

We arrived home at the Bibby's late that evening and Charlie and Mrs Bibby were waiting. They expected me home that night and we found a meal waiting. In those days a cup of tea or a meal was always on for a visitor. The Bibbys were pleased to meet Jack and after we finished our meal, they invited him to stay the night. Jack said he should go home that night, but he was very tired, and providing he could get away early next morning he would be glad to stay. I was also very tired. The two days had been very exhausting. I had travelled sixty-four miles by horse and sulky as well as the coach and the cart. Travelling in a cart can be very monotonous and tiring. Next morning we were up early and Jack left for his home.

22

Goodbye

While I was away Charlie had started chopping and burning down timber and scrub on another piece of land that would be cropped in the next cropping season. He wanted to get one hundred and sixty acres ready for burning and clearing, so for the next month or so we would be very busy. The land we were getting ready didn't have many big trees on it. The timber was small but there was a lot of it. We had to chop most of the trees off at ground level. I could use an axe very well by then and we got along fine.

I had my fourteenth birthday while we were doing this work. Nobody bothered about it.

The first week in September my brother Eric came to see me. It was on a Sunday morning, just after my birthday. He told me that our mother had written to him telling him she had shifted from Kalgoorlie to Subiaco and would like us boys to visit her. She had said she would love to see us (especially me as I was the baby of our family). She said in her letter that she had two children to the man she married after our father died – one boy and one girl and their names were Jack and Mollie.

I asked Eric what he thought about going to see them and he said that he and Roy were going down to Subiaco at the end of the month. He asked me to go with them. I said I would have to see what Mr and Mrs Bibby thought about it. I reminded him that she hadn't been much of a mother to us. (What Grandma told me came to my mind: 'Watch your money, Bert. Don't let her know how much you have, for she will find some way of getting it out of you.') Eric said, 'I think she may be trying to make up for what she did to us when we were younger. Anyway, we are going to see her. You think it over and make up your mind. If you decide to come we will be leaving Wickepin by mail coach on the last Monday of this month.' He left after a few more minutes.

He and Roy were still working doing contract work for settlers in the Wickepin district. They were both much older than I. Eric and I never got on, but Roy and I were like twins – we always got along fine. After Eric left, I wondered why our mother suddenly wanted to see us. Did she have a guilty conscience after all this time? Or did she hope to get money from us?

When we finished our midday meal, I told Charlie and Mrs Bibby the reason for Eric's visit. Eric hadn't been to see me since I started work over four years ago at Cave Rock. The Bibby's were very quiet when I told them. Then Charlie said, 'What do you think of the idea?' I said, 'I don't know what to think. I'd like your opinion on it. I'm not very happy about it.' Charlie looked at Mrs Bibby and then he said, to my surprise, 'She is your mother, Bert, and you can only have one mother. No matter what she has done in the past, she is still your mother. You must make up your mind about this. If you want to go and see her it is okay with Mrs Bibby and I. We would like you to help us with the burning and chopping down but we should have enough done by the end of the month for me to be able to finish all right.' I said, 'I'll think it over and let you know in the morning.'

Next morning at breakfast, I told them that I had I decided to go and see my mother. I said, 'I haven't seen her for nine years and she may have changed. When I did see her nine years ago it was only for a few minutes.' It was then that Mrs Bibby said, 'I think we missed your birthday Bert. It was in August, wasn't it?' I said, 'Yes, it was the thirty-first – I was fourteen.' She said, 'Oh, I'm sorry. We forgot all about it. We were going to give you a birthday party. Oh, I'm sorry.' I said, 'That's all right. I've had the last six birthdays and nobody has remembered them so don't worry. In fact, I'm glad you forgot it if you were going to give me a party. That would have made me scared. I wouldn't have known what to say or do.'

I told them from then on, until I went, I was going to work on Sundays as well, to get as much as possible done. Charlie said, 'If you do, I will pay you an extra five shillings a week for working on the Sundays.' He then said, 'You have made a wise decision, Bert. I would have been disappointed with you if you had decided not to go.' So that was settled. I worked long hours every day to do as much as I could for these lovely people.

I received the school books from Jack and they were just the very thing that I wanted. I could learn to read and write with the books as a guide. One was all about how to write capital letters and small letters and how to put them together to make words. Now I had something to do at night. From then on I put in two hours every night before I went to bed. Mrs

Bibby was very helpful and wrote the letters for me to copy. In three weeks I could write my name quite good. So good that Mrs Bibby remarked, 'You'd have no trouble signing your name now, Bert.' I must have written it over a thousand times in the next week or so.

I finished working for the Bibbys on the last Saturday in September 1908. About four days before that, Charlie rode into Narrogin. He had some important business to attend to and he wanted to do it while I was there as he didn't like Mrs Bibby being alone. She was a very timid person at night when alone. Charlie arrived back on the Thursday evening before I left on the Saturday. He gave me some good news. He had seen the Police Sergeant at Narrogin and was told that the cattle stealer had confessed to stealing the cattle and to passing bad cheques. The Sergeant told Charlie to tell me that I wouldn't be wanted as a witness. The man would be sentenced by a Perth judge in due course. This was good news as I was feeling a little scared at the thought of appearing in court. Charlie also said that tests had shown that the two cows had died from York Road Poison.

So I finished work for these lovely people. That Saturday evening Charlie paid me in full and I asked Mrs Bibby would she drive me over to Uncle's as I would like to see Grandma before I went to see my mother. She agreed to do this. I said that I would stay at Uncle's place on Sunday night, and Aunt Alice would drive me to Wickepin on the Monday morning so I could catch the mail coach to Narrogin as arranged by my brothers.

Next morning Charlie asked me what I was going to do in the long term. I said I didn't know until I saw my mother. In her letter to my brothers she had said she would like me to stay with her until I was older and she told them to be sure to bring me with them. Charlie said, 'All right Bert, but if you don't get along with her you can always come back to us.' I said goodbye to Charlie, and Mrs Bibby drove me over to Uncle's. I took my rifle and a tin trunk with what clothes I had in it, and strapped the travelling rug and blanket that I had to the trunk.

On our way to Uncle's place, Mrs Bibby told me about the trouble that they were having paying their way. She said that they were depending on the crop they had in to see them through and that the crop badly needed rain. I had been too busy thinking about my trip to Perth and learning to write to be bothered about the weather. Then I remembered we hadn't had any rain since August. I cheered her up as best I could and said, 'The rain will come, don't worry about it.'

We arrived at Uncle's at about eleven o'clock. Grandma was so pleased to see me. Uncle Archie and Aunt Alice were also pleased to see me and made Mrs Bibby very welcome. They asked her to stop and have some lunch with them. My cousins and I watered and fed the horse, then, after I had answered about a thousand questions about what I was doing and where I was going, we were called to lunch.

Mrs Bibby had lunch with Grandma, Aunt and Uncle and I had mine with my cousins. Bill wanted to know all about my rifle and I promised to show him after lunch. They all wanted to know more about where I was going. When I told them they said how lucky I was to be going to the big city. I told them I was frightened and didn't know why my mother wanted to see me after all this time.

When lunch was over, Mrs Bibby was ready to go back to her home. Bill and I put her horse to the sulky and fetched it to the house. She came to me, put her arms around me and kissed me two or three times. Then she got into the sulky and drove away. Uncle said, 'Well I'm damned, she is crying.' Grandma said, 'She's very fond of you, Bert.' I replied, 'She's a lovely woman. I wish that she was my mother.'

23

TRAVELLING HOME

I got a shock later when Uncle told me that my brothers had gone the day before. He said, 'They didn't think that you were going to go, and their job cut out on Thursday so they left yesterday. They will be there by now.' This made me feel bad and I said that if I had known before Mrs Bibby left, I would have gone back with her. Then to my surprise, Grandma spoke up and said, 'Don't worry. You will be able to go to Perth by yourself all right. When you get to Narrogin you go to the railway station and wait for the train. There is a waiting-room there and you can get a sandwich and a cup of tea anytime you like.'

Grandma and I sat in the kitchen and had a long talk. I asked her if she thought I was doing the right thing and she never answered for awhile. Then she said, 'Well it is like this: she's your natural mother and until you are twenty-one she is your legal guardian and can claim you no matter what, unless the Court of Law says otherwise. So I think you should go and see what she wants you for, but don't forget what I have told you about money. Don't let her know how much you have because when she was younger, money was her God. She may have changed of course.'

Then Grandma told me that the man my mother had married was a widower whose first wife died at childbirth. The baby had lived and was still with them – his Christian name was Harry. That was how my mother came to meet this man – she looked after the baby for him. Mother had had two children by him – a boy called Jack and a girl called Mollie.

Grandma then said, 'If it is not too personal to ask, how much money have you got?' I told her I had sixty pounds that I had saved from my wages and made from animal skins. I told her that I had bought a rifle, tin trunk, travelling rug and blanket and a few other things, and that the Bibbys had bought all my other clothing. I had offered to pay them but they wouldn't hear of it. Grandma said that I had done well saving that much.

I then asked Grandma if she would like to come with me to see her daughter – I would pay her expenses. She said, 'No, don't go putting me on a spot. I'm over twenty-one.' She said this jokingly. Then she said, 'No Albert, it's up to your mother to come here to see me. I'm too old to go travelling much now. Are you taking all that money with you? Sixty pounds is a lot of money.' Then I explained what I intended doing. When I got to Wickepin the following morning I would go to the Post Office and put most of my money in the State Savings Bank, and keep only enough to pay my fare and keep me for a few weeks in Perth. 'I won't tell anyone how much money I have in the bank,' I said. 'I'll hide the bank book and then if I want more money I will draw it out down there.' Grandma said that was a good idea. I offered her ten pounds to spend on herself but she refused saying she was all right. All she wanted was for me to be careful and to make my money last as long as possible. 'Just as hard to spend as it was to earn,' she said. 'If you remember this you will be all right. Now you go and see your mother and give her my love, and tell her I would like a letter now and then from her and that I still think of her.'

After this long talk with Grandma I went out to join my cousin Bill who wanted to see my rifle. I showed it to him and he looked at it with envy. He wanted to have a shot with it but I stopped that because I knew what Uncle would say. I rolled it up again in its bag wrappings and put it away. For the rest of the evening all Bill could talk about was the rifle.

Next morning Grandma was up bright and early. She was always up first in the mornings. I got up a few minutes after Grandma and she made an early cup of tea just for us. She told me Uncle was busy making dirt bricks to build a new house.

These dirt bricks were made with a special kind of earth. The earth was dampened to an exact dampness, then put into a mould and stamped in with a special stamper until it was packed tight. Then the mould was lifted up and away, leaving the brick which was twelve inches by eight inches, and six inches thick. This process was done on a very level portion of ground especially prepared for the job. When one brick was done the mould was put on the ground alongside it, and the next one was made. The finished bricks were left on the ground for a day to dry. When they dried out they were very hard and could be stacked ready for use.

Uncle intended building the new house himself when he had enough bricks. Grandma showed me the plan of a six-roomed house with a verandah all around and a corrugated iron roof.

After breakfast that morning I said goodbye and received another warning from Grandma about my money. Then Aunt Alice drove me to Wickepin. I went to the Post Office there and booked and paid my fare to Narrogin. Then I enquired about how or what I had to do to open a State Savings Bank account. The Postmaster got some forms and showed me what to do. I told him I could sign my name but couldn't fill in the forms, so he said he would fill in the forms for me and that all I would have to do was sign them. I told him I wanted to bank fifty pounds and that I was going to Perth and may want to draw out some money there. He said that would be all right and that he would need a specimen signature to send to Perth. So when I boarded the coach I had ten pounds in cash in my pocket and fifty pounds in the bank. I felt quite rich and very pleased with myself.

The trip to Narrogin was very quiet. I had to sit in the back seat as there were two other passengers – a woman and her daughter – and they sat in the front seat with the driver. The mail coach was a kind of buggy. It had two seats, one in the front and one at the back. There was enough room for five people as well as luggage.

The coach always stopped at the Post Office in Narrogin. It was really a mail coach that was allowed to carry passengers. It wasn't far to the railway station so I carried my tin trunk and rifle to the railway station and labelled them as passenger luggage to Perth. To do this I had to pay my fare. The usual fare was one pound, but the Station Master asked me my age and I told him I was fourteen. Then I remembered that the police at Narrogin could verify this. The Station Master rang the police, and then he said it was all right. I asked him what he wanted to know my age for. He said that children under sixteen were only charged half fare, 'So you see, it is lucky that I asked you because now you can go to Perth on half fare which is ten shillings. The train leaves here at midnight.'

I thanked the Station Master. He became curious and asked, 'How come a lad like you is travelling alone. Don't think I'm nosey but it is not the usual thing.' I told him why and that I hadn't seen my mother for nine years. He seemed surprised and became quite friendly. The time was now getting on to seven o'clock. He said, 'Have you had your evening meal?' I replied, 'No, I haven't. I've been too busy travelling and thinking about my trip. I even forgot to have my lunch at midday. My Grandma said I can get a cup of tea and something to eat at this station.' He told me that the tea-rooms were closed between trains and that I would have a job finding a place at this time of night for a meal. He said that if I liked to wait for awhile until he was relieved at eight, I could go to his house and have a meal with him and his wife. He was sure his wife wouldn't mind. I thanked him and said that I would like that, so we talked until his relief came at eight o'clock. Then we went to his home, which was only about a hundred yards from the station.

The Station Master's wife made me welcome and said that she had cooked a stew and there was plenty for an extra one. She served me a large plate of stew. It was the nicest I'd ever tasted and after the meal I thanked them and said that I appreciated their kindness. They asked me to stay with them until later in the evening, as I would be more comfortable waiting there than on the station all alone. So I helped to wash the dishes and clean up, then they took me into the sitting-room.

They had a gramophone. The lady played some lovely music. I hadn't heard anything like it before. The music and singing was coming from a small, round-shaped thing, about the size of a jam tin, only black. They called it a record. All the voices and music sounded just like the real thing. It was marvellous. This invention fascinated me beyond all, I cannot explain how it made me feel. They must have played the records over and over because it only seemed a short while after that that I had been there three hours. It was eleven o'clock and these people were past their bedtime. I thanked them again for their kindness and told them that I had never enjoyed myself so much before.

The train from Albany to Perth was on time. I found an unoccupied seat and settled in for the trip. It was nine years since I had ridden in a train. The carriage had only one other passenger in it and he was lying full-length on the seat, sound asleep. He must have been used to travelling in a train. I was too excited to sleep. I was thinking about what it would be like living with a real mother. Would she boss me around and make me do all the work around the place, and what about my stepfather? What was he like? I hadn't even seen him. Would he be a bully or a kind man? Did he drink or get drunk? What were my half-brother and half-sister like? Would they like me? All these things were troubling me. I had mixed feelings about all this. Why didn't I stay in the bush where I had hundreds of friends? There were the birds and the animals. There was no loneliness in the bush and nothing to harm you.

Now I was on my way to the unknown. Oh well, I thought, I could always go back to the bush. Or could I? Grandma said my mother could make me do as she bade until I was twenty-one. This didn't seem right to me. Where was she when I was nine and sent out to work? Where was she when I was horse-whipped and very sick? Why hadn't she come to me then? Perhaps she wasn't told about my plight. Yes, that was it, I thought, she hadn't known. My thoughts went on and on along these lines.

Then all at once the man on the other seat sat up and said, 'Goodday.' I said, 'Goodday.' He said he was going to Perth and asked me how far I was going. I told him to Perth too, and from there to a place called Subiaco where my mother lived. He said that he knew where it was and that it was about three miles or so out of Perth. You could get there by changing trains at Perth or you could take a cab. He said that he would take a cab if he was me because Subiaco was a big place and I might have to walk a long way. A cab would take me right to the house where I wanted to go. I decided there and then to take a cab.

This man was very friendly. When the train stopped at Beverley and a man called out in a loud voice, 'Twenty minutes for refreshments,' he said to come and have a cup of tea and a sandwich. So we got out and walked along the platform to a large counter where most of the passengers already were.

Then the man asked me what my name was. I told him and he said that he was called Duncan, but Dunk for short. A girl at the counter came to where we were and asked what would we like. Dunk replied, 'Tea and sandwiches for two please.' She was back in a few minutes and said as she was putting the tea down, 'Sixpence each please.' We paid her and had our cup of tea and sandwich. Dunk had double service. He said that he was hungry, as he'd slept all the way from Albany till just a few miles out of Beverley.

Just before the train pulled out, three other passengers got into our carriage – a man, his wife and daughter. They were going to Perth. This put me back into silence – I always went shy with girls, and this one was about my age. Dunk and the man got talking about all sorts of things and I spent the rest of the trip looking out of a window.

24

ARRIVAL

We got into Perth about ten thirty on Tuesday morning, the first day of October 1908. Dunk helped me get my luggage and put it into a cab just outside the station. I gave the driver the address of Mother's place and away I went to Subiaco.

I arrived at Mother's at about eleven thirty and knocked on the door. There was no answer so I went around the back and knocked again. Still no answer. The cab driver had waited to be sure it was the right address. He suggested that I ask a neighbour. 'Yes,' the neighbour told me, 'your mother and two youths left this morning at about ten o'clock.' Her guess was that they had gone to the city. I went back to the cab, got my luggage and thanked the driver.

I carried my tin trunk and rifle around to the back of the house, then undid the travelling rug and spread it out to lie down. I was very tired. I hadn't slept for over twenty-nine hours and they might not be back for a while. I folded my coat against the trunk and in a few minutes was sound asleep.

I was awakened later by someone shaking me and calling out, 'Come on, get up and shift yourself out of this, you young vagabond.' When I opened my eyes, I saw that it was a policeman. He grabbed me by the scruff of my neck, stood me up and ordered me to put my coat on, pick up my things and get out. I was dazed and for a few seconds I couldn't understand what was going on. Then the policeman said, 'What's your game? Haven't you got a home? What's your name?' I said, 'This is my home now. I only arrived here a little while ago. This is my mother's place.' Then I noticed three children. They were standing outside the back path – two boys and a lovely little girl. The girl was only about eight years old. The policeman laughed and said, 'Don't tell me any tall tales. This is the home of these children.' I replied, 'Yes, they are my mother's children. My other brothers came down on Sunday.' Then the eldest boy said, 'Oh, Constable, we have made a mistake. We forgot about it. The others came on Sunday and they said Albert, that is this boy, was coming down later.' With that the policeman said he was sorry. Then he turned to the children and said that next time they must make sure of their facts about tramps sleeping on their back verandah, before they went bouncing down to the Police Station. With that he turned to me and said, 'Sorry lad.' He stamped off, slamming the front gate behind him. When he had gone the children started to laugh and I joined in with them. It was frightening while it lasted but we could see the funny side of it now.

So these kids were my relatives. They explained how the policeman came. They had all come home for lunch. Mother locked up when she went out and planted the key. The kids knew where the key was and let themselves in to have lunch, which was left prepared for them by Mother. When the little girl, who arrived first, saw what she thought was a tramp asleep on the back verandah, she had run to the Police Station and reported it. So that was my welcome home, or at least what I was supposed to call home from now on.

The three children had their lunch and I ate with them. Then they showed me where my brothers slept. There was a bed made up for me in the room, they said. When the kids went back to school I made myself at home, put my trunk under one of the beds, lay down, and in a few minutes I was asleep again.

I was awakened by one of my brothers shaking me. Dinner was ready and it was about half past five. When I walked out into the dining-room all the family were there. My mother ran to me, put her arms around me and kissed me many times. She said that she was so pleased to see me. Then she introduced me to my stepfather. I had already met the others. My stepfather shook hands with me and said that I was a big boy for my age. He told me that I was very welcome and to make myself at home. My stepfather is what I called 'a little big man'. He was only about five feet eight inches tall and weighed about sixteen stone. He had been a top class sportsman when younger. He had played league football on the Goldfields and later played league for Subiaco Football Club. After that he was an umpire. He told me to call him Bill and said, 'That is what all my friends call me.' I said that I would like that. With that we all sat down to dinner.

This was the first meal I could remember having with my mother. After dinner my mother, Harry and Bill cleared the dishes away. I volunteered to do the washing-up but my mother wouldn't hear of it. She said, 'Not tonight, you must be tired. Jack and Henry (Harry) can do it tonight.' Harry was about twelve years old and Jack was nine.

So Mother, Bill, my two brothers and I all went into the sitting-room. My mother and Bill asked a lot of questions about my work and how I had been treated. They were amazed at what I had been through, and how I had been robbed of my wages and flogged. They were shocked. To prove my story I took off my coat and shirt and showed them the whip marks which were still very clear over my back and upper arms. I explained that the lower part of my body and legs were worse.

I was told that my sister Myra, who was left with Mother when we first arrived in Kalgoorlie from Barkers Creek in Victoria, had taken ill just before Mother came to Perth, and was in a sanatorium at Coolgardie. She had been suspected of having consumption. Mother told me that she hoped to get transferred to a hospital for infectious diseases at West Subiaco. She hoped it would be soon so that Eric, Roy and I could see her. It was something I looked forward to as I loved my sister Myra. We were always together when we were little in Victoria. I hadn't seen her since I was five years old.

Mother also told me that my oldest brother Joseph was in the wheatbelt somewhere, still working for a firm of surveyors. My other brother Vernon was also still in the Royal Australian Navy and was at that time attending a naval school in Melbourne. I hadn't seen either of them since they had come west with our father when I was a baby. So I really didn't know them at all – only as names.

Bill said that he may be able to find work for my two brothers. He was a Master Plumber and taught plumbing two nights a week at the Perth Technical School. He had his own business in Perth, doing contract plumbing, and he said that he might be able to use my brothers on this contract work. He would see what he could do. He then turned to me and said, 'I'm afraid you are too young to be considered for the work I have to offer, but we may be able to find some light work for you, such as a messenger boy or something like that. I am not allowed to employ anyone under sixteen years old.'

We talked about many things until bedtime.

25

MOTHER

Next morning we were all up early. Bill went to work about seven and my brothers and I decided to go and have a look around Perth. We found our way around, as Perth wasn't a very big city then. There weren't any moving pictures during the day – the only amusement was the Wax Works, the parks, river trips on the ferry, the beaches or fishing. At night there were dances or variety shows. That evening, after walking around Perth, we were dog-tired and went to bed a few minutes after tea.

Next morning our mother woke us at about eight o'clock. Bill had gone to work and the kids were ready for school. Mother prepared some breakfast for us, then when we sat down at the table she said, 'Now I have something to say to you. It's about the position I find myself in with you three boys. As you know you have a stepfather and he is only a working man with limited means. He's trying to work up a business but it is a battle and he has been very good to me. He never complains but I cannot expect him to keep you boys. He is not your real father and has three children of his own.' She suddenly stopped talking about Bill and said, 'How much money have each of you got? She looked straight at me. I felt myself blushing and looked at my brothers and said that I had enough to pay my way for a few weeks. Eric said he had enough to do him until he got his wages and he continued, 'I'm starting work on Monday next.' Roy said the same. We were keeping our financial position to ourselves. Mother then said that board and lodgings would cost each of us one pound a week. 'That is what you would be paying in a boarding-house. The only difference is that I will do your washing and ironing, and at a boarding-house you would have to pay extra for that. Now that may seem hard to you but from tomorrow I want one pound a week from each of you, and each Friday thereafter, whether you are getting wages or not.' Eric remarked that she was being a little hard on Punch (my brothers always called me

Punch). He said, 'He is only a kid and not able to go to school. He'll have a hard time getting a job.' Mother replied that if I could not pay my board, I would have to go back to the country – I was fourteen years old now and they couldn't send me to school. Eric and Roy looked disgusted and I knew then that I didn't like my mother. What Grandma had said was right. If you had money for her everything was fine. She had showed her feelings to us, no doubt sensing that we were not prepared to reveal our true financial position.

After breakfast we walked to the railway station at Subiaco, boarded a train and went to the Port of Fremantle to have a look around. While in the train my brothers and I discussed our mother's attitude towards us. Roy said, 'She only took four days to put the screw on us to know how much money we had.' He then said to me, 'How did you avoid telling her what money you had?' I said, 'Grandma warned me about her liking for money. That is what made me careful.' Eric let himself go and said that she had no love for any of us and that he had a good mind to clear out and not bother to see her again. So we talked about her all the way to Fremantle.

After seeing all we wanted to see at the port we went by train to Cottesloe beach. We lay on the sand at the beach, then hired some bathers and went for a swim. We didn't go home until late in the evening.

On the train on the way home we again talked about Mother. Roy made the suggestion that if I was unable to find work, he and Eric would pay my board between them. Eric agreed to that. I told them that I would be all right for about two months and surely something would turn up in that time. At that moment I felt that it was a terrible mistake to have come from the country. Everything was so different. In the country the people were more friendly and I felt like I was wanted, and I was happy.

The next three weeks were a nightmare to me. Besides paying my board, I had to split up enough wood blocks to keep the fire going. Mother would send me out in answer to ads in the morning paper to try and find a job. I had little knowledge of Perth and surrounding districts and got lost trying to find the places. When I did find them I would be too late or would be told that my reading and writing was not good enough to do the work.

Then one Friday evening I was walking home from job hunting down Rokeby Road, the main street of Subiaco. A storekeeper, who was standing outside his grocery store, stopped me and said, 'Are you the boy who is looking for work?' I replied, 'Yes, sir.' He then asked me what work I could do. I told him, 'Anything. If you show me what you want me to do, I'll do my best. I don't mind what it is.' He said, 'It will be cleaning up in the mornings and evenings, filling up the grocery shelves and bringing in fresh supplies from the storage places at the back as they are required, and delivering small orders in and around Subiaco. Do you think you could do that?' I said that I could. He thought for a moment then said, 'All right, I'll give you a week's trial and you can start Monday morning at seven thirty. Now, what about wages. How much a week do you want?' I said I hadn't worked in town, only in the country, and I was receiving up to fifteen shillings a week and my keep. The storekeeper said quickly, 'I cannot pay anything like that, but if the job is any good to you, I'll pay you one pound a week and you must make arrangements to keep yourself.' I thought for a moment. The wages would at least pay for my board. I decided to take the job.

I hurried home to tell Mother. When I told her she said, 'What are you going to do for pocket money? I cannot reduce your board because you eat as much as a full-grown man.' I said I still had enough to keep me going for a week or so and something might turn up. I would try it for a few weeks and keep learning to read and write.

I had been learning every chance I could get and sometimes I got on Mother's nerves asking questions. She was good at helping me at times, but she was also impatient, so I had to find a quiet spot somewhere to study as best I could. I was coming along nicely and could write very well and sign my name without any trouble. In fact, last time I made a withdrawal at the bank, they came and questioned me about my signature. When I explained about my improved writing and learning to read they were very nice, gave me a pat on the back and said, 'You keep on son, you'll come good. We are glad you told us because your writing has improved noticeably since you opened your savings account.' (It was five weeks since I opened it.) 'We would like you to give us another specimen signature.' This made me very pleased and it was an inspiration for me to work harder.

The first week in my new job was not a happy one. The sweeping, dusting and re-filling of shelves was all right, but the delivering of stores was not so good for two reasons. Firstly, I had to learn to ride a cycle with a large cane basket strapped onto the handle-bars to carry the groceries. It was hard to manage this bike and when the basket was full I found it even harder. I doubt that I could count the number of times that I fell off and tipped the groceries out onto the road – spilling sugar, breaking eggs and numerous other things. And also, not being used to the city, I had a problem finding the places to where the groceries were to be delivered. I expected to be sacked before the week ended but although he growled and threatened me many times, my boss also gave me a lot of encouragement and said, 'Never mind, lad, you will learn in time.'

At the end of the second week the boss told me I was doing fine and he was very pleased with me. But I didn't like the job. My brothers told me that there was no hope of advancement. 'You are only working for your keep,' they said. 'What will you do when you want more clothes or boots?' This disheartened me and I decided to go back to the bush. I thought any condition in the bush is better than this hustle and bustle of the city.

I got Roy to write two letters for me; one to Grandma and one to the Bibbys asking would they like me to come back to work for them. My Grandma wrote back and said that things were very bad in the country. The crops were a failure because not enough rain had fallen during September and October to bring them to maturity. Most farmers would be lucky if they got enough wheat for their seed for the next crop. A few days later I got a letter from Mrs Bibby and her story supported Grandma's. She said that they would gladly have me back but they wouldn't be able to pay me. They thought their crop would strip about one bag (three bushels) per acre. This news upset me. I felt sorry for these people doing all that heartbreaking work for nothing. I got Roy to write a letter to tell them how sorry I was and thank them, and wish them better luck next year.

After I had been at the store for nearly four weeks, Bill came home one evening and said he had been talking to some cattle station owners he had met in a hotel in Perth. They had told him that cattle stations up North were looking for lads who could ride a horse, for mustering around Christmas time. They told him that the lads could get up to thirty shillings a week and keep all year round. This appealed to me and I got Bill to make enquiries about how to get up there and where to go for a start. The station owners told Bill that I should go to Geraldton or Carnarvon (two seaports on the Western Australian coastline, north of Fremantle). Bill also found out that the best way to get to these places was by boat from the Port of Fremantle.

Roy, who was working in the city, made enquiries for me at a shipping office during his dinner hour. I would have to book my passage to get to Geraldton on the small steamship *Kanelpy* or one of the other small boats that went north calling at all ports. So the next day Roy booked my passage to Geraldton on the *Kanelpy,* sailing at four o'clock on the first Monday in December. I felt pleased with myself as I didn't like my job in the city. Give me the bush where I could be with the things that I liked, and I liked horses.

My mother was very annoyed with me and said, 'What will you do if you don't find a job up there?' Then Roy said he would help me if I got stuck and that I was to send him word and he would lend me the money. My mother turned on him and told him he would want his money to buy clothes and boots. He replied, 'Punch will send it back as soon as he gets settled in a job.' I had told Roy that my financial position was all right but not to tell anyone else, especially Mother.

I finished up with the grocer on the Saturday and Mother washed my clothes and got them ready for me. Early on Monday morning I went into the city and withdrew some money out of the Savings Bank, enough to last for a month. I arranged with the bank to send my specimen signature to the Geraldton branch. I had thirty pounds left in the account, and considering that I had been in the city for nearly nine weeks I hadn't done too bad.

Before my brothers and Bill left for work that Monday morning, they said goodbye to me and wished me luck. The three kids said goodbye to me before going to school. I knew that I wouldn't see my mother again for a long time. Mother didn't seem to worry. She asked me a lot of questions. One thing she asked was, 'Don't you feel afraid going away all on your own?' I told her I wasn't afraid and that I would be quite at home in the bush. Everything was so quiet and free there, I wished I hadn't come to the city.

After lunch I finished packing up my tin trunk. My mother said she would come with me and see me off at Fremantle. So, carrying my trunk, we set off to the Subiaco Station. We had to walk about half a mile, then we boarded the train for Fremantle. We walked from the Fremantle Station to the wharf. Now I got the biggest surprise of my life! The ship, *Kanelpy,* was very small. So small that we had to go down a ladder to get onto it from the wharf. This was strange to me as I remembered the old tramp ship the *Coolgardie* that we came over from Melbourne on. She was called small but she was many feet above the wharf. But this boat? I didn't feel so brave now.

A man in uniform met us and I showed him my ticket. He looked at my mother and she hurriedly told him she was seeing me off. He seemed satisfied and showed me my cabin. It had four bunks – two below and two above. My bunk was one of the lower ones. I put my trunk under the bunk, then Mother and I had a look over this boat that was called a ship. It was bigger than it looked from the wharf and was fairly long. I felt a lot better after I had seen it from end to end.

We went back to the railway station, and as I had plenty of time before the ship sailed, I sat with Mother until her train came. She said goodbye to me and kissed me, and I noticed a few tears in her eyes. As I went back to the ship it seemed to me that that woman who was my mother showed she had a little feeling for me – enough to shed a tear. That was something I had to remember her by even if I never saw her again.

JOURNEY

1908–1909

It was a feeling of wonder — not lonely, not afraid —
a feeling of independence.

26

TRAVELLING NORTH

The boat sailed a little after four o'clock in the afternoon. There were five other passengers on board. The water was very calm and the little boat ploughed its way out to sea. I sat on a hatch cover and watched Fremantle get further away, wondering what was ahead for me. I felt free. It was a feeling of wonder – not lonely, not afraid – a feeling of independence. Here I was, only three months over fourteen years of age and free to go and do as I pleased.

The Captain of the boat asked me if I was enjoying the trip. I said, 'Yes, it is nice and calm. I hope it stays that way. When the water is like this I'm a good sailor.' He told me that it would get rough later but I'd have no worries as we would be in Geraldton early in the morning. Then he asked me if I was going to my people or to a friend at Geraldton. He was surprised when I told him I was looking for work. 'What is a kid like you doing on your own? Where are your parents?' I told him how I came to be on the boat. He said, 'We are not allowed to carry kids under fourteen without a parent or guardian.' I told him when my birthday was and he sighed and said, 'Thank God for that.'

We were now out of sight of Fremantle and although the sea was only a little rough, I felt squeamish. When the dinner gong went I didn't feel like a meal. That night the sea got into what they call a swell and I got very seasick. I spent most of the night vomiting over the side and by the time we arrived at Geraldton I felt really ill.

When I got off the boat I spread my travelling rug on the ground under a big shrub and lay there for over an hour before I felt well enough to bother about finding somewhere to stop. I didn't know what time it was. All I knew was that it felt better on land than on that small bouncing boat.

When I stood up the ground felt like it was rising and falling under me for a while. I managed to carry my trunk and rifle up to the main street of Geraldton, where I saw a sign in front of a fairly large building that said 'Coffee Palace'. I remembered the Coffee Palace at Narrogin, and I knew people could get lodgings and meals there. I went in and a large lady came to me. I told her that I wanted somewhere to stay and she said, 'You've come to the right place. Come in.' She took me into an office and asked me my name, age and what I was doing in a place like that. I explained my reasons and she said that I should have gone on through to Carnarvon where I would have a better chance of getting a job on a station. The large station owners mostly traded through Carnarvon. I told her that if I had gone any further on that boat I wouldn't have been alive to want a job. She said, 'Were you seasick? You don't look too good. How long do you think you will be stopping? The board and lodgings will cost you one pound a week in advance, or if you are staying a day or two, we charge a little more by the day.' I agreed to pay one week in advance and see what turned up. I said, 'You never know. I might get lucky.'

I was shown my room. It was a small room at the back of the building and I had it all to myself. The lady said that she would let anyone who may come there know that I was looking for work on a station. I told her that any sort of work would suit me, no matter what kind. Sometimes one kind of a job leads to another.

She seemed a kind lady. Her name was Mrs Stafford and she and her daughter Jean ran the Coffee Palace. They employed another girl to do the cleaning and wait on the tables. Her name was Mary and she was about twenty years old.

Then Mrs Stafford said, 'I have some cold meat and a cup of tea. I bet you could do with that.' I thanked her and said I was hungry.

Mrs Stafford was a very big person but nicely spoken and seemed to understand people's feelings. We went into the kitchen and it took her only a few minutes to make the tea and sandwiches. As I ate she asked me questions about myself and how a boy like me was alone in the world. I explained the best I could about my position and all the cruel people I had been unlucky enough to meet up with, and also the nice ones I had met.

After the tea and sandwiches, I became tired and sleepy, so I asked Mrs Stafford to excuse me as I wanted to go to my room and have a sleep. She said, 'You do just that. You look all in. We have dinner at five thirty. If you leave your door unlocked and you don't waken, one of us will call you.' I had no sooner laid down on the bed than I was sound asleep. The next thing I knew, someone was shaking me and saying, 'Come on, dinner is on.'

Mrs Stafford and the girls were sitting at the table having their dinner as I came down. Mary jumped up and said, 'I will bring your dinner into the dining-room for you.' I said, 'Could I have my meals in here with you? I don't like strangers and I don't understand the names you put on the menus. My reading is limited, you see. I never had any schooling.' Mrs Stafford said that they would be pleased to let me have my meals with them in the kitchen. So Mary sat me at a place at the table and served me my meal there. This made me pleased.

After dinner I helped the girls to wash up and then I walked around Geraldton for about an hour. It wasn't a very big town. Some of the streets had lights. As night came they were lit by a man on horseback. They burned on some kind of gas. When I went back to the boarding-house, Mrs Stafford and her daughter were playing cards with a strange man and woman. I didn't go into that room but went up to bed.

I must have slept soundly because when I woke up the sun was shining. I jumped up, got dressed and went into the kitchen. Mary was there and she said, 'You're just in time, I was going to call out to you. Mum's out chopping wood.' She always called Mrs Stafford, Mum. I went out to the backyard and there was the lady swinging an axe like any man. The wood was in lengths of three to four feet. I asked if I could cut the wood for her. She replied that she didn't think I could manage, as the wood was very hard and should be cut in one foot lengths so it would be easy to split. I said, 'Let me have a go, I have used an axe often.' She handed me the axe and stood and watched me, no doubt thinking that I would soon be convinced that she was right.

My way of cutting the lengths to oven size was different from Mrs Stafford's. The pieces that were three inches thick or less, I cut into foot lengths. The thicker pieces, I split down to two or three inch strips, then cut these into lengths to fit the oven. After watching me for a few minutes, Mrs Stafford went back into the kitchen. A few minutes later she opened the door and called me to breakfast.

I picked up an armful of wood and took it into the large wood-box she had in the kitchen. After washing my hands and face in the laundry I joined Mrs Stafford and the two girls for breakfast. As I sat down at the table, I asked Mrs Stafford how she liked the wood. She said, 'Lovely, where did you learn to cut wood like that?' I told her I had worked for a new settler in the wheat-belt and that he had shown me how to use an axe. Mrs Stafford said, 'Do you think you could cut me enough wood each morning to fill that box while you're here?' I said that I would be glad to. She then said, 'If you do that, I will give your board to you for fifteen shillings a week because cutting that wood is killing me.' So I filled the wood-box each morning. It took about one and a half hours. After that I used to go for walks around Geraldton.

At this time of the year everything was dusty and showing the effects of the beginning summer. On one of my walks into the country, I came across a camping ground. It was about one and a half miles out of Geraldton in an easterly direction near a Government well. I was standing looking down the well when I was startled by two large half-breed stag hounds coming towards me, barking and looking as if they were going to tear me to pieces. Then I heard a man's loud voice calling the dogs off, and to my relief, they obeyed. To me the man yelled, 'They won't hurt you. They always make a big fuss when they see a stranger but they won't bite you.'

He was a big man with a large black beard. He lived in a tent pitched under a shady tree, and he also had a large tarpaulin stretched over a pole, with each side tied down to make a nice shady place for meals. He invited me to come to his camp and have a chat. I did this and he told me he was a kangaroo shooter and that he always came into Geraldton around December to sell his skins and get some extras for Christmas. He said, 'I never stay here for Christmas though. I like the quiet of the bush. Geraldton is too rowdy for me at Christmas time. I like my beer, whisky and wine but not all in one week. I take whatever I need into the bush and have a little whenever I feel like it. It acts as a tonic to me that way, I never drink enough to make me drunk, so I have my Christmas cheer all over Christmas and into the New Year. Sometimes the supply I take with me lasts into the end of January. I buy the same amount each December.'

He then asked me to have a drink with him. I said I was sorry but I could not drink intoxicating liquor. I said, 'I am under age for that. And another thing, I promised my Grandma that I would not drink it, ever, as long as I live.' He looked at me suddenly (I thought I had made him mad), then he said, 'Son, I drank every drink that there was by the time I was ten years old and I bet you are older than that, aren't you?' I said, 'Yes, I'm fourteen.' 'Then you're not too young to drink. But making a promise is another thing. Now, once you make a promise, no matter what happens, don't ever break it. You no doubt think that I am a rough, untidy and don't-care person, but I like a body with principles.'

This rough, bearded man was something out of the ordinary. He made me feel good. I liked him. He asked me, 'How did you manage to come to Geraldton. Have your folks moved here or are you living with friends?' I told him all about my past and how I came to Geraldton looking for work, and that I was stopping at Mrs Stafford's place. He was quiet for awhile and then he said, 'You've come to the wrong place. You should have gone further up north to get a job on a station. The station managers and owners generally go to Carnarvon and get on a boat there for Fremantle. Sometimes they come into Mullewa, that is about sixty miles in an easterly direction from here. I'm going out there next week. That's my starting place for my kangaroo shooting.

Then the man told me all about his work. He was going to work the station commencing some hundred miles north-east of Mullewa. Sometimes he stayed from one month to three months on each station. The station owners and managers all gave him his supplies free while he was shooting 'roos to encourage him to continue. The skins, he kept and sold. The station owners also paid him a bounty of one pound on any dingo scalps. They branded the scalps and then got one pound from the Government as well, so a dingo scalp was worth two pounds to him. He also got a two shillings bounty for each goat he shot and he sold the goat skins for three to four shillings each. The stations paid a two shilling bounty for every emu's head he brought in. (He could sell all his skins at Mullewa but the dingo scalps had to be brought to a Police Station and there wasn't one at Mullewa. He came into Geraldton once a year.) 'So,' he said, 'taking all these bounties into account with the kangaroo skins and the free stores, I make good money.'

'Now,' he said suddenly, 'if you like, you can come with me. I'm going out to Mullewa next week. You may pick up a job there. What made you want a job like that? Can you ride a horse?' I replied. 'Yes, and I love the bush and horses. A man from up North told my step-father there is plenty of jobs for lads up North on the stations. Things are bad this harvest down in the wheat-belt.'

This kind man told me that his name was Bill Oliver and he said that he would like me to call him Bill. I agreed and told him my name. We shook hands on that. I made my way back to town after he had made me promise that I would come out to his camp in a day or so, and let him know if I was going with him to Mullewa.

On my way back to Mrs Stafford's Coffee Palace, I wondered how I would like kangaroo shooting. It seemed exciting. I had my own rifle and wondered how many 'roos it was possible to take in a week, not forgetting that each 'roo had to be skinned, the skin taken back to camp, pegged out to dry and then painted with weevil paint to preserve it. I had seen Uncle do this when he first killed 'roos for the meat and skins. I liked shooting and I knew I was a good shot.

When I arrived back at the Coffee Palace I asked Mrs Stafford if she knew Bill Oliver. She said that he was a kind, honest, and respected man. I told her that he wanted me to go with him to Mullewa next week as he thought I would have a better chance of getting a job on a station from out there. She thought for a while, then said, 'I think he's right. If you don't get a job, you can come back with the mail coachman. He goes out there every fortnight and carries passengers either way.'

Next morning I fully made up my mind to go with Bill if no job turned up before he left for Mullewa. I went out to his camp that afternoon and told him. He seemed pleased and told me I could camp with him at Mullewa. He expected to be there at least a week before he moved out to his kangaroo shooting. I went out to Bill's camp every second afternoon. And I walked a lot, sometimes along the beach and sometimes out into the bush.

A few days later, Bill made up his mind to move on. I hadn't found a job, so he asked me to camp with him that night so we could get away early next morning. He wanted to be in Mullewa for Christmas dinner with a friend, a lady whose husband had been a good friend of his. Bill said, 'He was killed about three years ago. Thrown from a horse and landed on his head. The fall broke his neck.' Bill told me that the lady, May, worked at the hotel and lived about half a mile out, in a small house on her own. When her husband died Bill gave her money as a loan and helped her, so she made him promise to come and have Christmas dinner every year.

We decided that I should leave my tin trunk and rifle with Mrs Stafford in case I didn't get a job. So, about five days before Christmas, we left early in the morning, bound for Mullewa.

27

ROAD TO MULLEWA

Bill had two horses and they seemed to be part of his life. He loved his horses. He used one in the shafts of the cart and the other attached to the cart, outside the shafts. A horse used in this way was called the out-rigger. Bill had quite a nice seat on the cart with a back rest all nicely padded and covered with lamb skin. I asked him how long it would take to go the sixty miles to Mullewa and he said, 'About three days or a little more. I never hurry my horses, I let them go at their own pace.'

So we travelled very slowly. The sun as it climbed in the sky got hotter and hotter. The horses, although only travelling at a slow walk-ing pace, were perspiring freely. Bill looked at his watch and said, 'It's half past nine. There's a watering place about a mile further on. We'll stay there and rest for a few hours. It's better to travel in the early morning and late in the evening these hot days. It's much better for the horses anyway.' The two dogs walked in the shadow of the cart during the heat.

The watering place turned out to be a well. Bill said that it was over ninety feet deep and there was about ten feet of water in the bottom. When hauled to the top, the water was lovely and cold and fresh to drink. The horses and dogs enjoyed it. We lit a fire, boiled the billy and had a mug of tea and something to eat. Later we lay on the tarpaulin under a nice shady tree to rest. I went sound asleep and Bill had to shake me awake. He said that it was half past three. We had another drink of tea, then harnessed the horses and set off again.

We travelled on with the sun behind us. There was a long period of twilight, then night came and it was very dark. Bill kept the horses going. He asked if I was tired and I said, 'Yes, tired of sitting.' He had been telling me that he expected to finish kangaroo shooting soon. He had been at it for over six years and he thought he might give it away and have a change. He said, 'So you see, Bert, you aren't the only one that may be looking for a job. I very seldom mention my business or my intentions to anyone but I feel so happy about something I want someone to know. Of course, I may be counting my chickens before they hatch.'

At that moment the horses turned off the track (the road to Mullewa after it passed the outskirts of Geraldton was only a bush track). Bill said, 'They know where they're going. This is the twenty-three-mile well. It's where we camp tonight. Bert, I will tell you tomorrow all about my plans.' This well was only about twenty feet deep but the water in it was just like the last one.

After we had a meal, we lay down to rest for the night. The dogs were acting strange – they wanted to get near to us. Bill growled at them, and told me that they were scared of dingoes at night. The dingo smell makes a tame dog scared. There are very few tame dogs that will attack a dingo.

This dingo business not only scared the dogs. I didn't like them either, and for the rest of the night I had very little sleep. I didn't let Bill know my feelings. He hadn't been lying down long before he was snoring, but not me. Then one of the dingoes howled not far away and a funny feeling ran up and down my spine. The two dogs huddled in closer to me and I didn't mind a bit. All through the night the dingoes kept howling. So many things went through my mind. (You have to hear a dingo howl close by to know how frightening it can be.)

I was glad when daylight came. Bill didn't have to shake me to wake me – I was wide awake already. While we were having a bite to eat I spoke to Bill about the dingoes. He said, 'There's a large granite hill range not far from here. It's a breeding ground for dingoes. There's big caves going up under the boulders where they can have their pups and no one can get to them. They won't come close enough to hurt you. The only time a dingo will attack you is when he cannot escape. Then he puts up and fights for his life.'

We got on our way before sunrise, and what a sunrise it was. Everything was a golden colour – the hills, the trees. I hadn't seen anything like it before. Bill said, 'If you get a job on a station two or three hundred miles north-east, you'll see sunrises prettier than this, and some beautiful sunsets too. Some of the country up North seems to all come to life at sunrise and kinda slows off at sunset.'

As we slowly made our way along the track to Mullewa, Bill said, 'Now I'll tell you about my plans. This lady I was telling you about – the one I have my Christmas Day with – wants me to get a regular job such as a station hand or manager or something like that, and settle down. I think I brought this about myself because last Christmas Day I was so happy with her I had a little more to drink than I should have, and I asked her to marry me. She wouldn't agree because she wouldn't like me being away from her for long periods. She said she would be glad to marry me if I could be with her all the time. When I left her after last Christmas she told me to think about finding some way to be able to do this. She said to me, 'Bill, I love you, and I feel sure we could be happy together, but we must be together all of the time. I don't want a husband that I can only have once or twice a year.'

Bill then told me that when he arrived back in Mullewa about two weeks ago, the Postmaster had told him that a large stock firm in Perth was advertising for station managers or stockmen with a good knowledge of the North and an understanding of cattle. He said, 'I sent an application in the day I arrived in Geraldton this trip. I haven't received an answer yet. It takes about three weeks or a month to get a letter to Perth and return, if they answer straight away. The mail comes up through Narngulu to Mullewa. So I won't leave Mullewa until the Wednesday after the New Year – that is mail day. I don't want to build your hopes up too much, Bert, but if you haven't a job by the time I leave, you could come with me kangaroo shooting. If I get a favourable reply to my letter, I may be able to fit you in with me too. That's why I am telling you all this. Now you know what's on my mind.'

Then Bill started to talk about May. 'You will like her,' he said, 'she is a wonderful woman. No funny business. She is as straight as can be and very respectable, and honest as they come.'

The horses were walking very slow. It was a very hot day. After half past ten we stopped at a nice shady spot. There wasn't any place to water the horses. Bill said that there was a well further on, but we wouldn't get there until late that evening. We had three large waterbags with us, so, when we unhitched the horses, Bill put half the contents of one of the bags into a flat canvas bag and gave them a drink. We made a small fire and using water out of another waterbag, filled a billy can to make a billy of tea. Bill gave the dogs a drink by turning his felt hat inside out, and filling the crown with water. After we had something to eat and drank our tea, we spread the tarpaulin out on the ground in the shade and rested.

We were up and away again about three o'clock and travelled along slowly. I walked for a few miles, I was tired of sitting for so long. We arrived at the watering place that evening. Bill said, pointing to an area of green grass, 'That is what we call a spring formation of the ground. Water is forced up out of the earth and runs all year round. It is beautiful fresh water. The early settlers and travellers dug a large hole at this spot and stoned it up.' The hole was about eight feet wide, six feet deep, and raised about two feet above the surface of the earth. The water had filled the round hole and was running over the top and down into a creek. Bill said, 'This is a wild animals' watering place. You will hear some frightening noises tonight. Wild horses, kangaroos, dingoes will all be here after the water.' We made camp about two hundred yards from the water-hole. Bill said that there was nothing to worry about.

When we unharnessed, watered and fed the horses, Bill said, 'We are only about eighteen miles from Mullewa. We will make it tomorrow easily.'

The weather was much cooler that night. I was very tired and went to sleep a few minutes after we turned in. I slept right through and when I awakened, it was daylight, and Bill had the billy boiled. He asked, 'Did you hear the dingoes last night?' I said, 'I didn't hear a sound. I must have slept right through the night.' He said, 'You must have been very tired because there was a terrible din. I was wakened several times and you hadn't moved. The dingoes came very close and the dogs were barking. There were a lot of wild horses galloping about too, and neighing. Sounded like the mares calling their foals, no doubt protecting them from the dingoes.'

When we got under way Bill said that this would be the quickest trip he had made. It usually took three and a half days from Geraldton to Mullewa but we would be there in less than three. The sky was overcast and it looked like a storm was coming up.

Bill seemed to be happy in himself. He talked a lot about May. 'You'll like her,' he said. 'When her husband was killed, she was left all alone. I came in from the bush and stayed with her. She sent word to me by a black stockman. He rode over two hundred miles to get me. Her husband and I were good mates. I used to work with him wellsinking when I first came to Mullewa. His name was Jack Prang. He could do almost anything. He specialized in horse-breaking, well-sinking and stockyard building, and he wanted me to give in kangaroo shooting and go into partnership with him. I almost did once. I wish I had – it may have saved his life. He was on his own when he got killed. Horse-breaking is a two man job.'

I noticed as we travelled along that the country was changing. The timber was smaller and more open, and the scrub was thicker. We had passed through some very rough granite hill country and deep valleys, but now the country was flatter and more even. During the trip Bill had pointed out many new settlers' places and he remarked, 'The poor devils are having a battle, I think they're only wasting their time and money. They don't know enough about farming in this country to be able to make a living.'

Bill let the horses take their own time. He said, 'We will give them a spell at about eleven o'clock, then we should arrive in Mullewa by three or three thirty. If a storm breaks we will keep going.' He said that the clouds were too high for a storm, although they looked very black and threatening. No rain came, and after giving the horses a rest for about an hour, we moved off on the last six miles.

This trip reminded me a lot of the trip with Uncle Archie from York to Wickepin in 1902. I often wondered what was ahead for me. I hadn't been able to carry on with my schooling since I left home at Subiaco. Now my school books were in my tin trunk at Mrs Stafford's place at Geraldton.

After travelling for about an hour and a half, we came up onto a large hill, then all at once Bill said, 'There she is.' He was pointing towards two or three buildings some three quarters of a mile away. 'That's Mullewa.' he said. This made me feel sad – I had expected to see some sort of town. As we got near I could see there were three buildings – a fairly large one, and two small cottages. There was also a railway station. This was Mullewa. The large building was the hotel, store and Post Office all in one.

When we arrived at the hotel, it was half past two in the afternoon. Bill stopped the horses just outside and said, 'You stay on the cart, Bert, and mind the horses. I won't be long.' With that he got down out of the cart and went into the hotel. A few minutes later he came out again, took the reins and said, 'We will camp at May's place. It's about half a mile from here.'

28

ANOTHER CHRISTMAS

May's house was built of granite stone. It was only small, two rooms with a verandah back and front. She used one room for a bedroom and the other was a dining-room – kitchen. She had a huge fireplace. Just off from the house was a shed. One end of this was used for a stable and the other was enclosed. In the middle of the shed there was a space large enough to put the cart in. Bill said we would camp there for the time being and have our meals in the house. He went on to say that May worked at the pub but came home to sleep every night. He knew where the key was, so we could get into the house.

We unpacked all the things off the cart and stacked them in the shed, then unharnessed the horses and let them loose. Bill said that there was plenty of feed and water in the paddock. The paddock was a home-stead block of one hundred and sixty acres. Bill found the key, unlocked the door of the house and lit a fire. The time had moved on to after four o'clock and we made some tea and had a meal. Bill said that May wouldn't be home until a little after six. She started work at seven in the morning and worked until six at night. Bill said that she had all her meals at the hotel, except on Sunday when she didn't work.

After we finished our meal, Bill left me to clean up, saying that he was going up to the pub and would walk back with May. At about twenty minutes past six, May and Bill arrived home. Bill was as pleased as a man who had just won Tattersalls. As they entered the kitchen he said, 'This is the lady you have been hearing about Bert.' She looked at me for a moment then came over to me and said, 'You are very welcome to stay here, Bert, and I am so glad to meet you.' I said, 'Thank you, Mrs Prang.' Then I told her that she was all Bill had said she was. She thanked me and said, 'You can call me May, Bert. All my friends call me May and I feel sure that you and I will be friends.' She was a small woman, about five feet two inches tall, with a dark complexion – a very nice looker. My first impression was that she was an honest and kind person. I liked what I saw in that first few minutes.

She said to me, 'You look very young Bert. How old are you?' When I told her my age she said, 'You are big for your age. Bill tells me you would like to work on a cattle station.' When I agreed, she said that it would be hard for me to get that kind of employment, because the station hands that are sought after are older and much more used to camping out for weeks at a time on their own. She said, 'I believe that the life is very lonely. I've met a few of the station hands passing through. But if you get a job at or around the homestead you will be all right. Anyway we will see what happens. I'll keep my eyes and ears open for you. One never knows what's around the corner.'

May had a gramophone (an Edison), and dozens of different records. The records were about the size of an ordinary jam tin, like the ones the Station Master at Narrogin had had. The gramophone had a handle and a large spring-like clock that had to be wound up, and it would play two records without having to be re-wound.

Bill and May were in a deep conversation sitting in the two easy chairs by the fire. I amused myself by playing records on the gramophone. May had many lovely waltz tunes and also some beautiful songs. That evening was one of the most beautiful to me. At eleven o'clock May made some supper, then we all retired to bed. Bill and I slept out in the shed.

The next day was Christmas Eve. When I awakened, Bill was up lighting the fire. May had gone to work. We had breakfast, then Bill told me that May had arranged for us both to have our meals up at the pub. 'Of course, we will have to pay for them. They will cost us one and sixpence each meal, but don't worry, I'll fix yours.' I objected to this as I had enough money on me to pay for my meals. Bill said, 'Okay, if that's what you want, Bert.' He then told me that May always had Christmas Day off, so we would have our Christmas meals with her.

Christmas Eve went by and Christmas Day came. The overcast clouds had gone and Christmas morning came with bright sunshine. Bill was up and had the fire burning. Later I heard Bill and May wish each other a Happy Christmas. Then a few minutes later, Bill called me in to breakfast.

After breakfast I washed the dishes while May set about preparing the Christmas dinner. She had two dressed cockerels to cook. Bill was getting the vegetables ready, and as we chatted and joked with each other, we all seemed very happy. Bill no doubt showed his feelings towards May. He couldn't take his eyes off her. They had several drinks together that morning. May hadn't forgotten me – she had lemonade and ginger ale, as well as lemon and orange squash. I hadn't had such luxuries before. I played a few records on the gramophone and each time a waltz was played, Bill grabbed May and waltzed her around the kitchen.

May had the table set and decorated with all kinds of bush flowers which were beautiful at that time of year. They were something you would have to see to believe. So we had Christmas dinner and it was the nicest I had had. When it was over May and Bill had some drinks and Bill was getting unsteady on his feet. It didn't seem to affect May. She explained to me that Bill, after going so long without strong drink, then letting himself go, was easily affected. He was, at that moment, sound asleep in one of the armchairs in the kitchen. I helped May do the washing and cleaning up, then she went into her room. She said she felt sleepy and would have a sleep also. I went for a walk into the bush for two or three hours and when I returned they were still asleep.

29

SIGNING ON

Two days later I had a visitor. A man on horseback came at about ten in the morning. (Bill had gone up to the pub to help May as he did nearly every day.) The man said goodday to me and I said goodday to him. Then he said, 'I was talking to Bill Oliver up at the pub and he said you were looking for a job on a station.' I replied that this was so. He said, 'I'm looking for a lad to go with me and my gang on a cattle drive. Every year I arrange to drive cattle to the coast for shipment to the markets. I have a contract with the station managers to drive their cattle to various places – mostly Geraldton every second year. One year I drive them down to the Ashburton River route then the next year I do another route.'

The man told me that his name was Bob McInnis, 'mostly known as Baldy'. He took his hat off and said, 'The crop of hair you see on my head explains why.' His head had only a few hairs, just above his ears. The top of his head was shiny like it had been that way for years. He was a small wiry man about fifty years old and weighed about ten stone. Although he had no hair on the top of his head, he made up for it with a big black bushy beard, about eight inches long.

He told me that the job would be for some five to six months, depending on how the weather and Mother Luck held out. Once we started there would be no turning back. 'Your job,' he said, 'would be cook's assistant. The gang is made up with four white men and myself, and if you join up it will be six whites, and eight blacks. We will all be on horseback. We take four pack mules and five spare saddle horses.' He then asked me my full name. I told him and said that everyone called me Bert. 'All right,' he said, 'I'll call you Bert. If you take the job you can call me Bob. I'll pay you one pound a week and keep. You will be paid from the day you take the job up to when the drive is finished. It's not hard work, only the monotony is hard to take, and for awhile you will get very saddle sore. Once you get used to riding and the saddle, it is not too bad.'

He hadn't mentioned anything about the wild blacks. I didn't say anything either, but I had been told some terrible tales about them. I wondered if there was any truth in the stories. When Bob left me he said, 'You think it over and let me know within two days. If you don't want the job I will need time to find someone else.' I promised him I would let him know the next day. As he left he told me where his place was and said that Bill would direct me.

A few minutes after Bob went, it was time for me to go to the pub for dinner. While we were having our dinner, I asked Bill all about Bob McInnis and the job. Bill said that the job should suit me as I loved horses and I would have a horse to ride to myself. I was puzzled about being at least six months on the job, and said that they must go a long way to take that long. Bill said, 'Did he tell you the name of the drive?' I said he had mentioned the Ashburton route, then Bill said, 'Oh, yes, you will take about four to five weeks getting from here to where the drive starts. It's somewhere up near the Ophthalmia Ranges, over six hundred miles from here, through Meekatharra, right up to above the head of the Ashburton River near Mundiwindi.'

After giving the job a lot of thought, I decided to take it. Next day, after our midday meal, Bill and I drove over to Bob's place and I told him that I would take the job. He seemed pleased and said, 'You won't regret it, Bert. We are a happy mob and we will see that you fit in with us.' He then told me what I would want for the trip and he said, 'I will supply you with a horse, saddle and bridle. The horse is the prettiest little thing you have ever seen. It is a filly and she is black, with four white stockings and a white face. She was born on a drive about four years ago. You will love her, Bert. She is very quiet and when she gets used to you she will never leave you.'

Bob McInnis had a lovely home; a large house built of mud batts, with an iron roof, and a verandah all around it. It was called a bungalow type. I told Bob I would shift to his place the next day. Bill said he would bring me and my things over. On our way back, I spoke to Bill again about taking the job and he said he would have liked me to be with him, but his position was uncertain. As things were, he didn't know what he would be doing. He said, 'I cannot make up my mind until I get a reply about the station manager's job. You're doing the right thing, Bert. You will have a job for at least six months, and one pound a week and keep is good wages for a fourteen-year-old boy.'

Then Bill told me a secret. He said that he wouldn't be going 'roo shooting anymore. He had been offered a job as a yardman by the owner of the pub. He was also to put up some more stables at the pub, and milk the cows and deliver the milk. 'Of course,' he said, 'I cannot take this job if I get a manager's job. But in any case, Bert, the secret is that May and I are getting married, but don't mention it within May's hearing. She might tell you herself now she knows you are going with Baldy.'

The next morning Bill got up to see May off to work. After breakfast, I put my belongings into the cart and drove up to the pub, where I bought two pairs of riding trousers, two shirts, an extra pair of riding boots, two large handkerchiefs (Bill told me to get them to put around my neck at night) and a broad-brimmed hat. I also bought a mosquito net, ground-sheet and a rain cape.

Having put these purchases in the cart, I went to say goodbye to May. She said that she was sorry I was going but she thought it was the best thing I could do. Suddenly she put her arms around me and kissed me hard. I noticed she had tears in her eyes. That was the first time anyone had kissed me like that besides Grandma. I went all hot and cold. Bill was watching, too. While May still had her arms around me she said, 'Bert, Bill and I are getting married in about four weeks time. Isn't that wonderful?' I recovered enough to say, 'Yes, that's fine and I wish you all the luck in the world. When I get back after the drive I hope to see you both again.' With that I broke loose and went and got into the cart. I felt I would have cried if I didn't get away quick. A few minutes later, Bill came out and off we went to Baldy's place.

When we got going Bill was very quiet for awhile, then he said, 'May was quite upset when you said goodbye. She has a heart of gold, Bert. She thinks it's a shame that a boy your age has to battle along on his own.' He looked at me and said, 'What do you think of her, Bert?' I didn't answer him for awhile, then I said, 'Bill, I have only known her for one week but I feel as if I have known her for years. She is a wonderful person and I think you are a very lucky man. What knocked the stuffin' out of me was the way she kissed me. It made me feel really happy. I have never been affected like that before. I don't know what I looked like, but I felt stunned.' Bill said, 'All the time I have known her – before her husband died and over the three years since – she wouldn't even let me put my arm around her, let alone kiss me, until two days ago when I decided not to go kangaroo shooting any more.'

A few minutes later we arrived at my new boss's place, and after unloading my belongings, Bill said goodbye. He made me promise to see him and May when the drive was over. Then he got on his way back to May and happiness.

CATTLE DRIVE
North-West of Western Australia

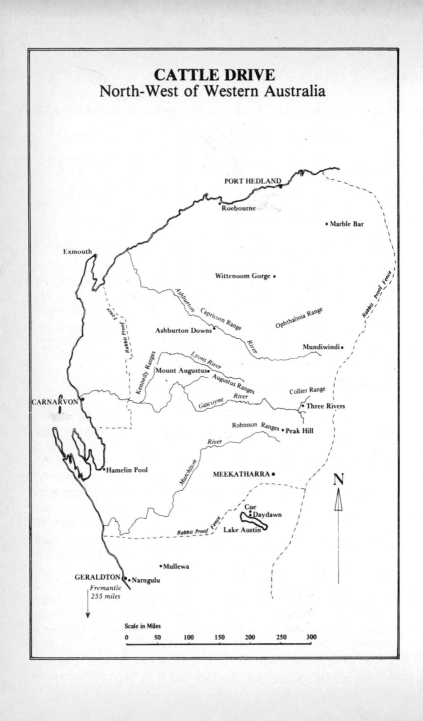

PORT HEDLAND

Roebourne

Marble Bar

Exmouth

Wittenoom Gorge

Ashburton River

Capricorn Range

Ophthalmia Range

Ashburton Downs

Rabbit Proof Fence

Mundiwindi

Kennedy Ranges

Lyons River

Mount Augustus

Augustus Ranges River

Collier Range

Gascoyne River

CARNARVON

Three Rivers

Robinson Ranges

Peak Hill

Murchison River

Hamelin Pool

MEEKATHARRA

N

Cue
Daydawn
Rabbit Proof Fence
Lake Austin

Mullewa

GERALDTON Narngulu
*Fremantle
255 miles*

Scale in Miles

0   50   100   150   200   250   300

30

PREPARATION

My new boss showed me where I was to stay until we set off to start the cattle drive. I had a room to myself for the time being. Bob said, 'When Arthur arrives back, he will share this room with you. He's the cook and you will be with him all the time we are away, so if you're sleeping here together, you will get to know each other a little.' Bob showed me around his place, and when we came to the horses, he pointed out the filly I was to ride. She was the loveliest and prettiest pony I had ever seen. She was a black-and-white, four years old and very quiet. Bob hadn't exaggerated when he told me about her.

Bob had an eight-stall stable and a large stockyard built around it. The stockyard covered about half an acre, and there were several large shade trees in it and feed mangers around it. The mangers were very strongly made out of some hollowed logs with the ends boarded up and a portion of the top cut out for the horses or cows to put their head in to get feed. Bob also kept some cows for milk.

The next day Bob gave me the job of oiling the saddles, bridles, saddle-straps, cruppers and reins. All the leather straps had to be scrubbed in warm soapy water, and then put out into the sun to dry. When they were properly dry I had to rub raw linseed oil into them until the leather became soft and pliable. Bob said this would preserve the leather because it would have to be out in all sorts of weather, and the softening also made it easier to ride in the saddle.

Bob came and talked to me the second day, while I was oiling the saddles. He told me he was a widower and that he had lost his wife a few years ago. They had only been there a year when she died. They had no children. He said that it took him a couple of years to get over her death. 'The old man that you met yesterday,' he said, 'is my wife's father.' (The man Bob was referring to, I knew as Jock. He was a Scot and did the cooking and looked after the place while Bob was away droving.) Bob said that the old man used to go droving with them, but his age now was against him for roughing it.

So, 1908 went out and 1909 came in. The weather was hot and sultry. I had finished the oiling and Bob and I cleaned out a soak. It was the only water supply on Bob's property, and it hadn't been cleaned out for three years. Bob said it was beautiful water, just like rain water from a tank. (Bob had several thousand-gallon rain-water tanks for the house supply.)

We not only cleaned out the soak, we deepened it another three feet, and stoned the sides up to stop side soil from falling into the water. This took us three days and when we finished, it filled up to the top in a few hours. We did this work on the soak so that Jock wouldn't have any trouble with the water while we were away.

At night, after our evening meal, Bob used to ask me all about myself, and was surprised when I told him that I hadn't any schooling. One night I asked him was there any truth in the stories I had heard about the blacks up North. He told me that there were some blacks still very hostile to whites, but he hadn't had any trouble with them. He said, 'Some of the stations had trouble on account of them killing cattle. Of course the poor beggars have to live the same as we do and they do knock off prime bullocks now and again. I don't think that's so bad, when you remember how station people shoot hundreds of kangaroos and leave them to rot because they are living on the station grass. The kangaroo is the black man's main meat supply. No, Bert, you won't have any trouble with the blacks. Just be friendly to them, they have feelings just like we have, and I'm sure they won't worry you.'

Two days later Bob's place became a hive of activity. The four white drovers turned up: Arthur Rose – the cook, Stan Smith, George Pogson and George Morgan (they called him Darkey because of the other George). Then later that evening the coloured men arrived – six part-blooded Aboriginals and two full-bloods.

The next day was a day of getting ready. Bob went up to the store for supplies for the trip and he told Stan and Darkey to bring the horses into the stable. I asked Darkey why Bob wanted the horses in, and he said, 'This is what he always does a day or so before starting the drive. We'll feed the horses on chaff and oats. It hardens them up a little. When we go, some extra feed will be strapped onto the spare horses and pack mules, so that we can give all the animals one feed a day of hard dry food. This stops them from getting gripe and stomach pains. After a few days of travelling they will be all right, but at first we have to go steady.'

That night, when we were having our evening meal, Bob announced that we would be leaving the following afternoon. He said that we would be travelling as much as possible in the evening, night and early morning while the weather was so hot; and resting up during the day. He said, 'Tomorrow morning, finish your packing, strap your bed-roll onto your horse, then rest up for the rest of the day. We will have a meal about four thirty and be ready to leave at five.'

We all went to bed early that evening. I felt very excited. While Arthur and I were getting into bed, Arthur said, 'Bert, tomorrow and the next few weeks will be bad for you. It takes about two weeks to get over saddle soreness if you're not used to riding. Us others take only two days after we have been away for a few weeks. It's six weeks since I rode a horse so I expect a little trouble. Ask Bob for some of his ointment tomorrow. Rub it on your bottom and the back of your legs from the knees up in the early forenoon and again just before midday. Then keep the treatment going every day, it will help a lot.' Next morning I didn't have to ask Bob. He came to me with a four-ounce bottle of ointment and gave me the same instructions. He said, 'This is going to be your biggest worry for awhile, Bert. Saddle soreness is very trying, so you will have to overcome it. After that you will be okay, so good luck.'

31

THE RIDE NORTH

So, on the tenth day of January 1909, at almost five o'clock in the afternoon, we set off on the long trip to a place unknown to me, some six hundred miles away. As well as our own saddle horses, we had five mules loaded with food, pots and pans, and a camp oven. Five spare saddle horses were carrying feed, nose-bags, ropes, hobbles and other gear. The five pack mules were hitched together by a lead, and led by Arthur, all travelling in Indian file. Stan led the spare horses the same way. He, George and Darkey agreed to handle the spares until I got over the expected saddle soreness. We were all in Indian file, our boss taking the lead, and the black men at the rear. We made quite a long line, twenty-four horses in all.

We started off with the sun behind us. The horses were very fresh and walked at a fast gait. Bob didn't follow a track of any sort during the day, but as darkness came we came across an unused track and followed this until well into the night. There had been heavy rain the second week in December up where we were going and down to Mullewa. The small water holes had plenty of water in them and Bob remarked that the early rains had given the natural grass a good start.

Finally the Boss said, 'We'll camp now for a few hours, then get going about three o'clock in the morning.' We all unsaddled our horses, and hobbled them or let them go to graze. The spares and mules were hitched to long ropes so that they could graze. One of the men took the first turn looking after the horses and mules and the rest of us had a mug of tea and a meal that Arthur had made. Then we slept until about three o'clock in the morning, and were on our way again soon after.

This was the procedure for the first four days. We travelled from five to ten thirty in the evening, then from four to nine in the morning. This made our travelling time about ten hours each day, and we covered roughly thirty miles a day.

On the morning of the fifth day we came to a water hole in a creek. The grass was extra well grown so Bob gave the horses a whole day's rest. We had passed through the first rabbit-proof fence about an hour before. The next day was overcast – heavy black cloud covered the whole sky and the weather became cooler. Just after daylight we loaded up and set off again. The day's rest had done my sore bottom and legs good. I never let on to any of the men, but I had suffered hell for two days before we had a break. I rubbed on the ointment several times while we were resting.

Our food was mostly tinned food – tins of meat, jam, tinned milk – and Arthur used to make a baking-powder loaf in the camp oven. When he took the loaf out of the oven it looked like a grindstone and this was what Arthur called it. When we stopped for a few hours, or for the night, Arthur would leave his horses and mules for us to look after and say, 'I'll have to make another grindstone.' These loaves Arthur made were lovely. We never had any butter because of the heat, but we had plenty of golden syrup, tinned jam and cheese. Our boss used to take two of the horses and go into the station houses we passed to fetch back some home-made bread and fresh meat.

The camp oven was made of cast iron, round, and was twenty inches across and five inches deep. Arthur used to hang it on one of the pack mules where it was always handy to use. He had various billy cans of all sizes hanging on the same mule and used to make about two gallons of tea at a time.

Late in the afternoon of the sixth day, when we had been travelling for about three hours, it started to rain. The Boss came back from the lead and said that we were in for a downpour. He told us to make the horses hurry along because it was only a few miles to Lake Austin where we would camp the night. So we hurried the horses along, trotting them on the downhill stretches. We had put on our capes, and the food and rugs were covered with waterproof sheets.

Finally we arrived at Lake Austin. There was a large shed there that had been built many years before for boundry riders. We had room enough to stack all our saddles and gear, and still shelter in it ourselves. All the horses except one were hobbled out to graze. (We always kept one horse on a lead near our camp to round up the others the next morning. This horse would graze around as far as the lead would reach, then one of the men would get up during the night and shift it so it could reach more grass.) Next morning, it was still raining. We were lucky because the old shed had a fireplace in one end and we managed to find enough dry firewood to have a nice big fire.

The rain stopped early in the afternoon, and it was late in the evening when we moved off. We followed the bush track north-east. Stan said that this track was the Central Stock Route. The sky was cloudless and we kept going for about six hours. Well into the night we came to a valley; both sides towered hundreds of feet into the sky with large granite boulders showing like big monuments on top. We camped at this spot. A creek ran through the valley and there was plenty of grass for the horses to eat. We had a quick cold meal of tinned meat and damper owing to not being able to get enough dry wood or sticks to light a fire. There were many large overhanging boulders and we camped under these. In spite of the heavy rain the ground there was dry.

I was still very saddle-sore. When we were travelling after dark, I was able to take the weight off the sore parts by leaning and putting most of my weight on the bedroll strapped to the front of the saddle. I tried to hide my soreness because the men were all so sure that I would have to get off my pony and walk. So in the daytime I would grin and bear it, but under the cover of darkness I did all kinds of things to keep myself going and show them I could stand it.

The next few days were very hot, so we returned to our pattern of resting during the hottest part of the day and around midnight. Time lost importance to us as the days came and went. The Boss kept records of the days and the weeks. He and Darkey were the only ones who had reliable watches. Two of the black men had watches but they had to correct them each day with the Boss or Darkey, as one would always be fast and the other kept stopping.

We had no water problems as the creeks still had plenty of water. The country and scenery changed from day to day. The timber was only in the valleys and it was small; large trees were few and far between with none whatsoever on the hills or high ground. We saw thousands of anthills – some standing as high as fifteen feet – all over the low level ground, thousands of blackboys, and patches of mallee. The hills looked bald. Most were covered with granite boulders or scrub, and some were covered with a reddish soil which looked very pretty at sunrise and sunset.

The track we were following wound around the high hills and over the smaller ones. We came near to some homesteads, but although the Boss called into some of them with two of the pack mules, the rest of us never went near them. The names of the stations are hard to remember as most of them were names used by the blacks before white men came. With my limited schooling, I couldn't pronounce them properly, so was unable to remember them.

During the middle of the third week out from Mullewa we had to have all the horses and mules shod. Stan, Darkey, George and the Boss did the shoeing. We stopped at a boundary rider's hut that had a small forge.

My soreness had almost gone and I was feeling much better. Arthur told me that we were east of the Robinson Range, or Peak Hill as some called it. He said that we were nearly halfway from where we had started and that we had done well, but from here on the going would be harder and we would have to rest the horses every two or three days. The shoeing was completed in almost four hours, and we all had a good rest before starting out again.

I remember the names of some of the places Arthur told me as we passed through them: names such as Lake Austin, Day Dawn, Meekatharra. Arthur said that one of the waterways we crossed was the commencement of the Murchison River. He said, 'Down near the coast it is very wide and hard to cross at this time of the year with cattle, but by the time we get down there on the way back, we will be well into the dry season.'

The travelling became harder, the country more rugged, and by the end of the third week the Boss decided to give the horses a day's rest. We came to a large valley the blacks called Wonging Valley. (I was told that Wonging means 'noises' in the blacks' language.) Arthur said the whites called it Echo Valley. It did return the sound to anyone calling out.

This valley was beautiful. A small water stream was running along it, and the water was clear, fresh and tasted beautiful. To the north was a large granite outcrop, some two hundred feet high, overlooking the valley. This outcrop looked like it had been part of a large range of hills that had been washed away, leaving only the granite rocks. In between the boulders and under the parts overhanging the valley provided shade and shelter. The water came from under the boulders running down the valley, and there was an abundance of beautiful feed for the horses.

We camped there and rested the horses, intending to move on the next day. But next morning the sky was overcast, lightning could be seen in the distance and we could hear thunder. The Boss said we were in for heavy rain. We remained where we were as the shelter was good. About midday it started to rain, and didn't it come down – I hadn't seen rain like that before. We were high and dry and well sheltered, and the men brought the horses in under the boulders. The rain was so heavy that the valley had about three feet of water in it within an hour. It rained all that afternoon and well into the night, and the thunder and lightning were terrific. I had never liked lightning and this storm didn't help me to like it any better. I was scared stiff.

The next morning was fine and the clouds were lighter, although the sky was still overcast. At daylight the men turned the horses out to feed. They had been tied under shelter all that night and were very hungry. After the midday meal we packed up and got on our way again. The weather was cooler and travelling pleasant.

During our stay at Echo Valley, the Boss had asked me how I was liking the trip. I told him that my soreness was gone and I felt fine. He asked me how I liked my pony and I said that she was lovely. He then told me how he came by her. Four years ago, while on a drive, they came across a mare. She appeared to be very sick, and looked as if she had been lying in the position they found her in for two or three days. She had lain down to give birth to a foal and was then too weak to get up. As they approached the mare, the foal whinnied and staggered towards them. It was a filly and very pretty. The mother was almost dead and beyond help, so the Boss shot her to end her suffering. He was about to shoot the foal when one of the young black boys begged him not to – he suggested that, as they had a cow in the herd that had had a calf the day before (they had to kill the calf as that was the usual thing when a calf was born on the drive), they teach the foal to suckle from the cow. The black said he would look after the foal, and make a cradle out of bags to carry her on one of the pack horses for a few days, until she was strong enough to keep up with the herd herself. The men appealed to the Boss and the prettiness of her markings made him spare her life. The black said that once the foal learned to suck the cow it would follow it. Everything the black said came true. The foal got a taste for the cow's milk, and after a few days, the cow took complete charge of the foal. 'Now Bert,' the Boss said, 'that's the pony you have on this drive. I broke her in last year. We named her Dinnertime. She got the name on account of always knowing when it was meal time while she was little on that drive four years ago.'

After we left Echo Valley the whole country changed. On the level and flat country there were thousands of anthills, some huge and some small, and the trees were all butt. Some of the tree butts were three or four feet through at the base, with two or three small limbs growing out of them. They looked as if something had cut the limbs off when they got to be three to four inches thick. Arthur told me that storms were the cause of this, and also, that cyclones were the reason why there weren't any large trees. He said that the cyclones flattened all the trees, and there was a cyclone every year or so in that part of the North.

Although the men used to tell some fantastic tales about the blacks, we didn't come across any big tribes until four days out from Echo Valley – then we came to a very large tribe. There were hundreds of them. Their camp was at a place called Three Rivers near the Collier Range. The natives were of all ages and were dressed mostly with skins. The men wore kangaroo skin loin coverings, the women had most of their body covered. The little kids didn't have any coverings at all. They were all bare-footed and didn't wear any kind of head covering.

As we approached the camp they ran to meet us. I must have looked frightened because Darkey said, 'Don't be afraid, Bert, they won't trouble us. They're a friendly lot.' I replied, 'They might be a friendly lot, but I don't like the looks of them. They look anything but friendly.' Our horses didn't like all the noise, especially the din the dogs made. They must have had fifty or sixty dogs, all shapes and sizes, and all barking.

We were travelling behind each other Indian file and we didn't stop. Some two or three hours later we stopped and set up camp in a valley near the Collier Range. I had to believe what I was told about where we were because I didn't have a clue to our true position. All I knew was where the sun came up and set. The Boss said that we would rest the horses for a whole day.

We were in our fifth week and had travelled approximately four hundred and fifty miles, and had some two hundred miles or more to go. We got going again the next afternoon. All the animals were fed and seemed to be anxious to be moving again. The country was very rugged and hilly, and the weather was again very hot. The only shade was in the valleys, under scrub and small trees.

Arthur said we would be passing through a large station in about three days. He said it was one of the biggest cattle stations and it was called Mundiwindi. We would be collecting quite a big mob of cattle from there on our way back. The station hands would bring them out to meet us near the commencement of the Ashburton River.

The next two days took us to Mundiwindi. We passed about two miles east of the homestead. The Boss and one of the blacks took two mules and went into the homestead for supplies. The Boss gave Arthur instructions to continue to a watering place about three miles further on and camp.

We arrived at the watering place (a well) near midday. It had a windmill that pumped water into a large squatter's tank and from that into several long water troughs for the cattle and horses. It was beautiful water.

The weather was cooler. We unpacked and had a mug of tea and a cold lunch of tinned meat and damper, then damper with jam. After that, we all – except one man who had to look after the horses – spread our bedrolls out on the ground and went to sleep.

One of our big troubles on the trip was wild horses, or brumbies. There were hundreds of them. That was one of the reasons why we always had to hobble the horses and mules when we turned them out to graze, and why we always kept a horse handy on tether. The wild stallions would try to entice our mares away, and would bite and kick the geldings, so one of us had to take turns in watching the horses all the time.

I didn't wake until just after sundown, when the Boss returned from the homestead. He had managed to get a few loaves of home-made bread, a side of young beef and a large piece of bacon. Arthur didn't take long getting some of the choice steaks fried, and we had the meal of the trip. We gave that home-made bread and steak the treatment that hungry people would be expected to give it.

Owing to the horses being leg weary, the Boss ordered us to rest till the next day. He said, 'We have only about one hundred and sixty miles to go, so we can take the horses steady from now on. We take over the first lot of cattle on the first day of March, in fifteen days time, so we can take our time.'

We followed the track north-east for the next eight days – to a point north-east of the Ophthalmia Range – covering a little over one hundred miles. From the Ophthalmia Range, we turned direct east towards the sunrise, then five days later we came to a rabbit-proof fence.

This was the first rabbit-proof fence built across Western Australia, to prevent rabbits from migrating into the stock and wheat portions of the state. This fence was a failure and two more fences were built further south. We had passed through them earlier in the trip. They were shorter and only fenced in special sections. There were gates all along at intervals for travellers to pass through. The Government built these fences and employed boundary riders to take care of them and to see that the gates were properly shut. This fence was the starting point of our long drive.

32

THE DRIVE BEGINS

We had two days to wait until we took over the first lot of cattle. Near where we made our camp there was an old boundary riders' camp and a windmill. Arthur said the windmill was pumping water from a bore. Artesian water came up through a two-inch pipe into a large tank and from there into water-troughs for the stock. The flow into the troughs was governed by a stopcock so that a plentiful supply of water would always be there.

The two days we had to wait were just what we needed, and we rested most of the time. The only ones that had to do anything, apart from Arthur and I, were the men who took turns in looking after the horses and mules. They also re-shod them. Arthur and I got the meals. My job was to find wood and sticks and I also gathered dry cattle manure. We used this to keep our fire burning as the dry manure would smoulder and keep alight. In the morning we would have red-hot ashes, and when we started them up with small sticks and wood, we would have a good cooking fire in a few minutes.

As well as the problem with the brumbies, we were now pestered by thousands of pink and grey cockatoos. The men called them galahs – they also called them many other things, of course. I'd never seen anything like them before in my life. They would bite holes in anything, even the leather saddles and straps. We would wash our clothes and hang them out to dry on a bush, and these birds would make big holes in the shirts or anything else. They got so cheeky and bold that one of the men had to get a rifle and shoot a few of them to frighten them away.

About eleven o'clock on the first day of March, the first lot of cattle were taken over by the Boss – some two hundred and twenty of them. All sorts and sizes; bullocks with large, wide horns, and cows of all kinds and colours. They were in very poor condition. Arthur said that they had come off scrub country and would soon pick up on the good grass on our way down the coast. We all had an early midday meal, then packed up and started on the drive.

Arthur rode his horse and led the mules Indian file as before. I led the spare saddle horses the same way.

Arthur, who was actually my boss, explained how and what we had to do while on the drive. He said, 'We will go ahead of the cattle early in the mornings each day and prepare a meal. There are fourteen of us altogether so our job won't be easy. The stockmen will have their meals in relays. The first lot are those that were out night herding. They have their meal first, then the others. Then they all go out and start the herding and we clean up and cut sandwiches for each man for the day. One of the drovers gets them and delivers them. Then we pack everything up and set off and find a place to camp that night. As the herd gets bigger our job gets harder.'

Arthur explained that, as our stocks of food got low, the Boss would go to the nearest station and get more. The stations kept plenty of supplies on hand, so we could always get fresh meat as well as flour, potatoes, baking-powder, and home-made bread and butter. (The Boss was well-known to the station owners and their wives, and they always knew within a day or so of the herd passing and made bread.)

Arthur also told me how the drive was carried out. 'We always have scouts out in front of the herd and on both sides. This is done so they can look out for station cattle and drive them well away from the herd. The scouts out in front are always about a mile ahead so the station cattle can't hear the herd or smell them. The scouts have to change their horses often as they do a lot more travelling than the drovers. They can't rest their horses like the drovers or allow them to feed along at the same pace as the cattle.'

Arthur reckoned that we had the best part of two and a half thousand miles to travel from where we started until we reached Geraldton. This was because of the winding route we would have to take. 'As the crow flies, the distance would be somewhere around one and a half thousand miles. We should make good time for the first few weeks,' Arthur said, 'but after that it will be slower, as there would be a big mob from Mundiwindi Station which we should reach in eighteen days or so.'

With a small herd the average distance travelled was about twelve miles a day, but a large herd slowed the pace down. Arthur estimated that we would be about three and a half months getting to Geraldton. I asked him how many head of cattle we would finally have to deliver, and he said any number between fifteen hundred and three thousand. He said that the Boss expected to pick up from eight stations en route – some of the stations helped one another to do their mustering and branding and brought their cattle in together. That way the Boss sometimes got a lot more than he expected.

So we started on the afternoon of the first of March. I still hadn't much idea of what to expect, and if I had known what was ahead of me, perhaps I would not have ventured.

I liked all the men; the black men particularly were nice and helpful. The five white men frightened me when I listened to their terrible stories about wild blacks. My Grandma had read to me when I was a small boy about a gang of blacks in Victoria or New South Wales who went around killing people (their names were the Governors, Jimmy and Jacky), and this made me scared.

For the next two weeks we settled into our job. The cattle were good travellers and we did several miles that first afternoon. Arthur and I were most of the time together; the only time we saw the others was at night and early in the mornings.

My pony, Dinnertime, and I got along fine. She was never far away from me, and she seemed to know that everything was strange to me and kept close. We sometimes let her off the tether unhobbled at night, and she would graze around not far away, then come as close as she could to where I slept, and lie down to rest. I thought this was wonderful. The men noticed it and called her my 'girl'. The Boss said he had never seen anything like it in his life. He remarked to me one morning, 'That pony loves you Bert.'

The men, black and white, hadn't shaved since we left Mullewa and all had beards. Darkey used to cut their hair but none of them had brought a razor. They all trimmed their beards but they looked like a wild mob. I used to get Darkey to trim my hair but I had no whisker troubles.

We had been on the drive for two weeks, travelling about twelve miles each day and were south-east of the Ophthalmia Range, when we got our next lot of cattle. Arthur and I had passed around the herd one morning – through a beautiful valley with a small creek in the middle of it – and travelled some distance, when we came across a large herd of cattle being driven by several station hands. One of the men came to meet us and asked how far back the herd was. Arthur told him that they would be along in about two hours. The man told us that the cattle were from Mundiwindi Station and two other stations further south. There was nearly five hundred head all together, a mixed lot, most of them young, about one and a half years old.

My biggest worry at that time was finding somewhere to start a fire for Arthur to do the cooking. I used to gather any dry sticks or wood that would do for making a fire, and also dry cow manure. I had two bags tied together hung over one of the spare horses, and I would put anything suitable I came across into them.

We were having hot, sultry weather and the sky was sometimes overcast. Near the end of March we met up with another small herd of cattle. They came in from the north, about one hundred and fifty of them. Arthur used to estimate the numbers and he was never far out. He was very pleased with the way things were going and said that the next lot of cattle we met would be at the Ashburton River, a little over a week away.

The weather became even hotter and the overcast skies had gone. By the time we reached the Ashburton some of the cattle were feeling the heat and our progress had slowed down to about eight miles a day. During the midday heat some of the older cows didn't like leaving the shade of the large granite boulders and the small trees in the valleys.

Arthur and I arrived at the Ashburton River on the second day of April, and waiting on the other side, was a fairly large herd of mixed cattle. The river here was very wide but the water was shallow. One of the stockmen from the other side came across to show us how deep it was. Arthur and I waited until our herd came up. It was about ten o'clock in the morning when it arrived. One of our men rode into the herd as it was bunched up near the water, lassooed a cow and pulled her out into the clear. Another one of our men got behind the cow with a whip. Then the first man tied the end of the lasso rope to the horn of his saddle and pulled the cow towards the water. After a few cuts with the whip the cow was persuaded to go into the water and hadn't gone more than twenty yards when the herd commenced to follow. An hour later they were all on the south side of the river and by the time we got across, the new cattle and our herd had mixed.

The man in charge of the cattle gave our boss a piece of paper with the particulars, then he and his men rode away. The herd was now about eleven hundred head. Arthur and I moved on to prepare a camping place for the night. We found a nice spot some four or five miles further on. Arthur said that he thought that that lot of cattle had come from a station called Ashburton Downs.

Arthur, besides doing the cooking, had to attend to shoeing the horses and mules whenever they required it. He was an expert at this. I learned a lot about shoeing horses and many other things about them, such as what to watch when they were feeding on natural grasses, and the type of scrub that was not good for them to eat. Some of the scrub would make the horses scour badly and they would go off their feed, become lifeless and get very thin.

After crossing the Ashburton River we headed south-west towards the coast and Hamelin Pool, some three hundred miles away. Ten days on from the Ashburton we would reach the Lyons River, which was only a small water-course, Arthur told me. Arthur estimated that we had travelled three hundred and eighty to four hundred miles since we had taken the first cattle. To the north, in the distance, we could see the Capricorn Range, and to the south was the Augustus Ranges.

It was now past mid-April. The country we were crossing was more open and flatter than usual. There were a few granite outcrops, some very large anthills and an occasional clump of huge granite boulders. These boulders stood hundreds of feet high, like statues, as if there had been a flood that had washed all the earth away from around them.

The sky was overcast and a gale was blowing. Arthur said he thought we were in for some rain. As the clouds became lower and darker, we could hear thunder in the distance and see flashes of lightning. We made camp that night near an outcrop of granite boulders where we would be able to keep dry should it rain. A small valley just beyond the boulders, with a sharp rise at ground level beyond that, would be a good place to bed the cattle for the night. They would be protected from the wind. Arthur told me this when he picked the spot and he said that rain didn't bother cattle unless they got a fright. The herd came in at about sundown.

The Boss was very pleased with the camping spot. He said that the weather looked ugly and we might have a rough night. I managed to get a good fire going for Arthur with the sticks, wood and dry manure I had picked up along the way. Arthur cooked a nice stew. The cattle settled down early as they were very tired. The Boss had made them travel faster because of the weather, and they had covered a good twelve to thirteen miles that day. This was the usual pattern adopted by experienced drovers when the weather was threatening: make the cattle as tired as possible to calm them down.

Leaving three men to ride around the cattle, the rest came in to camp. They had our stew, then three men rode out and relieved those riding the herd. It was getting very dark and the thunder and lightning were more frequent and close, and very loud. Arthur and I cleaned up our pots, billys, enamel plates, and soon we were all very tired, so we rolled into our rough beds on the ground.

The men out herding the cattle would have two hours on, then they would be relieved. This was so they would all get a break of six hours to sleep. Arthur and I didn't do any herding but we had to look after the horses and mules during the nights. Nights like this one, we couldn't let the horses off the tether, so we had to shift them two or three times to be sure they got plenty to eat.

About midnight Arthur called to me and we shifted the tether ropes for the second time that night. Arthur put some more dry cattle manure onto the fire and we went back to our beds. The storm was very close.

The next thing I knew, Arthur was shaking me violently saying, 'Come on, the cattle have stampeded, we will have to go after them.' I ran to Dinnertime and saddled her, and rode her towards what I thought was the cattle charging through the bush. The thunder and lightning were terrific. I followed the sound I was sure was the cattle – it seemed to be a crashing, galloping noise. The rain commenced to come down in bucketfuls – I was wet through to the skin but I was sure I could hear the cattle, so I kept going. The lightning was flashing every few seconds but I couldn't sight the cattle. I had no idea in what direction I was travellng. All I knew was that the storm and I were going in the same direction, and as the storm was from the north-west, I must be going south-east.

33

Lost

The rain continued and daylight came. There were no cattle and I couldn't find any tracks. I came across a high ironstone hill so I tied Dinnertime to a bush and climbed up to the top, about two hundred feet, to see if I could see where I was. It was still raining and there was running water everywhere. I was sopping wet and freezing but climbing up the hill warmed me up a little.

All I could see from the top was mountainous looking country in all directions. The sky was thickly covered with dark cloud. It was impossible to see the sun so I had no idea what way I was going. So at last I knew the worst. I was lost. I was also cold, wet and very hungry, and I was frightened.

I scrambled down to my pony, climbed on her back and gave her her head. I had been told that if you get lost while on horseback, you should give the horse its head and it will take you home. But this theory was no good with Dinnertime – she took me where there was plenty of feed and she fought for her head to eat it. I let her eat as much as she wanted and I walked for a time to get the warmth back into my legs and body. Then I rode to the top of some high hills, but still to no avail.

The rain was tumbling down. It hadn't let up since the cattle broke. And now it was getting late – the sun must have set without me knowing. I felt very scared but I didn't panic. I kept Dinnie going until we came to a gorge with large granite boulders on each side. There were large caves running up under the boulders, big enough for a horse to walk into.

It was nearly dark so I decided to camp there for the night. I unsaddled Dinnie, and tethered her near the cave (we always carried tether ropes on the saddles). Thank goodness I had the rope because without Dinnie, all would be lost for me – I had to be sure she couldn't wander away. I put the saddle down in the cave to use as a pillow, and covered myself with the saddle cloth. I lay there listening to the rain still pelting down outside. Dinnie pawed the ground and came inside the cave and lay down to rest. I felt happy about this and some of the fear left me. After awhile I went to sleep.

When I woke it was daylight and still raining. Dinnie was standing in the mouth of the cave. Outside there was a lot of running water, the gorge had a stream running through it like a little river. I was still wet and cold. The sun was completely hidden so it was impossible to know which way to go. I was unable to tell north from south, or east from west. After giving Dinnie a longer tether rope so she could reach some grass, I sat thinking what to do. I remembered that the storm had been travelling from north-west to south-east when I left the camp, but what about the wind changing? If I could only see the sun I'd get some idea.

I watched Dinnie cropping grass and noticed the sort she liked best. I thought, if the grass is good for Dinnie, it is good enough for me. I put some in my mouth and chewed it. The juice tasted nice but no matter how hard I tried to swallow the grass, I couldn't. I tasted the leaves of some of the scrub. Most of these were awful but I found one scrubby looking bush that was nice to eat – it had a salty taste.

When Dinnie stopped eating, I saddled her up and set off to try and find some place or person. I rode all the rest of that day towards what I thought was the west. I rode up on to high hills and peaks along valleys, but the only things that I saw alive were kangaroos by the hundreds, a few emus and a few wild horses. Not a sign of anybody or any made place. Not even a track or an old road.

As the day drew to a close the rain was getting less, but the sky was still overcast. The rain stopped just before dark. The wind stopped too and everything was still and quiet. I stopped and listened. All I could hear was a dingo howl and another answering in the distance.

I wondered where I would stay the night – I didn't like the idea of travelling in the dark.

Water was running everywhere in all directions. At least I had no water troubles. It would be terrible to be lost like this with no water. Dinnie was in clover; she didn't seem to mind if we were lost forever.

I came across a very thick patch of scrub and decided to camp there for the night. The scrub was wet but it was too dark to look for something better. To get warm I stood with my body close to Dinnie – she was lovely and warm and she didn't mind. After awhile I broke off a pile of scrub and made a place to lie down. I was very hungry now as well as cold and wet. I again used the saddle for a pillow and put the saddle cloth over me. I piled some scrub underneath me and I also put a pile of scrub up on top of the saddle cloth. I tethered Dinnie and spent my second night alone.

When I awoke it was still dark. A dingo's howl close by sent shivers down my back, as it always did. Several dingoes answered back but they were further away. I would have liked to get up to change Dinnie's tether rope so she could get some fresh grazing but the dingo howls made me too scared to move. I lay there keeping very still until daylight.

In the morning the rain had stopped and the sky was clear. I moved out of my bush bed and walked about. My legs were stiff with the cold. I shifted Dinnie to where she could get plenty of grass, and I tried again to eat some myself. Although I could swallow the juices I couldn't swallow the grass. The scrub that I had eaten and liked the day before didn't grow in this part of the country, or I couldn't find any.

I waited for the sun, looking to where I expected it to rise. Then I got the surprise of my life. It rose behind me. This confused me completely. I realized now that I was absolutely lost. I sat down on the saddle and wondered what I should do. Then I decided that if I kept travelling in one direction, I must come across some road or river that I could follow back and out of this hopeless situation that I had got myself into.

I saddled Dinnie and rode off in a south-west direction, or at least what I thought was a south-west direction. Dinnie walked at a very lively pace, like she knew where she was going. We went along valleys and over high hills and flat scrubby country. Then, when we were emerging from a small valley up onto a rise, Dinnie pricked up her ears. She stopped still, looking, as if she had spotted something. I got off her back, led her back down into the valley and tied her to a clump of scrub. Then I sneaked back up to the rise to see what was there, being very careful not to be seen. Luckily the wind was blowing towards me so whatever it was wouldn't be able to smell me. I got up close to the spot, keeping very low and staying behind clumps of scrub. Then I saw something. For a few minutes I couldn't make out what it was. I moved closer until I got into a position to see clearly. Then I was scared stiff. It was a black man, very wild-looking, with a long bushy beard. His only dress was a loin cloth – a real wild one if I ever I saw one. He was doing something on the ground, bending down on one knee. I stopped where I was, behind a thick bunch of scrub, watching. After a few minutes, he picked up the hind-quarters of a large kangaroo and put it over his shoulder, then picked up a bundle of spears and set off over the rise.

When I was sure he was gone I went and had a look at the spot where he had been. There I found the front half of a kangaroo that he had just skinned. The 'roo was probably too big for him to carry whole. I noticed that he hadn't taken the liver, so, being starving hungry, I took it out and ate it all. Then I took the rest of the carcase down to where I had left Dinnie, tied it to the saddle and walked, leading the pony.

It was now well into the afternoon. I felt much better and my appetite seemed to be satisfied. I came across a small running stream and followed it the way the water was going. I first had a drink of the water and it was fresh and clear.

All of a sudden I became very ill and commenced to vomit. I felt as if I had been poisoned. I put the tether rope on Dinnie and lay down near a large granite boulder. I was so sick I was unable to unsaddle Dinnie. I just lay there and vomited – I couldn't stop. My stomach was empty but it kept on heaving. I felt too weak to do anything. Finally, when the vomiting stopped, I managed to get up. I untied the kangaroo from the saddle, took the saddle off and rested it against a boulder. Then I tethered Dinnie to where she could get plenty of good feed. I lay down after putting the carcase up as high as I could on top of the boulder. I was glad to lie there and let come what may. Funny, I wasn't frightened – I just didn't care what became of me.

It was hours before I went to sleep. The noise of running water helped to deaden some of the night noises. The weather was fine and warm. In fact, during the day it had been quite hot and my clothes were dry. Finally I fell asleep, and woke just before daylight, on the fourth day, with terrible pains in my stomach. Daylight came and I was still in shocking pain. I rolled on the ground with the pain and felt very faint. It was nearly midday before the pains eased.

Dinnie stood looking at me. She couldn't understand why I hadn't shifted her tether to fresh grass. When the terrible pains left me, I had a bad attack of scouring and was not able to do anything until late in the afternoon. When I was well enough, I put the saddle on Dinnie – although very weak I managed – then I had a drink of water and felt a little better.

I pushed the kangaroo carcase off the boulder, and getting some sharp-edged stones I set about bruising pieces of the flesh of the carcase, and putting each piece as I broke it off into my pockets. You would have thought I had a swarm of bees around me, there were so many blow-flies. The carcase was badly fly-blown, but that didn't matter to me. I wanted to chew the kangaroo meat into small pieces later, when I felt better. By the time I had finished getting all the meat off the carcase that I could, the sun was close to setting. I saddled up and followed the stream hoping to find a better camping place.

This fourth day the sunset was beautiful. I came across very high ironstone cliffs on both sides of the water-course, and in places I had to make Dinnie walk in the water to get through. Just before dark I came to a place where the cliffs were wider apart; this made a beautiful wide valley with the water-course almost big enough to be called a river. Some of the cliffs were overhanging and protected from the weather, so I camped there.

On the verge between the cliff and the river there was plenty of feed for Dinnie. I unsaddled and tethered her and made myself a place to lie down for the night. I tried chewing some of the small pieces of kangaroo meat. After chewing for quite awhile and venturing to swallow, I was afraid of another vomiting bout, so I ate only two or three pieces. As I lay chewing I couldn't help thinking that perhaps I had made a mistake in hiding from that black man. He may have been able to help me – almost anything would be better than what I was going through now. I swallowed a few more pieces of well-chewed meat and still had no ill effects. Finally I dozed off to sleep.

I awakened the next morning before daylight, and as I hadn't vomited during the night, I started chewing the meat again and swallowed some more well-chewed pieces. When daylight came I shifted Dinnie's tether rope and had a drink of water out of the stream. I think I was feeling a little better.

I was in the fifth day now and no sign of anything that would help me – no tracks, no cattle, no way of knowing how far I had travelled or in what direction. I made up my mind that no matter what happened, I would not leave the water-course. I would keep following the direction of the flowing water. It must eventually take me somewhere.

I saddled Dinnie and set off again. I felt very weak and discouraged. I kept on chewing and eating the small pieces of meat, and whenever I stopped to rest or have a drink, I would chew grass or the leaves of the scrub bushes. My stomach had settled down and didn't revolt against the scanty food it was getting.

It was terribly hot so I had to rest every two or three hours. The flies were very bad and during the nights the mosquitoes took over, but the nights were much cooler. As I travelled, following the water-course, the country changed somewhat towards sundown. The going was very rough – mountains with huge boulders all over them – then a valley would open out into a large, flat scrubby plain with the everwinding water-course travelling on and on.

The next day was very similar to the fifth. The sun was very hot – so much so I was forced to lay up for about five hours in the middle of the day.

That night I slept close to the bank of the water-course. I found a sand patch that was nice and soft to sleep on. I was still chewing kangaroo meat but my supplies were getting very low. I felt a little stronger although the raw meat was all that my stomach had had, except a lot of juice from chewing grass. Near the sand patch were two large boulders close together, and in between them was a strip of sand. When I unsaddled Dinnie and tethered her to graze, I put the saddle at the end of the sand patch in between the boulders, and lay down. It was a long time before I went to sleep. All sorts of frightening thoughts came to me. A person would have to be lost like I was to really know what it was like – it was dreadful.

34

DELIVERANCE

When I awakened in the morning of the seventh day I got a shock. Dinnie was over the other side of the stream. I could see her from where I was lying. I sat up and at first thought she must have got off the tether, then two black men jumped me, one from each side. I was unable to offer much resistance. I yelled, 'Let me go!' and tried to struggle free, but they held me and one of them called out to a third man who was on the other side of the stream with Dinnie. They could not understand my language. They spoke to one another but I didn't know what they were saying either. The one with Dinnie brought her back over the stream, then they put the saddle on her and one of the men made signs to me. After awhile I realized that they wanted me to get on Dinnie's back. I did this, then one of them took the reins and led her. One man was in front of him and the other one came up behind. We left the water-course and travelled north.

These black men looked very wild to me. They wore only a loin cloth – no hat or boots. The loin cloths were made out of kangaroo skins. They all had beards. I had been scared many times in my short life, but nothing like I was now.

The black men ran on their bare feet, and Dinnie had to trot to keep up with them most of the time. They travelled towards a large hill. It had a gradual slope and it took us about two hours to get to the top.

When we arrived at the top they made signs to me that I took for wanting me to get off Dinnie's back. I did, and one of them unsaddled Dinnie. The other two gathered some dry sticks and scrub into a pile. Then one of them squatted and did something with the pile so that, after a few minutes, smoke started rising, and a little later, flame. They gathered some green scrub and bushes and heaped them near the fire. I don't know how the man started the fire – I didn't see him with any matches – but when they got the fire going properly I was sure my time had come!

I asked one of them what they were going to do, but they didn't understand and took no notice of me. The three of them piled all the green bushes and scrub onto the fire which made a thick white smoke. Then one of them took the saddle cloth from Dinnie and kept putting it on and off the fire. The other two stood looking in different directions. It was at this moment that I realized, with relief, that they had built the fire to make smoke signals.

After awhile they built up the fire again, put more green scrub and bushes on and made more smoke signals. Then they stood looking in a north and westward direction. The whole operation must have taken at least a half hour. Suddenly one of them gave a shout and seemed very excited and pointed to something in the distance. The other two looked and then they all came over to me and one patted me on the shoulder and pointed at something in the distance. For awhile I couldn't see anything to get excited about, then I saw it. Little clouds were going up into the air at small intervals from a hill top to the north-west, some three or four miles away.

One of the black men put the saddle on Dinnie and the other two put the fire out by throwing earth on it. When they were sure the fire was out, we set off towards where the smoke signals had been. They ran when going down hill and on the level ground but walked up the hills. It was amazing how they could travel over prickly scrub and stony ground with their bare feet.

We stopped about every two or three hours for the men to rest. Every time they stopped they would let Dinnie feed. I still had some small pieces of 'roo meat in my pockets and I slipped them to my mouth and chewed them while we were travelling. The fear had left me now, and I knew the blacks were my friends.

This kind of travelling went on all the rest of that day until after dark. Apart from stopping for a drink of water when we came to a small water-course, the blacks had no food, and how they kept going I'll never know. They were the blackest men I had ever seen – their hair and skin were jet black.

After dark they slowed to a walk. Then, while travelling on a rise, they stopped and one of them pointed to a small light in the distance. He put his hand on my leg and squeezed it. I couldn't see his face in the dark but the gesture conveyed to me that we were close to the end of our journey.

An hour or so later we arrived at a large blacks' camp. About thirty dogs came towards us barking. There were several large fires burning and in the dark these reminded me of a lot of small pinnacles.

We were soon surrounded by dozens of blacks and then, to my surprise, out walked Stan Smith. Some of the blacks took Dinnie and Stan said that they would look after her. 'Bert, you come with me,' he said. He took me to a fairly large mia-mia. Inside there were several older natives and they were all very pleased to see me. Stan asked how I managed to keep alive but before I could answer him a middle-aged native woman came in. She had a bowl like a drinking vessel with some kind of dark fluid in it. She handed it to me. I looked at Stan and he nodded his head and said to drink it, it would do me good. I didn't like the look of it but it tasted fine.

Stan could talk the blacks' language and understood their ways and customs. He spoke to the natives in the mia-mia and said to me after I had finished the food, 'You better not have any more Bert after not having any for so long. You'll have to be careful and start with only a little at a time for now.' Stan had a rug and insisted that I have it. He lay on some skins that the natives had put there for him. I lay down on the skins in the place prepared for me, with the rug spread over me. I was dog-tired and was soon sound asleep.

When I awoke next morning the sun was high in the sky and it was very hot. Stan wasn't there. The native woman came to me again with some more liquid like soup. I was hungry and drank it. Then Stan came into the mia-mia and asked me how I felt. I told him I was still very tired but felt much better, although I had a bad cold. While we were talking the woman came back in. This time she gave me some kangaroo steak that had been grilled on hot coals. She also gave me some kind of damper. I ate the steak and damper and it tasted beautiful. I also drank some water she had fetched me. Stan spoke to the woman and she looked at me and smiled. I asked Stan to thank her and the three men that found me. Stan replied, 'That is what I was just saying to her.'

After awhile we left the mia-mia. You would have thought I was a special king or something, the fuss they made. The three men that had found me came and shook me by the hand and patted me on the shoulders in such a friendly and jolly manner. Then the boss, a large man (Stan told me later he was the chief), took me by the hand and wished me well. He could speak English in a way. He could make me understand what he meant, and one thing he made clear was that he and his people were my friends. A few minutes later they fetched our horses and Stan strapped his bedroll onto his saddle and said we must get back to the herd. He asked me if I felt well enough to ride. I assured him that I did. Then, after shaking hands with dozens of the blacks – men, women and children – we rode away.

We didn't speak for quite awhile. Then Stan said, 'I have some food in my saddle-bags, Bert. We'll rest up later on and have some lunch.' The day was very hot and Stan said that the extra heat this time of the year was unusual – it could mean another storm. I said, 'I hope not. I've had enough storms to do me the rest of my life.' Then Stan asked me how I had managed to live. I told him about the kangaroo carcase and the black man that left it there, and how I had taken pieces off the carcase and kept chewing them. He thought for awhile, then he said, 'If you had approached the black he would have saved you then. All the blacks were on the look out for you. They're all friendly. Don't take any notice of the tales that you hear. Those things did really happen but many years ago. It's different now.'

We camped for the night at a boundary rider's shack and had something to eat. The boundary riders' huts always had tea, sugar and some tinned meat in them so we made a billy of tea.

We sat talking for awhile and Stan asked me to explain what the country was like where I was lost. I did, and when I told him about deciding to follow the water-course no matter what, he said that it was good judgement and most likely saved my life. He also said that the kangaroo meat would have played a big part in keeping me going.

Stan was a good bushman and knew the country in the North like the back of his hand. He said, 'That water-course you followed was a branch of the Gascoyne River – the Lyons – only you came across it up near Mount Augustus where it starts. That country all around there is very rugged and rough. Our herd should be travelling close to the other end of the Lyons about now.

There were two rough bunks in the hut. We lay down and I was soon asleep. Stan awakened me just after daylight and we had more tea and finished our food. Stan found a pencil and left a note on the table to the effect that we had camped there and taken two tins of meat to eat during the day. He estimated that we should catch the herd some time that day.

Late in the afternoon we came across tracks made by the herd. Stan said that the tracks were a day old so we should catch up to them before dark. About sundown we reached the camp. They had set up for the night close to the bend of a river. Stan told me again that this was the river I had been following when I was found. 'So,' he said, 'you were on your way to safety although you were lost.'

We had now arrived at camp. Darkey and three blacks were out herding the cattle but the rest of the gang were there to give me a merry welcome back. They all ran to shake hands with me, and to my surprise, the Boss grabbed me and kissed me like he was my mother. He said that I looked pale and had lost a lot of weight. Stan remarked, 'No wonder, with only grass to eat.'

When we had something to eat they all sat around, and I had to explain what happened and how I managed to stay alive. When I finished telling them my story they all agreed that the kangaroo meat saved me and also that I shouldn't have hidden from the black man. They said he would have taken me to safety. After the herders had gone out to relieve the four who took the first shift, Arthur and I put our beds down and turned in for the night. I was very tired and felt very weak. I was soon sound asleep.

35

BACK TO WORK

Next day I was back into my usual routine of leading the spare horses and helping Arthur. He made me take things easy, on the Boss's orders. Arthur told me that they had lost about two and a half days getting the herd rounded up and back together again after the stampede. They had found eight head killed in the stampede, and three others had to be destroyed because they had broken legs. One of those was a young bullock which was butchered for meat and wasn't a complete loss. It wouldn't be known for sure how many they had lost until the end of the drive when there would be a final count. Arthur said that the herd was now around the two thousand mark (three stations had sent herds to join the drive while I was lost), and we had about five hundred miles to go.

He pointed to a rough looking mountain range ahead and said, 'That's the Kennedy Range. We go east of that and then it is good going except for the crossing of the Gascoyne and the Murchison Rivers.

I asked Arthur if he knew the date and he said he thought we were in May. The Boss told us that night that the date was the third of May. (He kept a diary of daily happenings.)

The Boss often came to me to ask how I was and to tell Arthur to look after me. He told me that he was very worried while I was lost, but now that I was back with them safe and sound he felt good.

Six days later we came to the Kennedy Ranges. The weather was very cool and travelling was pleasant. The cattle were all looking fine. The Boss said he was very pleased with the way things were turning out.

The next week brought us to the junction of the Gascoyne and Lyons Rivers. The Boss sent Stan on ahead to see what the crossing would be like for the cattle – he hoped to take them across the following day. Stan returned that night and reported that he had found a place to cross where the river was about two feet six inches deep and about three quarters of a mile wide. On this report the Boss decided to camp near the river and take the herd over in the morning. So, on the seventeenth day of May, we crossed the Gascoyne with just over two thousand head of cattle.

Arthur told me that we now had about ninety miles to go to the Great Northern Coast stock route. From there on there would be two or three small water-courses to cross, then the Murchison River which was our only real worry. If the weather held out we should have no trouble, Arthur said. If we had another rain storm like the one when I got lost, we might have to wait until the water level dropped. Arthur said that cattle don't mind water so long as they don't have to swim and as long as they can touch the bottom. They will walk across with a bit of coaxing, but when they have to swim they turn to the nearest way out, which is mostly back to where they have just left.

The next few days went well. However, we were crossing through cattle country so the Boss had put two extra men on the scouting team to help clear any station stock. Our progress was very slow. (When the herd was spread out grazing it was at least one mile wide and a mile long. This will give some idea of the big job the drovers had.)

Towards the end of May we arrived at a point inland from the sea near Hamelin Pool. We were now on the Great Northern Coast stock route. The weather was fine and cool and we hadn't had any storms since I was lost. The small water-courses were back to their normal level, the cattle were all looking fine and I was feeling quite strong again.

The scouts' job was a little easier now. With the sea a few miles to the west of the route, they had only the east side and the front of the herd to watch. We had only one drover on the coast side looking for strays.

One evening in early June, the Boss asked Arthur to limit our day's travel to eight miles. He said that the cattle were getting near prime condition and we must keep them that way. He expected us to be in Geraldton near the end of the month. We were twelve days covering the next hundred miles. The stock feed was plentiful and the cattle looked in tip-top condition. Another small herd had joined us and the Boss said that it was the last we would take. He didn't expect any more.

We reached the Murchison River and Arthur picked out a good camping spot. Then he took his horse and rode along the river to have a look at the possibilities of crossing. He left me to tether the mules and spare horses, and build a fire. A few minutes after Arthur returned the Boss came in. They decided that we would have to take the cattle east along the river for about four miles to where the river was very wide and shallow enough to take them across.

The next morning the herd was driven along the river to this spot. We had a job getting the cattle across. In fact, it was almost sundown that day before the crossing was complete. The trouble was that for the first few yards the water was deep – up to the cattle's backs – and they didn't like it. I had never heard so much shouting and swearing in my life. The men were swearing at one another and at the cattle, and this went on until the Boss made them cut it out. He ordered them to cut off a hundred or so head at a time, and drive them across as a group. Some men were left watching the main herd, then as each mob got across, two men were left to mind them until the next lot came across. That's how we crossed the Murchison River. As usual we used a lead cow. The cow on the lead had to go back and come over in front of each lot to show them the way – she must have crossed eight or ten times. At first a hundred came over with her but later on three to four hundred at a time would follow.

That night we camped close to where we had crossed, and next day went west on the south side of the river, back to the coastal stock route. From this point we were about eighty miles from our goal, Geraldton. The men herded the cattle that night in a large bend of the river just below where we had crossed. The bend was like a big elbow – the river wound and came back within a quarter of a mile of itself, forming a place where the cattle could graze, and the herders only had to ride back and forth across one side.

Next day everything went well. We let the cattle make their own time. We hadn't crossed the Murchison any too soon, because two days after the crossing we got heavy rain. It rained all one day and half that night and even the small creeks were in flood.

Five days out of Geraldton we had to take the cattle about four miles inland from the stock route on account of the railway that ran along the coast from Geraldton to a tin mine. The trains made such a noise it might have made the cattle stampede.

The day before we were due to arrive in Geraldton, the Boss rode ahead to make arrangements for the delivery of the cattle. He stayed in town that night and rode out to meet us early the next morning. Arthur and I were about two miles ahead of the herd when the Boss came back. He told Arthur where to go and make camp – in an old barn-like hut in a paddock. Arthur said this hut was about two miles out of Geraldton and that the cattle would be put into holding paddocks. The firms that handle the sale of the cattle have these paddocks and the cattle stay there until they are sold and shipped away or disposed of.

So that night the drovers delivered the cattle into several paddocks. The herd was divided into different lots, each lot being put into the paddock most suitable for them. That night the Boss explained that our job wasn't finished until the cattle had been classed, valued or sold, and he expected that it would take about two or more weeks to complete our contract.

My job was now easy – all I had to do was help Arthur. All our mules and horses were tethered out in a paddock of their own. The Boss told us we were not to go into Geraldton without his permission. Then he said, 'The only one who is allowed into Geraldton is Bert. He will have to go for fresh meat and bread first thing in the morning, so anything you need Bert can get it for you. I have fixed it up with the storekeeper, he will book it all up to me until we have disposed of the cattle.' He said, 'Anyone that goes into town without my permission will lose his share of the bonus.'

The bonus was paid to the boss based on the number of head considered to be in prime condition on delivery, and also a percentage of the price paid above the set amount for each head. The Boss was also allowed one head of cattle per hundred as a loss. If he lost more than that he had to make it up before settlement. Also, any cattle that managed to stray into the herd unbranded or not earmarked were considered the Boss's property and could be sold by him. All these payments together made up the bonus, and the Boss agreed to divide equally the total amount received, among the white drovers that stayed through the whole drive. There were five white men including the Boss and me, but I didn't think that I would be in the bonus as the Boss had never mentioned it to me. Arthur was sure that I would be included in the sharing. Anyway, I would have to wait and see.

36

THE DRIVE ENDS

We all had a wonderful night's rest, and the next morning I caught Dinnie and one pack mule, saddled up and set off to town with a long list of stores and other things that the men wanted. Arthur wrote everything down for me. On arriving in Geraldton I went straight to Mrs Stafford's Coffee Palace. She was delighted to see me and said I had to tell her all about the trip. I didn't have time to tell her very much but I promised to try and get one evening off. She invited me to come to dinner one evening and have the talk of our lives. She said my tin trunk and things were still there and were all right.

I arrived back at camp about eleven o'clock that morning. Arthur was busy getting ready for the lunch and the Boss and the drovers were all out with the cattle. They had to sort out the bullocks from the cows and also the prime beef from those not yet in prime condition. When the cattle were sorted into their various grades, they would be put into paddocks of their own so they could be easily driven to the sale-yards. Near where we camped there were large stockyards and a crush for handling and marking. (They used a kind of paint for marking and there were many different colours.)

The sorting, grading and marking took four days. We were all very busy while this went on – I had to go to Geraldton twice, help Arthur, and also help with driving the graded and marked cattle into their various holding paddocks.

Then, on the fifth day of July, roughly six hundred head of prime bullocks were taken into the sale-yards. Just before midday, when they were all counted and ready for the sale, we all went to Mrs Stafford's Coffee Palace for lunch (all except Arthur and one of the blacks). It was while we were having lunch that I plucked up enough courage to ask the Boss for an evening off to put in with Mrs Stafford. He gave me the next evening off.

The sale started that afternoon at two o'clock but we didn't stop for it. The Boss and Stan stayed but the rest of us had to go back to camp and start preparing another lot for sale. They expected to hold three sales each week until the lot were sold.

Darkey was in charge when the Boss and Stan were away. Stan was the Boss's right-hand man and was always the head man when the Boss was away. Darkey was next in charge. I heard him tell George that the Boss was extra pleased with the whole drive – it was the most successful drive he had ever had. The Boss had said that, 'Only for the kid getting lost and the stampede it would have been perfect.' Hearing myself referred to as 'the kid' made me feel bad. I didn't think it was my fault about the cattle stampeding and I didn't get lost on purpose.

That night I told Arthur that the Boss had given me permission to have the following evening with Mrs Stafford. Arthur gave me a list of stores he wanted the next day, and told me to go in early and get the things before the store closed, and bring them back with me when I came back to camp that night. The next afternoon I left camp about three o'clock got the stores and strapped them onto the pack mule. Then I put the mule and Dinnie in the stable at the back of Mrs Stafford's place and by the time I had done this, dinner was on. I went into the kitchen and had my meal with Mrs Stafford, her daughter Jean, and Mary.

They wanted to know all about how I got lost and found, and how I lived – a hundred questions. When we finished dinner I helped the girls to wash up. Then we retired to the sitting-room and I explained all about the drive, the storm, getting lost and getting found. They just sat and listened and hardly said a word until I finished. I was usually very shy when talking to ladies but with these people I felt quite at home and had no shyness at all. When I had told of my experiences they asked me all sorts of questions.

After awhile, I asked Mrs Stafford if she had seen or heard anything of old Bill and May at Mullewa. She told me that they had married and that Bill had got that job managing a cattle station about one hundred miles east of Mullewa. She said that they were very happy. I told her that I had promised to go and see them when the drive had finished but there was no way to getting to where they were, as I intended going back to Perth when I finished with Bob McInnis. I asked Mrs Stafford did she know how I could get a message to them. She said that if I liked, she would write a letter for me before I left for Perth. I thanked her and she said, 'You can tell me what you would like me to write.' She knew I hadn't any schooling and that while I had been on the drive I hadn't had a chance to learn any more about reading and writing. All of a sudden I looked at the clock on the mantelpiece and the time had gone like a few minutes. Believe it or not it was half past ten. So I thanked them for the lovely evening and promised to come again another time.

It was close to midnight when I arrived back at camp, and Arthur got out of bed and helped me to unload the mule and put the stores away. He said, 'They're taking another lot of bullocks to be sold in the the morning, so it looks like a busy day. You better get some sleep.' Then he asked me if I had a good time. I told him that the evening went so quick we didn't realise how late it was. I said that I enjoyed myself and that Mrs Stafford was a lovely woman.

We were all woken early next moring when it was still dark. The blacks got our saddles and horses and Arthur and I prepared a beautiful breakfast of eggs and bacon, and bread and butter – this was something we all enjoyed after the rough and ready meals on the drive. We all had to help except Arthur. The Boss told him that all who were taking the cattle in today would have lunch at Mrs Stafford's Coffee Palace so he could have a rest. We took about nine hundred head in, some five hundred bullocks and about four hundred prime cows. The delivery took us until midday and after lunch we all went back to camp, except the Boss and Stan, who stayed to watch the sale.

On our way back to camp Darkey told us that we should finish early the next week. George asked me what I was going to do. I said I hadn't made up my mind yet but I thought about going back to Perth for a few weeks, then make up my mind from there. The men were growling about not getting any money until all the cattle were sold. I told Arthur about this when we arrived back in camp and he said, 'If them blokes get their money now they won't be able to do anything because they will be blind drunk, and it would be weeks before they would be any use to the Boss. He knows that. He's had trouble before over booze.'

Arthur asked me if anyone had told me how successful the drive had been. When I said no, he told me that the cattle delivered to us on the drive (according to the statements handed to the Boss by the head man in charge of each herd that joined our drive) amounted to two thousand four hundred and sixty-one. 'But,' Arthur said, 'on the tally we have two thousand four hundred and ninety-one, so we have a surplus of thirty-eight head, and twenty two of them are clean skins (unbranded). He continued, 'Has the Boss said anything to you about being included in the bonus?' I said, 'No, why?' 'Oh,' he said, 'we was wondering. The boys and I think you should be.'

On the fourteenth of June we delivered the last of the cattle, mostly cows. That day we stayed at the sale-yards to see the cattle sold. There was a big demand for cows on account of the hundreds of new settlers down south. Two large stockbroker firms conducted the sales (Elder Shenton and Company and Dalgety's Company Limited). All the cattle were in demand. Stan remarked that the prices they had fetched were the best he had ever known.

So, two days later the company agents came out to the camp, and they and the Boss and Stan sat around a table. They were all there for about two hours and when they went away the Boss called us in and we got our pay. The blacks were paid first, then Stan, Darkey, George and Arthur. Then the Boss called me up to the table and said, 'Well, Bert, this is the best day of them all – pay-day. You've been twenty-eight weeks with me. That makes your wages twenty-eight pounds. Now the other men and I think you should be included in the bonus so I added twenty-two pounds. That makes your total fifty pounds. Are you satisfied with that?' I said, 'Oh yes, Boss. That's fine and thank you very much.' Just think of my amazement when he counted out fifty sovereigns onto the table. I stood there sort of stunned. I had never seen so many sovereigns all at once before. The Boss broke the silence saying, 'You've earnt it Bert. You are a good lad and if you like you can come and work on my place in Mullewa. Think it over and let me know tomorrow.'

I went out and all the men had already left for Geraldton, except two blacks. I had some lunch and cleaned up the dishes we used and the Boss said, 'You and I have a job to do in Geraldton Bert. After that you are free to do what you like.'

This puzzled me. What is there he wants me to do, I thought. As we rode along he said, 'I suppose you are wondering what this is all about. Well I should have told you before. We have to give the Police Sergeant at Geraldton a full report about you being lost. Stan has to be with us too. Don't worry, it is only a formality. They were arranging a search-party, but you were found before they could get started. As you know it rained for nearly three days after the stampede and we were not able to get a message through. It was five days before the police were notified, and then they had to get a black-tracker. On the seventh day, just before the search was due to start, a policeman at Carnarvon sent a message through to say that a black man said he had seen a smoke signal to say you had been found. So now the police want a firsthand statement to show their superiors.'

We arrived at the Police Station and Stan was already there. The Boss introduced me to the Sergeant and the Sergeant said, 'So this is the boy that was lost. He doesn't look to be any worse for seven days without food.' The Boss and Stan told him about the storm and the stampede and how I was found. The Sergeant wrote it down on paper and the Boss and Stan signed it, and so did I, in my own way. The Sergeant witnessed our signatures and then he thanked us. The Boss and I left and went back to camp but Stan stayed in town. He said that Darkey, George and Arthur were at the pub and that they would stay in town and see us tomorrow some time.

The next morning I went to the Boss and told him that I wouldn't be taking the job he had offered me. I said, 'I will be going back to Perth for a few weeks, then I may come back if that's all right with you Bob.' That was the first time I had called him Bob for a long time and it seemed to please him. He remarked, 'I like you calling me Bob, but thanks for the respect to me while I was your employer. In answer to you wanting to go to Perth, you just do what you like Bert. If you have trouble finding suitable employment just pack up and come to my place and you will have a job. I will treat you like my own son.' I felt sure that he meant it. I thanked him again, then went and packed my few things together, intending to walk into Geraldton. Bob wouldn't hear of it and he sent one of the blacks to bring in Dinnie and another hack, then he said to him, 'Take Bert into Geraldton, then bring Dinnie back.' With that he shook my hand and I rode away.

We arrived at Mrs Stafford's place just before lunch. Charlie, the black man, wouldn't stop for lunch but went straight back to camp. The hardest thing was saying goodbye to Dinnie. I cried and hugged her and when I went back into Mrs Stafford's I had tears in my eyes. She noticed that I had been crying and she hugged and kissed me and said, 'I understand. You can become very close to a faithful horse.' She gave me the same room I had when I first came to Geraldton.

I had lunch that day in the kitchen with Mrs Stafford and the girls. Mrs Stafford asked me what I intended doing. I explained about the job Bob had offered me and told her that I wanted to get some more learning on reading and writing. I said it was impossible to learn anything at all on the drive and I hoped if I could get a job of some sort in or near the city, that would give me a chance to take some sort of lessons in that direction. I said, 'I feel terrible out of place in any kind of company.' She said that she understood and she thought I was doing the right thing.

After lunch I went to the shipping office and made enquiries about when the next ship to Fremantle would be calling. The officer in charge said that I would have to wait six days as one had left that morning. So I went back to Mrs Stafford's and told her. She said, 'That's good. If you like you can stay here on the same terms as before, when you were here. Just keep the wood-box full. We are so glad that you will be staying here for a few days.'

So for the next six days I had a nice holiday. I had all my meals in the kitchen with Mrs Stafford and the girls, and I tried my hand at fishing but was not successful. I caught a few small ones but felt sure I wouldn't make a success as a fisherman.

There was a rail running from Geraldton to Perth but I was advised that the rail was terrible and it would be better to go by boat. I saw Stan, Darkey and George several times but nothing of Arthur. When I asked Stan what became of Arthur, Stan said, 'He hasn't been sober since he got paid and he won't sober up until he is broke. That Arthur has troubles. When he is sober you couldn't find a nicer bloke alive but when he is drunk there isn't a worse one.'

Finally, having put forty pounds in my State Savings account, just keeping enough to pay my board and boat fare to Fremantle, plus some pocket money, I left Geraldton on the twenty-fourth day of July 1909 on the *Kenalpi*, the same boat that I had arrived on nearly eight months before.

Knocking About

1909–1914

'Just call me Punch.'

37

CITY LIFE

The sea was calm when we sailed but became very rough towards evening. The Captain and crew members recognised me and they all wanted to know about where I had been, but before I was able to tell them much I got very seasick. All through the night the sea was rough and it tossed that little boat about like a cork. How it managed to keep afloat I will never know.

Next day, near midday, we sighted Fremantle, and it was early in the afternoon when we came into the harbour. Wasn't I glad when I stood on firm ground again.

I hadn't written home since I had left eight months before. I made my way to the railway station and paid my fare to Subiaco. On arriving at Subiaco I put my trunk into the care of the Station Master and went to Mother's address. But when I got there I found that she wasn't living there any more. I hadn't counted on that. (My mother had never owned a home of her own – our stepfather always rented a house. This was something I couldn't understand. He was a good, first-class tradesman and always had plenty of work. Well, that was his concern but my grandma used to say that people should own their own home because paying rent was just throwing money down the drain.)

Anyway, my worry at the moment was: where was my mother? I went to the local butcher and to the store where I used to work, and was told that she had shifted to West Perth. No one knew where but it was suggested that I go to the Post Office as there was certain to be a forwarding address there. I made enquiries at the Post Office and they gave me the address. I then hired a cab (in those days cabs were horse-drawn carriages) and went to Mother's new home where I got another surprise – she and my stepfather were renting a large store with a top storey.

The ground floor of the building consisted of a lounge-dining room, kitchen and a large double-fronted shop, and there were two bedrooms upstairs. The shop was stocked with all sorts of ironmongery for sale. My mother was looking after the shop, besides doing the cooking for all the family and the housework. She was so pleased to see me. She reminded me that I hadn't written to her to let her know where I was. I explained that I couldn't send her my address because I had no way of receiving a letter while I was on the move all the time. She told me why they had shifted and said that my two older brothers were working for Bill, my stepfather, and that they were doing well.

The time was four thirty in the afternoon. Mother showed me where I would sleep – I would share a room with my stepbrother Harry. I put my things in the room and lay down. I was dog-tired and hungry. I hadn't had any sleep since I left Geraldton, and had been too sick to eat on the boat.

I fell sound asleep and the next thing I knew Roy was shaking me to wake me up. When I came into the dining-room they were all sitting at the table having dinner. I said, 'Goodday,' and they started asking questions all at once until Bill said, 'Just a minute. Let him get inside and settle down. He'll tell you all in good time where he's been and what he's been doing.'

My mother was a good cook and this dinner was no exception. We had grilled fillet steak and I thought it was delicious. I was too busy with the steak to talk, although I knew they all wanted to know where I had been and all about the cattle drive. As I unfolded my story they all sat and listened in silence. Then I was flooded with questions until bedtime.

When I awoke the next morning my stepfather and brothers had gone to work. Mother was waiting for me in the kitchen and she and I had our breakfast with the three kids.

When the kids had left for school my mother told me some bad news. My sister Myra had been brought down from the hospital at Coolgardie to the Infectious Diseases Hospital at West Subiaco. She had got worse and died two months ago. Mother said that she had tried to find me but couldn't find anyone that knew me or where I had gone. This news about Myra shocked me and Grandma's remarks about how my mother treated us came back to me. It left me speechless. I felt terrible. I felt that I hated my mother. Without saying a word I got up from the table and went to my room and had a good cry. Myra was only two years older than me and we were always together when we were living with Grandma in Victoria. She was a pretty girl and had lovely long, dark hair. She must have died during the time that I was lost.

Later that day my mother came to me and said how sorry she was and claimed it wasn't her fault. She said that when she married Bill he made it very clear that he wouldn't have any of the children from her first marriage living with them unless they could pay board, and as Myra was to go to school, she had to put her into a home under the care of a religious group. That was where she developed pneumonia and then the consumption that finally killed her. Mother told me that when Myra got old enough – the people managing the Home used to take in washing and ironing – she and the other little girls had to work. Mother said, 'Myra used to tell me about this when I went to see her, and I used to complain about it but all they would say was, "If you don't like what your daughter has to do then take her away." I begged your stepfather to let me bring her home but he wouldn't agree, so what could I do?'

After hearing my mother's story I felt a little better towards her, and the damage was done – Myra couldn't be brought back. I told Mother that she should have let Grandma know because she would have done something to save Myra's life. I was sure of that.

I spent the next few days having a holiday, then Bill gave me a job helping two men dig drains to lay sewerage pipes and put in septic systems. He paid me three pounds a week and out of that I had to pay my mother one pound for my board. After a few weeks he paid me three pounds ten shillings a week and told me, 'If anyone asks your age tell them you're sixteen.' (The Union insisted that boys under sixteen weren't allowed to work at the job.) I worked Monday to Friday from half past seven in the morning until five in the evening with one hour off for lunch, and Saturday mornings.

I got along fine on this job. The two men I worked with treated me well and wouldn't let me work too hard.

Every evening after we finished dinner I would study my books, and Roy and Eric, who had had some education, used to help me. Eric went out a lot of the evenings. He was at the age to take out girls and he was always short of money. Roy was different. He only went out on Saturday nights and I used to go with him sometimes.

At the end of August one of the men I worked with found out I was a good boxer. From then on he used to tell me all about boxing and about the boxing school he was helping to run. His name was Ernie Hickland and he told me that he used to help teach boxing with a one-time champion heavyweight called Charlie Burns. He invited me to come down to the school and see how it was done and said that, if I would like to learn to box, I could join the school for five shillings and pay two and sixpence a lesson.

I decided to join after seeing how it was done. They taught me to skip and to do ball punching. There were about thirty boys attending, some three to four years older than me and some younger. After a few visits my shyness wore off and I really did enjoy myself. The boys were put into age groups. I was big for my age so I was put into the fifteen to sixteen age group. I turned fifteen the first week that I joined.

I had no idea how to box properly but Mr Burns, who did the teaching for my group, soon showed me how to go about it. He was very strict and would not allow any boy to smoke, and he made all the boys go straight home after lessons each night. He was one of the nicest and kindest men I had met. If something turned up so that one of us couldn't make it to a lesson. he never charged us but always wanted to know the reason for not attending. He considered that defence was the first and most important thing about boxing and we had to practice foot-work, side-stepping and the art of avoiding being hit without having to use your gloves to block punches. Mr Burns insisted on practice and more practice until each movement was perfected.

Bill kept my two brothers and I in a job and I stuck with him until February 1910. During this six months, I also stuck with Mr Burns' boxing school and kept on learning to read and write. I also learnt a lot about money matters and arithmetic. It was easier for me to learn about figures than about reading and writing.

Bill finished the contract he had been handling and he had nothing for me to do, so I tried to get a job. One day Mr Burns told me about a job at a foundry in West Perth. He said he knew the boss there and gave me a letter to take to him. The next morning I went to the foundry, saw the man and gave him the letter. After reading it he asked me my age. I told him the truth – that I was fifteen years old – and he asked me all about myself and what work I had been doing. He then asked me to follow him to the part of the foundry where they made parts of various kinds. He said, 'We will give you a trial for a few weeks and see how you go.'

The parts were made of cast iron and moulded in damp sand. My job was damping the sand, and packing it firmly around a sample part before it was lifted, leaving an impression for melted iron to be poured in. A man about fifty years old was working with me, pouring the iron. His name was George McDonald and he was a very nice, understanding, well-mannered man and wouldn't let me lift anything very heavy. He would say, 'Don't do anything that will cause strain. It could be the undoing of you physically.'

I had been working at this job for about six weeks when the boss sent for me. He asked me, 'Would you like to be an apprentice to a trade here with this foundry. We are very pleased with you and your work and there are several good trades you could be apprenticed to.' I told him that I would love to learn a trade but I would like to know what my mother thought about it before anything was agreed to. He then asked me what grade I had made at school and was shocked when I told him that I hadn't ever been to school and was trying to learn all I could myself. He said, 'Well, without proper schooling you wouldn't be able to take a trade.' He said he was sorry and asked why I didn't go to school. I explained the reason and about my life up to then and he remarked that he was afraid I would have a hard time. With that he got up and showed me out and said he was looking for a lad like me but he must be educated.

So that was that – out again in the cold hard world. I went home and told my mother the sad news. She wasn't very well and asked me to look after the shop for her for awhile, which I did. I liked the shop work although my mother couldn't pay me wages. I stayed in the shop for over a month until mother recovered – she suffered from what was said to be appendicitis and at time she was in great pain. I had to put hot packs on her stomach where the pain was most severe and this relieved it.

One morning in May, Mother drew my attention to an advertisement in the newspaper for a lad to work on a farm at a place called Lake Yealering, only a few miles from where I had worked for Charlie and Mrs Bibby. The advertisement was for a firm called Coad and Tindle. I went straight away that morning to the address given – an office in Perth. Mr Tindle asked me some questions about stock and farming, and he also asked if I had any references. I didn't have references but I told him where I had been working at the foundry and that I had worked for a Mr Bibby. As soon as I mentioned Mr Bibby he said, 'What? Charlie Bibby?' I said, 'Yes.' 'Righto lad,' he said, 'you have a job. I know the Bibbys well. I've stayed there many times. We want you to go to Wickepin – there is a train out to there now – and our manager, Mr Kent will meet you. He is managing our property at Lake Yealering.'

Mr Tindle then told me that he, his brother and Mr Coad had taken up four thousand acres of land about four miles west of the lake and were running sheep on it. My job would be looking after the sheep, doing a bit of boundary riding and general work on the property. Mr Tindle then asked, 'What about wages?' I said, 'What do you think?' He replied, 'What about thirty shillings a week and keep?' I agreed to those terms and was told that I had to leave the following Monday morning.

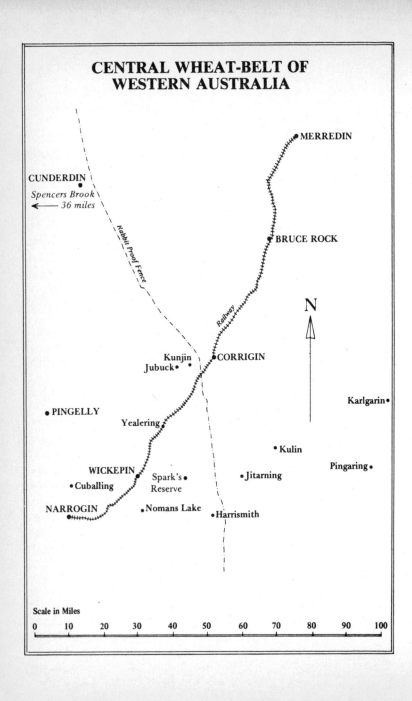

CENTRAL WHEAT-BELT OF WESTERN AUSTRALIA

MERREDIN

CUNDERDIN
Spencers Brook
← 36 miles

Rabbit Proof Fence

BRUCE ROCK

Railway

N

Kunjin
Jubuck
CORRIGIN

Karlgarin

PINGELLY
Yealering

Kulin

WICKEPIN
Cuballing
Spark's
Reserve
Jitarning
Pingaring

NARROGIN
Nomans Lake
Harrismith

Scale in Miles

| 0 | 10 | 20 | 30 | 40 | 50 | 60 | 70 | 80 | 90 | 100 |

38

BACK TO THE BUSH

When I arrived at the station Mr Tindle was there to meet me. He handed me a railway ticket to Wickepin with a pound note and said, 'You will have to stay at Narrogin overnight. The train gets there about midnight and the Wickepin train leaves at eight in the morning, so you can stay at the Coffee Palace just east of the station. The pound note is to pay your way.' He saw me onto the Albany train, then left saying that he would see me soon and that he hoped I would like the job. I couldn't help thinking how oddly things turned out. Here I was going back to almost the same place I had worked before I left to see my mother.

This job was good. Mr Kent was a single man and a terrible cook but we got along fine.

The property was fenced all round with a dog-proof fence, and I had to ride around the boundary every five days to see that the fence was intact. I carried an axe and a shovel with me, and I also carried my rifle. If the fence was broken or the limb of a tree had fallen on it, I had to put things right. The rest of my time was taken up looking to see that the sheep were all right. I learnt a lot about looking after young ewes, especially when the lambing was on. Mr Kent showed me how to help them if they had trouble when giving birth.

I liked this job. I felt that I was doing something important. There were fifteen hundred sheep on the property and I felt that I was responsible for them, especially when my boss told me that he was depending on me to look after them.

Wickepin was our nearest town and Mr Kent went there for stores every two weeks and sometimes he let me go with him.

In September the shearers came to shear the sheep. In those days shearing was done by hand with wide bladed shears like big scissors. This time there were three shearers and they sheared about three hundred a day between them. Mr Kent showed me how to class wool and throw it so it would fall spread out over a special wool-table.

In November that year, Mr Kent got leave to go to South Australia for a trip and said he would be away for six weeks, including Christmas. He asked me if I thought that I could look after the place while he was away. When I said that I could he asked. 'Are you sure? Because if you have any doubts about it I will employ someone to stay with you.' I assured him that I felt sure of myself and that I felt terribly important – manager of a big property like that – the sheep flock had increased to over two thousand with the lambs. So Mr Kent came to me about a week later and said he was leaving the next day. I drove him to Wickepin to catch the train. He was going to Fremantle and from there by boat to Port Adelaide.

Mr Kent wasn't one that could be called a talker – he said very little – and I never asked him anything of his business because if he wished to tell me, he would. At Wickepin that day, just before he got on the train he said, 'Now Bert, look after things while I'm away. You are in full charge and when I come back I will have two big surprises for you.' With that he departed.

I got some supplies from the store – tinned meat and tinned milk, jam, sugar, baking-powder, flour and some small tidbits. I had some lunch after feeding the horses. They were two lovely horses – Mr Kent always used two horses in a buggy when making a trip to Wickepin. It was sixteen miles away so the return trip of thirty-two miles in one day was a full day's work for them. On the way back home I wondered what the two surprises were. I couldn't think what they would be.

During the absence of Mr Kent I was kept busy. The weather was becoming very hot and I had to watch out for flies, as fly strike to the ewes was bad at that time of the year, and we had some twelve hundred ewes. I had to yard the sheep every week and spray them with oil. Mr Kent called it whale oil. It kept the flies off because they didn't like it.

We had two good sheep dogs and they were the only company I had while Mr Kent was away. I always tied them up when I went to town for supplies, but at home they followed me everywhere and were real pals. They were black kelpies, both males.

Just before Christmas Day I had a visitor – Jack Lander – and what a thrill it was. He was the man who had been a witness to the cattle stealing while I was working for Mr Bibby and who had given me the books for schooling. He wanted me to go to his place, about seven miles away, for Christmas dinner. He stayed and had lunch with me. While I would have liked to go for Christmas dinner I had to refuse, because I had promised Mr Kent that I wouldn't leave the place except to get stores. We had a long chat about the past and he was thrilled when I told him that I was in charge of the property. He remarked, 'Fancy a lad of sixteen years being manager.' I felt a thrill from his remark, and when he finally left to go back to his place he said that he would have liked me to come for Christmas dinner, but as I had promised not to leave the place he understood and admired me for sticking to my word.

The days, then weeks went by. I had a quiet Christmas. I got a pound tin of Christmas pudding and a pound tin of ham and that was all I bothered with. The quietness didn't trouble me – I liked it and being kept so busy helped. I had three windmills to look after as well as the boundary fence and the sheep.

About every eight days I had to change the sheep into a fresh paddock. They were divided into two flocks – the ewes and lambs in one paddock and the dry sheep (non-breeders) and rams in another. The property was fenced into seven paddocks and the sheep were rotated, so that the grass and scrub could make new shoots and be much nicer and fresher when the sheep were put back.

Time had passed quickly. It was now the middle of January 1911. I went to Wickepin for stores, and there was a letter there from Mr Kent to tell me that he would be returning to Wickepin on the last Saturday in January. I was to meet him with the buggy.

So on that Saturday I got the first of the two surprises. Mr Kent brought back a wife with him. He hadn't mentioned anything about it to me before. The first thing that came to my mind when he told me that the lady was his wife was, 'I hope she can cook.' She was tall and had a dark complexion – a good-looking woman about twenty-five years old and beautifully dressed, with the largest hat I had ever seen. The brim must have been three feet wide. Mr Kent fussed around her and every second word was 'darling' or 'ducky'. They went to the hotel for their lunch (Wickepin now had a hotel). I had my lunch at the usual place, the Coffee Palace.

After lunch I hitched the two horses to the buggy and drove to the station, where I got six large travelling bags (trunks). Then I went back to the hotel where the bride and groom were waiting. After getting an extra list of stores we set off for home. I drove all the way – he was too busy hugging and squeezing his bride. He told me that they had only been married a fortnight and the trip from South Australia was their honeymoon. They told me that a railway van was on its way from Perth with their furniture and that a carrier from Wickepin would bring it out as soon as it arrived. I had never seen so much hugging, kissing and lovey-doveying in my life. I thought it was sickening. I was very shy where girls were concerned.

The next few days I didn't see much of Mrs Kent. Mr Kent came with me to see the sheep and had a good look around. He complimented me on the way I had looked after the place and the stock. He told me that the big bosses – the Tindle brothers and Mr Coad – were coming for a holiday in about a week's time. They wanted to have a look around and do a little hunting and duck-shooting. Mr Kent said, 'They will be delighted with you Bert. You've done a mighty job while I was away and they'll see that you get something for being so thorough.'

The furniture arrived and I helped put it into place. Then, a few days later, the Kents went to Wickepin and came home that night with the big bosses. I got my first disappointment with these people. I was told that I would have to have my meals alone in the kitchen. Up to then I had always been one of the family, but all at once I wasn't good enough to eat with them. Mr Kent himself was an employee, the same as me, and before he got his wife he always took me places with him. Now I wasn't good enough. This hurt me and made me mad.

I kept away as much as possible. I had the two dogs and my work, 'So,' I thought, 'what do I care about those snobs.' That Saturday they all went into Wickepin. They took the buggy and didn't come home until Sunday afternoon. They didn't tell me where they were going or anything about it. I don't suppose they thought about me. This was one of the loneliest times of my life.

A few days later Mr Coad told me that, because I had done such a good job while Mr Kent was away, they had decided to pay me manager's wages during Mr Kent's absence. 'So,' he said, 'you will get the same wages as Kent for those eight weeks.' He then asked me how I liked the job and I said that before Mr Kent went away to get married it was all I could wish for, but since then it hadn't been so good. I said, 'Mr Kent seems to think that getting married places him above other people and I feel that I've been let down. I didn't think a wife could change a man so quickly. We used to share and share alike but now I feel as if I have been graded down to the level of the dogs.'

The manager's wage was, I found out, the second of the surprises that Mr Kent had spoken about before he went away.

The Tindles and Mr Coad finished their holiday and left. Then, about the end of March, Mrs Kent's brother arrived from South Australia. It appears that it was arranged by Mr Kent when he was over there, that he was to come over and work on the farm. I thought then that maybe this was why I was being treated so badly.

Mrs Kent was the worst cook for a woman I had ever met. After she came, the food – which had never been good – was awful. Our menu each day was: breakfast – cold boiled mutton, lunch – stew (sometimes she would fry mutton chops), evening meal – cold boiled mutton. This went on day after day and often the cold mutton would be fly-blown.

The first Saturday in April the Kents were going to Wickepin for stores. Now that Mrs Kent's brother (his name was Stamp) was staying, they always took him with them. I asked if I could go but Mr Kent said, 'If you want to go you can ride your horse in on your own.' I wasn't getting along too good with Stamp and I suppose that was the reason. Or it could have been that they thought I wasn't good enough to ride with them. Mrs Kent used to fuss over Stamp. He was useless as a farm-hand and very lazy.

On the Saturday I saddled Scarlet, the horse that I always rode around the farm, and was leading him out of the paddock ready to set off for town, when Mr Kent asked me to harness the two buggy horses for him. I hooked Scarlet's reins over a post while I fixed the horses into the buggy. Suddenly I heard a horse moving off into a wild gallop. Looking out into the yard I saw Scarlet galloping around madly with Stamp trying to hold onto the saddle. Then all at once the horse pitched him over a fence into a big clump of scrub. I ran over to Scarlet, patted him on the neck and hooked the reins over the post again. When I got to Stamp he was still lying on the ground. He didn't seem to be hurt although he was moaning and complaining about his arm and shoulder. I got him up on his feet and he said that, as he was getting into the saddle to ride around the yard (he had never been on a horse before), a large sheet of newspaper had wrapped itself around Scarlet's hind legs and made him kick and buck. I told Stamp that he had no right touching the horse, and for doing so he deserved to be thrown. He hurried over to the house holding his shoulder.

After awhile Mr Kent came out and said that I must not talk to Stamp the way that I had. Then the first harsh words came between us. I told him that if Stamp didn't stop interfering with the horses, especially Scarlet, I would put his nose out. Mr Kent just walked away. I coupled the horses to the buggy and drove it over to the house for them to go to town in. Then Mrs Kent came out and called me a brute and said that I didn't know how to speak to a gentleman. I tied the horses to the rail just outside of the house and walked away. I didn't say a word to her. I got Scarlet and rode off to town. I knew that my days were nearing an end as far as the Kents were concerned. I made up my mind to look for another job.

Well, that is the way of life. You think you know a person then some small thing happens: one day a manager, next day a tramp.

Arriving at Wickepin, I stabled Scarlet then went for a walk. Wickepin now had two general stores, two banks, one hotel, a hairdresser's shop and a tailor's shop. The hairdresser was a very popular man and he got to know everybody. I called in and had a haircut, and while he was cutting my hair he asked me how my job was going. I explained how things were since Mr Kent had got married. I said, 'At the moment I think I am very unpopular.' I told him about Stamp and that I was looking for another job.

He stopped cutting my hair and said, 'There's a man in town looking for someone. He's from the Goldfields. He and his brother have taken up land thirty-five miles east of here in the Jitarning District. He doesn't know anything about wheat and sheep farming and is willing to pay good wages to a man to come and work for him and show him how to go about it. It should be just the job for you. He is staying at the pub.' I asked what the man's name was. The hairdresser said, 'Let me think. His first name is Richard. The barman told me – you go and ask him.'

I went to the hotel and the barman told me that the man's name was Rigoll and gave me his room number. I went to the room and told Mr Rigoll that I had heard about him wanting a man who knew how to go about turning virgin land into a wheat and sheep farm. He said, 'That's what I want. Do you know where I can get such a man?' This made me a little narked, then I realised that I was only young and he wouldn't have thought that I was applying for the job myself. When I told him of my experience he sat up and became very interested. He had heard about my uncle being one of the pioneers of modern wheat and sheep farming in the Wickepin District. He asked when I could start if he employed me. I said that my boss would be in town that day and I would see him when he arrived. I told Mr Rigoll that I wanted to leave my job because I didn't get on with my boss's wife and brother, and that I would have to give a week's notice.

Mr Rigoll said, 'I will go with you and have a talk with him. He may let you go straightaway. It is thirty-five miles to our property and it's pretty wild country. My wife and three small children are out there on their own in tents and I can't leave them alone for a whole week.' We both walked out onto the footpath of the hotel and I saw the Kents drive into the back of the hotel. I introduced them to Mr Rigoll and said to Mr Kent, 'I'll go and fix the horses for you. Mr Rigoll would like to discuss something with you.' Mrs Kent and Stamp walked away into the hotel.

Mr Rigoll explained his position and Mr Kent agreed to let me go without a week's notice. I heard later that he had told Mr Rigoll, 'You will find it hard to get anyone better than Bert for the job you want doing. I'll give you a written reference if you like.' Mr Kent came to me – I had just finished unharnessing the horses and stabling them – and told me that I was welcome to take the new job. He admitted that I hadn't been treated very well since Stamp came. 'But,' he said, 'he is my wife's brother.'

Mr Rigoll told me that I had the job and my wages would start from Monday. He would pay me three pounds a week and keep. I said that I would have to go out to the Kent's to get my things and he agreed to drive out with me that afternoon and camp there the night. The next morning we would go straight to Mr Rigoll's property. Mr Rigoll said that if we got an early start we would make it home the same night. He had a very fine horse and a light springcart, and only a light load.

The Kents got home about six o'clock and they invited my new boss in to dinner. I was also asked into the dining-room for dinner which surprised me. Mr Kent paid me off after dinner. After a while my new boss and I excused ourselves and said goodbye as we wanted to get an early start. Then I got another surprise. Mrs Kent said for me to make some breakfast for Mr Rigoll and myself in her kitchen in the morning, and to help myself to whatever I wanted. She said goodbye and wished me luck. I shook hands all around and even Stamp wished me good luck.

39

SOLID ADVICE

It was seven o'clock next morning when we left. I had made Dick (Mr Rigoll told me to call him that) and myself a good breakfast of bacon and eggs. The Kents were still in bed when we set off.

We travelled very well, allowing the horse to walk on the up-grade sections and he trotted at a fast gait down hill. The horse's name was Boxer – he was a beautiful animal and trotted along like he knew he was going home. Dick said that he thought we had about forty miles to go.

The weather was nice and cool. We reached the Rabbit Proof Fence and turned south along it. (The fence had been built by the Government from coast to coast to try to protect the inner wheatbelt from damage by rabbits.) There was a good dirt track along the side of the fence. This was used by the boundary riders who rode along each day to see that the fence wasn't damaged and passable to rabbits. We came to a boundary rider's hut where there was water, so we rested Boxer for two hours and gave him a drink and a feed. Dick said we were more than half-way home.

We set off again at half past two by Dick's watch, and an hour later we came to the eighty-mile gate. From there it was sixteen miles to our destination. We travelled east letting Boxer take it easier.

We arrived just before sundown. Mrs Rigoll and the kids ran to meet us. Dick had three children – two boys and a girl. They were living in two tents with a covered area between them – a large tarpaulin swung over a ridge pole stretching from one tent to the other. They used the tents for sleeping in and had their meals under the tarpaulin.

Dick and I were very tired. Mrs Rigoll had a lovely beef stew cooked and we enjoyed it. She said, 'I'm worried about where you're going to sleep.' I said, 'Don't you worry about me. I'll spread some bags on the floor here under this tarpaulin and put my rugs on them, and before you say 'knife' I'll be asleep. We can arrange something more permanent tomorrow.'

As soon as we finished dinner I helped Mrs Rigoll to clear the table and wash up the dishes. Dick got me about four empty bags and I made up my bed at the back of the tarpaulin. Then, after I had talked to Dick and his wife for awhile, they retired to their tent.

The next thing I knew it was daylight. I got up straight away and in a few minutes Dick was up and out. He said, 'You seem like an early riser Bert.' I said, 'Yes, I am.' We went for a walk around the property near the tents. Dick explained as we walked that they (he and his brother Len) had taken up three thousand acres of conditional purchase land and they each had a homestead block of one hundred and sixty acres. All of it was first class land and the average rainfall was from twelve to fifteen inches per annum.

'Now Bert,' Dick said, 'what do you think is the most important thing to do first, or the three or four more urgent things? Of course you will want some time to think about it.' I started to consider the problem. I could see that Dick had been carting water and I asked him where he got it from. He replied that he carted it from a dam about four miles away – one hundred gallons at a time, which he put into a two-hundred-gallon tank near the camp. The tank was standing on two heavy cases about eighteen inches from the ground. It had a tap on it for Mrs Rigoll to turn off and on when she wanted water. As we walked back to camp Dick said he would have to go for some water tomorrow. Mrs Rigoll then called us for breakfast and while we were eating Dick asked me if I formed any ideas.

'Well,' I said, 'first we should get a permanent water supply on the property and I have an idea. Do you know anyone who will lend you a single-furrow garden plough, a quarter-yard scoop and three good strong horses with their harness and three sets of chains?' Dick thought for awhile and then said, 'Yes, one of our neighbours has a plough and some horses, and some others – the Lewis Brothers – have a scoop. What do you propose to do?' I said, 'Put a dam down in the valley.' (The valley was little more than a hundred yards from the camp and it started from the foot of a granite hill and ran down into a creek which was about half a mile below the camp.) My idea was to sink the dam in the valley, almost opposite the camp where it would have a catchment about a quarter of a mile long. It was an ideal spot. I explained this to Dick and said that we must get onto it before we got too much winter rain. Dick said he would go and see the neighbours.

I told Dick that the next most important thing would be to get about two hundred acres of good grassland fenced in for the horses. 'Then comes a decent house to put your wife and children in. These things will keep us busy for two to three months.'

Dick managed to get the necessary equipment – he borrowed some and bought some. While he was doing this I pegged out the site and grubbed out some trees and roots so we could use the plough and scoop without the risk of breaking them. We were four weeks putting the dam down and were lucky, as a few showers of rain fell but not enough to retard the work. In fact, the little rain that we got helped us, as it made the ground softer for us to plough and it stopped the dust. When we finished we had a dam of between one thousand and twelve hundred yards capacity.

We then went on to the fencing, enclosing two hundred acres of good grassland including the dam. The fence consisted of two barbed wires strung from tree to tree. Where the distance between trees was more than five yards, we put a post in. The barbed wire was nailed to the trees and posts. This kind of fence was called a 'lightning fence'. It took us two weeks to complete – we received heavy rains which held us up for three days. The rain put water in the dam – it half-filled it in fact – so Dick's water carting was over. He used to have to cart water three times a week.

Our next job was to build a decent home. We selected a spot and I suggested that we build the house out of bush timber with a galvanised, corrugated iron roof. My plan was for a structure with two ten-feet by twelve-feet rooms with nine-foot ceilings, a large kitchen twelve feet by twenty-four feet, making the overall size of the house twenty-four feet by twenty-two feet. The walls on the south and east sides were to be bush timber, and hessian whitewashed with a mixture of pipe-clay and lime with two percent English cement mixed with water. The north and west sides were to be made of iron because all the rough weather came from those directions. These walls would be white-washed too.

I told the Rigolls I had helped an Irishman (Moran) to build a house, and before that, I had seen my uncle build one out of bush timber. That is where I got the ideas from. I told them, 'A house like this will last at least ten years and by then you should be in a position to build a permanent home.'

The house that I suggested wouldn't cost a lot of money – one hundred pounds or less for iron and hessian, nails and an oven. We could get all the timber we needed out of the bush and could buy three cheap barn doors and four windows fitted with glass and fasteners.

Both Dick and his wife agreed to my plans but asked, 'Who is going to build it?' I replied, 'I will, with Dick to help me. We shouldn't take more than three weeks and while Dick is getting the materials, I will be out cutting and shaping the timber, and digging the holes for the posts, and carting the timber. It won't take long to put it up once we have everything on the spot.' I said that we could build the fireplace and chimney out of granite rocks, using cement for mortar.

I was a little puzzled about Dick's finance, and I asked him, when we were on our own, about how he would manage to pay for everything. He told me that his brother Len had a good job on the Goldfields and was financing the whole thing until it started to bring in enough money for both of them. Then Len would leave his job and shift down onto the farm. Dick said that at the moment they were okay – not rich but they had enough if they were careful and what I had suggested for the house was just what he wanted. He had written to Len and told him all about what we were doing. Dick said, 'Len says that he is all the way behind us and to go straight ahead. He is extra happy about the dam.'

We worked hard and long hours on the house and had it finished by the middle of August. I will never forget the day we shifted in. Dick and Mrs Rigoll had a home-warming and Dick bought a few bottles of beer and wine and got drunk. He tried hard to get me to have a drink with him but to no avail.

Mrs Rigoll was on top of the world. She said that after living in tents for six months the house was lovely. I was very proud of it, especially the chimney. I had never built a chimney before, but after a lot of working out and changing around, it worked fine – without smoking. It had a fireplace on one side and an oven built on the other. It took up about eight feet of the south wall of the kitchen.

Now Dick and I started to get some land ready for cropping. This was hard manual work – we chopped down small trees and burned down the big ones. The timber was then left, as on the other farms where I had worked, to dry out ready for the burning season starting in February. Dick and I worked only six days a week as our urgent rush jobs were over. (While working on the dam and house we had worked all day every day, and as much as we could into the night.) We completed one hundred and forty acres of felling in eleven weeks.

While the felling was going on, I wrote to Grandma and told her I had decided to go for a trip to Victoria to see my sister Laura, who was still living with our uncle at Campbell's Creek. I wanted to take Grandma with me and I told her that I would pay for her passage and expenses. Grandma wrote to me saying that she would love to go.

I asked Dick to let me go on the next trip to town for the stores, so that I could go to my uncle's place – it was only five miles out from Wickepin – to see Grandma. Dick agreed. Grandma was overjoyed to see me, and to have the chance of seeing again all her old friends and relations, and her home town.

I wrote to the State Steamship Company and sent them a deposit for two first class fares to Port Adelaide. (That is the way we agreed to travel because Grandma had some relations in the Mount Lofty Ranges in South Australia who we wanted to see.) When I got a reply to say we were booked to sail the first week of December, I sent Grandma twenty pounds for her to get some clothes or whatever she wanted for the trip. I told her in the letter what day we were to sail. I didn't get a reply but didn't worry because the only way we got our mail was when we went into town or a neighbour went in.

The end of the third week in November, I finished with the Rigolls and Dick paid me up and took me into Wickepin. He had asked me to give him a statement as to what he should do when I left, so I told him the following and he wrote it down: 'During the summer months, that is December and January, get as much ring-barking done as you can. That will kill the trees and give the natural grass a better chance to grow freely, increase the feed for the stock and also make the trees easier to burn later. And while you are doing the ring-barking, cut posts from all the suitable trees you come across, for fencing in the winter months after you get your crop in.

'Now you must be ready to start burning off the land we have chopped down, in February. You will want two or three men to help you do this, so each time you go to town try and make arrangements for them to start, or – if you can manage the finance – get a man just after Christmas. He can work on the ring-barking and post-cutting as well as helping with the burning – it would be money well spent. (Two pounds a week and keep would be good wages for this kind of work.)

'Now, when burning off, first of all burn all the stumps down to ground level and be careful that you don't burn all the other wood up before you finish this – otherwise you will have to cart more wood to finish burning the stumps. A good idea is to mark out an area, then go all over it and pack wood on all the stumps. When all the loose wood burns shovel the burnt coal off and pack more wood in. Keep doing this until all the stumps are burnt to the ground level, then you can pack whatever wood is left onto the fires and clear it all up.

'Before you start to plough the cleared land, you will have to go over it with a shovel and fill in all the holes that have been caused by some of the dry stumps that have burnt down into the ground.

'Now when the clearing is finished you will have to buy four good, medium draught horses (I advise to buy four young ones about four years old). Four horses will pull a three-furrow stump-jump plough. You will also have to buy the plough and you will want a drill. A sixteen-run drill is the best and four horses will pull the drill with the harrows behind easily.'

I told Dick that when he had done all of these things he would be well on the way to having a real wheat farm. I also advised him to write to the Agricultural Department for all the available books on wheat growing, which would have the times and kinds of wheat to grow. Then I said, 'I don't know what I will do when I get back from this trip but I hope to see you then.'

40

RETURN

I rode out to Wickepin to see when Grandma would be ready. The boat was to sail at eleven o'clock one morning in the first week in December. When I arrived at Uncle's place I got the shock of my life. Grandma wasn't coming. When I asked her why she said that she was too old to travel, and no matter what I said or did she wouldn't change her mind. After about two hours I went back to Wickepin, feeling very disappointed, and caught the next train to Perth.

The shipping company refunded me the money I had paid for Grandma's fare and although I was disappointed, I had a wonderful trip on the boat, the *Dimboola*. The sea was calm and a beautiful blue. I dined at the Captain's table.

I travelled through South Australia to Ballarat, then took a train to Castlemaine in Victoria. The train that went through Campbells Creek left Adelaide about five o'clock that evening (I sent Laura a telegram from Adelaide to say that I was coming by the train), arriving at Campbells Creek near midday the next day. To my surprise Laura was there to meet me. I was very excited. I hadn't seen her since I was four years old, and I had no idea what she looked like, but she knew me. She was about twenty and had grown into a beautiful woman.

I stayed with Laura until after Christmas and into the New Year of 1912, and we travelled around Castlemaine and Barkers Creek where Grandma used to live. I remembered the old place but I didn't know I had so many relations. We also went to Bendigo because we had relations there.

During this time that I was at Laura's I decided to travel up to Sydney to see the much talked-about Johnson-Burns fight that was being held up there at the Sydney Stadium.

I caught the train, first to Melbourne, and then up to Sydney. I didn't know a soul, but on the train to Sydney I met a young chap from Sydney, Peter Malone, who had been in Melbourne to visit an uncle.

He lived at Rushcutters Bay, not far from the stadium, and invited me to stay at his place. His mother was a wonderful woman, and his father was away working in the bush.

I stayed with them for a few days and they showed me around Sydney. The fight itself turned out to be a complete waste of time. I was never so disgusted in all my life. It wasn't sport at all – they were both nasty and spiteful. It was a vicious fight, and an absolute waste of my whole trip.

After I returned to Campbells Creek and the Christmas holidays were over, I took Laura down to our Aunt Lizzie's place in Footscray and we stayed with her until I sailed from Port Melbourne for the West again.

This was the best holiday I had ever had. I gave my sister a wonderful time – we saw all of Melbourne's suburbs and beauty spots, and all of the shows, pictures and everything we could think of. When I sailed from Port Melbourne on the S.S. *Orsova* Laura was very sorry. I wanted her to come back with me to the West, but she would have had to leave Uncle Best who was a cripple and she said she couldn't let him down. That was typical of Laura.

The trip back was very rough after we left Port Adelaide. Although the *Orsova* was a twelve thousand ton vessel, the sea tossed her like a cork. I got terribly seasick and was glad to arrive at Fremantle.

After getting off the boat I went straight home to my mother's place, and found that my brothers were still at home and were both still in work. I asked Bill if he had any jobs for me but he said that things were very slack and there were a lot of men out of work. He was very sorry, but he couldn't help me.

On the next Friday night I went to boxing school. They all said that I had grown and jokingly said I would be a heavy-weight in two to three years. I had a long talk with Mr Burns and he said that, owing to the number of unemployed, I would find it hard getting a job in Perth. He wanted to know if I had done any boxing since I'd been away. I explained that I had been in the bush and hadn't had a chance. I then asked him about a set of six-ounce boxing gloves and he offered me a good second-hand set with a platform punching ball and two skipping ropes – two pounds for the lot, which was cheap. The top platform board went with the ball and could be put up in a few minutes anywhere in a hall or shed. I bought the equipment as both Mr Burns and George Hickling advised me to keep doing punch ball, skipping and exercises whenever I could. They also told me to get someone to put the boxing gloves on and spar with me whenever possible, and not to forget to try all the things they had taught me. I promised them I would and then I left.

I stayed home for a few days, paying my board and helping Mother. Then one morning there was an advertisement in the newspaper. The Western Australian Water Supply wanted men to go into the country, fencing-in Government dams, rabbit-proofing, and fixing dam pumps. The ad said that only experienced men were wanted and that an under-standing of horses was an advantage. Applicants were to apply that day at the Water Supply Offices in James Street, Perth.

I got ready and went in straight away. I got there about eight a.m. but there must have been about thirty men there already. None had been called in for an interview up to that point, so I waited. I went to the office counter and gave the clerk my name. He looked hard at me and said, 'Only men with experience wanted, son.' I replied, 'That's all right.' He then said, 'The job's in the bush up in the outer wheat-belt.' I just nodded my head and went and sat down with the men who were waiting.

About half an hour later they commenced to call names (a lot had come since me). As each man's name was called he went into an office on the other side of the room, and a few minutes later came out and left. This went on for about an hour, then suddenly my name was called. It gave me a start. I went into the office and a man was writing something. He looked up suddenly and said, 'Yes?' I said, 'I want a job.' He looked at me and said, 'What do you know about horses and fencing?' I said that I was used to horses and I understood about fencing. He said, 'This work is in the bush. Have you any references?' I said, 'Not in writing but I have had a lot of experience working for farmers and new settlers and for my uncle who is a vet.' 'Oh,' he said, 'what is your uncle's name?' I told him, 'Archie McCall – he is at Wickepin and he has a farm there.' My uncle's name made him sit up. He looked at me and said, 'I know him very well.'

The man seemed interested now. He said, 'We have a gang of five men working east of Wickepin in the Harrismith District. They have two lovely-looking horses – I don't know what's happened but they won't pull the empty cart. By what we've been told they've become rank jibs. Do you think you could do anything with them?' I said that I would like to have a try and that I got along fine with horses. I said that perhaps the men were knocking them about – they become very nasty if they're treated cruelly. 'Well,' he said, 'if you wait out there I will see you again later on.'

A lot more men went in to be interviewed and came out and left, and finally there were only five of us still there. Two were called in for further questions, then one went away and the other sat down to wait further. I was called in and asked more questions about how I would handle the horses. The Water Supply man was happy with my answers and said that he had decided to give me the job.

Then he suddenly asked, 'What is your age?' I told him that I was seventeen years old last August. He then told me that his name was Sublet and he gave me an order to travel to Wickepin via Narrogin, leaving Perth on the Tuesday evening train. He said that a man named Johnson would be there to meet me with a buggy and pair, and drive me out to the gang. He told me that he had selected two other men who would be replacements for another gang. With that he shook my hand and said that he would see me soon as he made an inspection every few weeks.

'Now,' he said, 'remember that you will be completely in charge of those two horses. I hope that you're going to be a success.' I started to leave when he called to me. I turned back and he said, 'I never told you anything about wages. You will be paid ten shillings each day, Saturday and Sunday included, as the horses have to be looked after every day. How does that suit you?' I replied, 'That would be fine Mr Sublet.'

41

SETTLING IN

So now, with a job with the Western Australian Water Supply, I was going back to the Wickepin area. It seemed a strange coincidence that both the jobs I got through advertisements were in the Wickepin District. Although the actual place of my new job was Harrismith, the Water Supply Depot was two miles east of Wickepin.

I arrived at Wickepin on Wednesday and Tom Johnson was there to take me out to join the gang. We drove out to the depot and he said, 'We will have some lunch before I take you out to the gang. They're fencing a Government dam about twenty-five miles from here, so I will camp out there tonight and drive back tomorrow morning.'

We set off about one o'clock. Tom drove a buggy and a pair of beautiful horses. When we were well on our way he said, 'Do you think you will be able to handle those other two horses? They're a pair of devils. They take fits and starts. Sometimes they're good and then all of a sudden they'll get nasty and refuse to budge.'

Tom started to tell me a story about how difficult they were. He said, 'One day when the chap that is looking after them now came into the depot for wire and piping, we were a whole day trying to get those horses to budge the cart. All they would do is go around and around in a circle, and all the time they were doing this the wheels were cutting into the ground making it almost impossible to shift them. We dug trenches and put boards under the wheels; we belted them and done everything we knew to get them to move but they wouldn't. It became late in the evening so we unloaded them. The driver stayed the night. The next morning we put them back into the cart and drove them around with the cart empty, then loaded it again and they played up again for awhile. Then all of a sudden they went off without any further trouble, but since then they've been very hard to handle.'

Then Tom said, 'I'm glad it's you that's going to handle them and not me.' He asked me what I was going to do. I replied, 'I can't give an opinion until I see them performing. Horses are a wonderful creature and usually when they play up like you explained there is something causing it. Anyway, we will soon see.'

We arrived at the gang's camp just before sundown. The men had finished their evening meal and were sitting down talking. There were five of them – the ganger and four men. As we arrived, they all stood up and Tom drove right up close to them. They all knew him and he was very popular with them.

Tom introduced me to them all and said that I had been sent up there to take charge of the horses with no interference from anyone, by the request of Mr Sublet. The boss of the gang gave a grunt and said, 'What? A kid! What next.' His name was Harry Beet. Tom winked at me and smiled. (Later he told me that grunting was one of the Boss's habits when he wasn't very pleased.) One of the gang put the billy on, made Tom and me a cup of tea and gave us something to eat.

The man who had been looking after the horses had taken up a thousand acres and a homestead block and was leaving to start work on it. He said he was fed up with these 'jibs', meaning the horses. When we finished the meal this man, Maurice Green, asked me if I would like to have a look at the horses. He told me that he had come out from England about two years ago and didn't know much about horses.

We had come to where the horses were tied up and I looked them over. They were very nervous and trembled when I went to pat them. I held the rope each one was tied up with and patted both horses on the neck and fondled them in turn. Green was watching me. After a few minutes the horses didn't seem to mind being handled. They were beautiful horses – one was bay with a white star on her forehead, the other was shiny black with a white blaze down her face and four white stockings. They were in splendid condition and I told Green I would take them over right then. He said that he was going back to Wickepin in the morning with Tom.

We went back and joined the others and the Boss said he wanted to shift camp in the morning. They had finished the present job and the next one was fifteen miles out of Wickepin. They had to fence a dam, put a pump, troughs and stand pipe in, and clear the catchment. The dam was known as Spark's Reserve – it was named after the settler whose place it was near.

We sat around the fire talking and telling yarns until near nine o'clock. Tom, who always carried his roll with him, slept in Green's tent. After I fed and watered the horses (again patting and handling them), I made my bed in a tent occupied by a Scotsman named Jock

McKay. He asked me what I thought about the horses. I said that they were very nervous and scared. He told me that Green, the Boss and Bentley knocked hell out of them. He said, 'I have seen them knock them over the head with a shovel and bash them with a mattock handle in the ribs and on their rumps, and the more they belted them the worse they got.'

It wasn't long before I went to sleep. I was very tired. Just before daylight I awoke and lay thinking about what would be the best way to handle the horses. They had apparently been ill-treated so I decided that I would do just the reverse, and try kindness. I remembered my uncle Archie saying that you couldn't make an animal obey you with cruelty. He said to be firm, show them that you're boss and be kind to them. I decided that that would be my approach to the problem.

As daylight came I got up, dressed and went to the horses. They looked at me with a sort of nervousness, tension and suspicion. I walked straight to them, untied their neck ropes and led them to the water-trough. They came along without any trouble and had a good drink. I then tied them up back at the feeder and fed them. They seemed to have relaxed and started eating. I then got the brush and commenced to rub the dry sweat off and brush them down. This made them stand taut for awhile, then each one relaxed as I brushed them. I stayed with them for over an hour, and when I left to go back to camp they were both very quiet and had let me brush down their legs, manes and also their heads, and I felt that they didn't mind me.

At camp I told Jock that I had brought some stores out with me. He and I agreed to share the costs of our stores and living expenses while we were together on the gang, and to use the same tent for sleeping. We had our breakfast and packed up all our stores and beds, then took our tent down and had everything ready to move.

I went to the horses and put the harness on them. The bay mare worked in the shafts and the black worked in the lead – they were always driven in this tandem fashion. I changed this by putting the bay in the shafts, and hooking the black in front. Driving this way, there were two pairs of reins – one for each horse. I got into the cart, got a firm grip on the reins and gave a short sharp whistle and yelled, 'Come on! Get up!' and shook the reins at them. They started to prance so I called, 'Whoa' and they stopped prancing. I waited for a few seconds and again whistled and shook the reins and called, 'Come on! Get up!' in a loud voice, and they moved off without any further bother.

I drove them out onto a nearby road and along it for about half a mile. Then I turned them around and drove them back to where the gang was waiting to be picked up, stopping and starting them to get them used to me. When I got back I pulled up near where the men had their gear stacked, and told them to load it on. While they did this I made a fuss of the horses, patting them and seeing that the harness was comfortable.

When the loading was finished, two men sat on the back of the cart and the Boss and the other man sat in the front with me. When all was ready I asked the Boss and the man in front not to call out at the horses if they started to play up. I said, 'Just leave it to me. They're my concern.' I took hold of the reins and gave a sharp whistle and called to them to get up. They made to go, then the leader started to do a bit of a dance, stamped her feet and tried to turn around, so I called, 'Whoa'. The leader stopped and I got down, patted her and brushed the flies away from her eyes. Then as I walked back to get into the cart, I gave them both a friendly pat. The Boss was holding the reins for me while I was letting the horses settle down. I got back into the cart and tried again. To the surprise of all, both horses moved up into their collars and moved off as if there wasn't anything wrong.

With all our gear, stores and tools plus five men, we had quite a load. Tom, who the Boss referred to as 'Johnson', drove along behind us for a few miles and Green was with him. We still had ten miles to go to Spark's Reserve when Tom saw that the horses had settled down, and passed us. We didn't have any further trouble with the horses and they turned out to be two of the best I had ever worked with.

42

Taking Charge

I stayed with this gang and our job took us to many places in the wheat-belt, until all the dams were fenced-in and rabbit-proof. I was told that there were four or five other gangs doing the same work.

When the dam fencing was finished a message was sent to the Boss to take two men and me, and go to a place called Kunjin, a new settlers' district a few miles from the well-known Corrigin. There was a well at Kunjin – it was ninety feet deep and had a solid granite stone bottom. Beautiful fresh water was seeping into the bottom but the settlers and the men who were carting water supplies couldn't get enough water for their horses. There wasn't enough pressure to force the water up to make a large enough catchment.

This job took us six weeks and the work was hard. I had to take my turn going down the well and helping put holes into the granite. One man had to hold the drill, while the other struck it with a heavy hammer. The man holding the drill had to give it a quarter of a turn after each blow. It took hours to put a one-inch hole down into the granite to a distance of two feet for blasting.

We managed to blast eight feet of rock out of the well (we always did the blasting just before we knocked off in the evening so that fumes would have cleared by next morning) and there was fifteen feet of water in the well, so our job was well done. The last blast had broken through the granite.

We reconstructed the windmill that we had had to take down from over the well before starting the blasting. It pumped the water up out of the well into a thousand-gallon tank on a four-foot stand, and from there, the water ran down a pipe into a trough. The trough had an automatic water control that kept it full.

The day before we finished working on the well the Inspector called on us and camped with us that night. He was full of praise for the job we had done.

Harry, our boss, took ill with some kind of back trouble. He said that he had had Bright's disease some years ago, and working down in the dampness had started it again. The Inspector decided to take him to town to the doctor. That left only three of us – Jock McKay, Bentley and me.

The Inspector asked us if we would clean up a well – it was at Jubuck, which was a few miles west from where we were, and was very deep. The Inspector told us that it had been put down years ago by sandalwood carters who had shored it with bush timber. He didn't know what condition it was in but he said that it could be dangerous. The settlers, who had no experience with hauling water out of a well with a windlass and eight-gallon buckets, had let so many buckets fall down into the well that they had blocked it. They now had to cart water many miles.

'Now,' the Inspector said, 'one of you will have to take charge and of course will get boss's pay. You will have to decide which one.' I suggested Jock but he wouldn't be in it. Bentley said he wouldn't be in it either, so the Inspector said to me, 'It looks like you.' I said, 'I'll do my best but I haven't had much experience at this sort of work.' He said, 'All you have to do is one of you go down the well and fish the buckets out of the water. Hook them two or three at a time onto a grappling iron – there's a three-hook one with the tools – then the men at the top can just haul them up. You also have a long steel rod with a hook to fish the buckets out of the water at the start.'

He told us where the well was, then dropped a shock on us by telling us that it was about one hundred and forty feet deep. We looked at each other with amazement. The well we had just done was, we thought, deep enough.

The Inspector gave us our pay and made Harry comfortable in his buggy. Tom was with them. When they were ready to depart, I asked the Inspector what he wanted us to do when we were finished cleaning the well. He said, 'Come to the depot at Wickepin. I'll see you there. You should be there in about eight days.' Then they drove away.

We pulled our camps down, packed everything onto the cart, and set off for the bucket-retrieving job that none of us liked the sound of.

When we got to Jubuck we found a good place to camp close to the well, unloaded our gear, and went and had a look down it – we didn't like what we saw. It was dark but we could see some water. There was a two-man windlass on the well and a very strong wire rope with a hook on each end for buckets – the idea was that one bucket would go down while the other was coming up. The shaft was large - six feet by four feet – and the timbering was very rough, with four to six inch gaps in places, between the sets of timber.

Jock and Bentley refused to go down the well, so that left me. We fixed our camp, had some lunch, and talked about the well and how we would go about it. Then I gave instructions to the men about how to let me down so that I could have a good look at the condition of the timber. I had fixed a rope loop to put on the bucket hook to hold me. Taking a hurricane lamp we went to the well.

There were two eight-gallon buckets hooked onto the rope, so we took one off and put the rope loop on. The men lowered me down slowly. At about seventy feet there was a lot of water seeping in and running over the timber, so from there until the bottom I got very wet – the water was as cold as ice. I managed to keep the lamp alight by holding it under me away from the falling water. At the bottom there were three buckets which were partly out of the water. I had a good look at the situation, then called to be pulled to the top again.

When I got to the top I was shivering with the cold and wet through. There was no foul air in the well and the water – which I had tasted – was fresh and beautiful.

The seeping water made us alter our plans. I said that I'd change into some fresh clothes and put on a water-proof overcoat. I went up to the camp and did this, and when I went back I took a flat, solid piece of jarrah and a handsaw with me. The board was one and a half inches thick and eighteen inches wide. I cut the board the right length to fit in between the well timbers just above where I would be fishing out the buckets. This was to protect me from falling water and anything else while down there.

With all the necessary tools for my work, I was again lowered down. I still had to have the lamp, because without it I couldn't see a thing. I also took some matches in case the lamp went out. I told the men that when I got settled at the bottom, I would call out and they were to pull up the end of the rope I had come down on, fix the three pronged grappling iron onto it and lower it down to me. I would then hook the eight-gallon steel buckets on to the grappling iron to be taken out of the well.

Everything went all right and that afternoon we managed to get eight buckets out. When we knocked off at five o'clock I felt much better about the whole job. We had plenty of water now, as each time the dislodged buckets had gone up, an eight-gallon bucket came down and I had filled it with water. Jock and Bentley at the top, filled our camp bucket and cans, and put the rest into the trough for the horses.

The next morning we started at about eight o'clock. I took a length of rope to the well – it was about one hundred and fifty feet long and one inch thick. (We had used it with blocks to take down and reassemble the windmill at Kunjin.) I tied one end of the rope to the windlass stays and let it hang down the shaft. As the men lowered me down I used to steady myself, especially when passing the bucket that was coming up.

The buckets were now proving hard to lift. Because they had been down for so long they had wedged into the mud and clay at the bottom. I got two out after a lot of manoeuvring and pulling and had to send them up out of my way to give me room to work in. I called to the men to pull them up and to be careful, as there were only two buckets and the left hook was protruding. It was hard to make them understand from so far down with the noise of water dripping and the wind that was blowing strongly at the top.

Jock and Bentley commenced pulling and all seemed to be all right, so I started to fish for more buckets. Then, all of a sudden, there was a loud bang about half way up, then a rattling noise like something hurtling down the shaft. I swayed under the board that I had put above me for protection. All hell seemed to break loose and large lumps of timber and earth came tumbling down. The lamp was knocked from my hands and went into the water. Everything went dark . . .

I couldn't see a thing and the water was rising. I had been clear of the water when the accident happened but now it was up to my knees. The noise of falling earth and timber stopped just as suddenly as it started, but the plip, plip of occasional pieces of rubble could be heard – all else was quiet. I was sure this was the end for me. It was pitch dark and only a matter of time.

Then I remembered the matches inside my pocket. I got them out and struck one. The light showed that the board I had placed above me was stopping a lot of timber and earth from falling further. After striking several matches I thought I could see a way out. By pushing some timber sideways away from where I was, I thought I might be able to squeeze through and get on top of the fallen debris.

After awhile this worked – I got through. 'Now,' I thought, 'if there's another fall I'm a goner!' I struck some more matches and could see that the timber in the shaft was sound, so the fallen timber must have come from higher up. I decided to climb up by placing my toes in between the timber on each side of the shaft, moving up about a foot to eighteen inches at a time. I felt my way with my hands as I went, and about every twenty feet or so I struck a match to see if I could see where the shaft had caved in.

At last I came to the spot. I struck another match and what I saw was terrifying. All one side and one end of the shaft had broken away, and most of it had gone down to the bottom, leaving a cavity on the west side, roughly seven feet deep and eight feet high. It looked like more would go at any minute.

I climbed into the cavity and looking up, I could see the top of the shaft – the cave-in was about sixty feet from the top. My matches were getting less but I chanced striking another. Then I saw my only chance of getting out of this death trap. The rope I had tied to the stay on the windlass was hanging down on the east side of the shaft, still intact. My hopes mounted. I stepped gently across and got hold of that precious rope and pulling on it, I went up and out in a few minutes.

When I was well away – about twenty yards or so – I couldn't help it, I cried bitterly and couldn't stop. Yet while I was down the well in great danger and scared stiff, crying was the furthest thing from my mind.

There was nobody around when I got out of the well so I went to our camp, stirred the fire up and put the billy on to make a cup of tea. It was somewhere near midday. The tears had stopped and I felt a little better but I still had that awful sick feeling in my stomach. I was later told that it was shock.

While I was waiting for the billy to boil, a man came galloping up to our camp on his way to the well. When he saw me he jumped off his horse and said loudly, 'Have you seen or heard anything about that bloke that's down the well?' Then without waiting for a reply he went on, 'He's done for. I wouldn't go down that damned thing for a thousand pounds.' And while he rambled on about the dangers, three men came up in a horse and cart. Jock was one of them. He jumped out of the cart and ran over to me, put his arms around me and said, 'How in the hell did you manage to get out?' The man that came on the horse stood back dumbfounded and said, 'It was you! How did you get out?' They all looked at me in amazement. I said, 'Don't talk about it, not now.'

Jock made a big billy-full of tea and they all had some. Then Bentley arrived with three men in a cart and was just as surprised to see me. He asked the same question, 'How did you get out?' I asked them all to excuse me and said I didn't feel very well. I had that terrible feeling in my stomach still and now I felt as if I was going to vomit. I went to my tent and lay down on my bunk. After awhile Jock brought me in a mug of tea and a thin slice of buttered damper. I drank the tea and ate the damper and felt a little better. I didn't feel like I was going to vomit any more, but I couldn't get rid of the sick feeling in my stomach – it was a fainting feeling.

I told Jock that we couldn't do anything about the well – it was too dangerous. I said that we would stop where we were until tomorrow and that I thought we should cover the well with logs in the morning, after taking the windlass off. 'I don't feel like doing any work this afternoon,' I said, 'so you both better take things easy for the rest of the day. Get yourselves some dinner. I don't feel like any at the moment. I may be better later but all I want to do now is lie down until this awful feeling goes.' I asked them not to go near the well. We had plenty of water to drink and the trough was full for the horses.

I lay there thinking about the whole dangerous business – how things can happen and how lucky you can get. When I thought about how close to death I had been, a cold shiver ran down my spine.

Then, Jock and Bentley came running to my tent and Bentley yelled, 'The windlass has gone.' I jumped up and went outside and sure enough the whole top part of the well had given away. We went to the well to have a look and saw that the top part had slipped down into the well and the windlass was about six feet down the shaft. There wasn't a thing we could do about it. I said to the men, pointing to the well, 'It's a complete write-off. We'll pack up tomorrow and start for Wickepin.' I would have to report to the Inspector. We had the eight buckets that we fished out – they were good steel buckets so we would take them with us.

We left the next morning after pulling and packing our tents and gear. It was some thirty miles to the depot at Wickepin and we let the horses take their time. I still hadn't recovered properly from the shock and the scare I got down the well. Jock and Bentley asked me a couple of times how I managed to get out but I still didn't feel like talking about it. I put them off, saying that I would tell them all about it later.

We arrived at Lake Yealering at one thirty that afternoon after covering about eighteen miles, and we camped there for lunch. It was a lovely spot with a fresh-water lake covering about two to three hundred acres – there was about five feet of beautiful fresh water. We gave the horses about two hours rest and then continued our journey to the depot.

We arrived at about six thirty that evening and there wasn't anyone there – it was a Saturday. The Inspector was to meet us, but as he wasn't expecting us for another four or five days, he might have gone off on an inspecting job. So, as I told Jock and Bentley, we would have to wait until he returned.

We put our gear into an unused room. There were several of these because the depot was once a public school building with classrooms. When the railway line was built out to Wickepin, the town soon took shape and a State School was built and the Water Supply took over the old building.

The following day there was still no sign of the Inspector or Tom, his driver, so I put the two horses into the cart and told Jock and Bentley I was going to visit my relatives and I would be back that evening. My grandma was still living with the McCalls, on their property three miles north of Wickepin, and I hadn't seen her for awhile. She was so pleased to see me and said that I had grown into a fine big man. She said that I was the image of my father. I had lunch with them and then we all had a long talk. Uncle Archie came home just before lunch and he wanted to know what I had been doing. They were all taken by the two horses. Uncle said that he would have liked a team like that.

Uncle Archie and Aunt Alice had gone ahead with their farm and were doing fine. I never mentioned the near-tragedy at the well as I knew it would worry Grandma. At four o'clock that afternoon I left and drove back to the depot.

There was still no sign of the Inspector or Tom. Jock and Bentley didn't mind doing nothing and getting paid for it. The following morning the Inspector and Tom turned up at about ten o'clock. I had just finished telling the Inspector about the cave-in when Mr Sublet and Harry arrived. They had come by train to Wickepin and were driven to the depot in a friend's car. Harry had been in hospital in Narrogin for a few days. They had patched him and he said he was much better. We were glad to see him despite his grumpy ways – he was a good boss and gave credit when it was due and didn't forget to let you know if he wasn't pleased with your work. (He had noticed me writing and learning to spell one day and from then on he helped me and told me many things.)

Mr Sublet and the Inspector retired to the office and after awhile I was called in. The Inspector had written down my report as I had told it to him and when I went in Mr Sublet was holding it. He had just finished reading it and he looked up and said, 'What do you think went wrong?' I replied, 'It's hard to say. I can only guess water was coming through the west side all the time I was down there before the cave-in.' I told him that about a week before we finished at Kunjin we had had heavy rain and that may have caused the water to come. It could have been that the water continually seeping through was too much for the timber which must have been rotten in places. I gave them some more details of the accident.

Then Mr Sublet said, 'Did it occur to you that the men on the top may have been careless?' I replied, 'No. Jock is very careful and very reliable and I would also trust Bentley with my life.' That satisfied them and Mr Sublet said, 'All right, you had a very lucky escape. I am going to recommend to the Government that they put down a two-thousand yard dam for the settlers at Jubuck.'

43

DINGO KILLER

We were told that afternoon to get ready to go out to a place some sixty miles east of Wickepin, to fence and put pumps and water troughs onto two dams. We would also put in drains and clear catchments.

Harry gave Jock a list of the materials required, with instructions to get it all together ready for loading early next morning. There was rabbit-netting, pipes, troughs, pumps and fittings. He told me to make out a list for enough stores and supplies to last us seven or eight weeks. Bentley and Harry gave me their list for stores and Jock and I made out our list together. We were the only ones sharing a tent – Harry camped in a tent by himself and so did Bentley.

I drove into Wickepin and got the stores and supplies. The men had given me the money for their orders. They all trusted me to handle their money matters and it was good schooling for me and I liked doing it.

The following morning we were all up bright and early and after breakfast we loaded up – and what a load it was – tents, bedding, stores, materials and four men. It was the biggest load I had ever put on the spring-cart in fact. It was so heavy I suggested that we cut the centre out of a blackboy to make two bumpers, then wire them onto the top of the springs at a centre position to stop the springs breaking should we have to travel over any rough roads. (The blackboy is a grass-tree and has a tough spongy centre that is light in weight – it has a fair amount of give and is ideal as a bumper.)

We had a long way to go and wanted to get to the first dam by the end of the second day. We travelled roughly forty miles the first day and camped at a place called Kulin. That left us roughly twenty miles to go the next day. The first dam we were to service was south-east of Kulin near Pingaring road and the second dam was some fifteen miles north of that.

We arrived safely and made camp about a hundred yards from the dam, which was half-full of water. There were several new settlers who had just settled on their land and were busy putting up huts made from bush timber, with bark rooves and bag sides and room dividers. Some of these huts were pretty crude. The Boss said he wouldn't like to start like these people. 'Sixty miles from the nearest town', he said, 'and not much hope of schooling for their children. What a life.'

We made our camp and built a large fire. We always pitched our tents close together so we could use the same fire for cooking. We often made a stew and we all had to cook our dampers.

I don't think any of us will ever forget the first night we camped at this spot. We were pestered by dingoes – there must have been hundreds of them. Jock and I always kept our meat and bread inside our tent in a bag safe which we hung on the ridge pole. Believe it or not we were kept awake all night chasing the dingoes away from trying to get at the safe. They howled all night long and all around. Bentley was scared out of his wits. He hadn't had any experience with dingoes like that before. He came to our tent and said that they had taken his meat. It had been in a camp oven with the lid on and they had knocked the lid off and taken it. He was shaking with fright, and brought his rugs into our tent and slept on the floor – or at least, he tried to sleep.

I got my rifle and tried to get a shot at one of them but it was too dark. Daylight came and I got out of bed. Peeping through the tent flaps I saw a large dingo standing in front of Bentley's tent. I shot him and when the bullet hit he sprang into the air, then fell dead. The report of the shot woke up the rest of the men and they came out to see what had happened. Bentley was quite excited. For several days I shot the dingoes – I killed four and some got away wounded. This frightened the others and we weren't troubled so much, although they still howled all night.

We were just about three weeks fencing the dam, clearing the catchment area and ploughing the drains. When we knocked off the last evening we had only the rabbit-stop to erect on the main drain where it entered the dam, to finish the job. (The rabbit-stop was a timber frame built across the main drain where the fence crossed it – a sheet of heavy flat iron was hinged to the frame and the iron would rise with the flow of water and fall back into place when the water stopped. This stopped the rabbits from getting into the dam.)

We were all sitting having our evening meal as the sun was setting when the Boss called out, 'Look, there's a dingo in the dam.' There it was, standing on the bank looking at us. Jock realised that it must have got through the rabbit-stop, and grabbing a pick handle he ran to the opening. Bentley and I followed. Bentley grabbed an axe and I picked up a handy piece of wood about two inches thick and about three feet long. Jock said to me, 'Get your rifle.' I said, 'We don't want a rifle for this one.' Then I said, 'Bentley, you go around one side of the dam with the axe and I'll around the other side. When the dingo sees he's cornered he will go for one of us so be ready to hit him – one good blow will do.'

The dingo ran to the fence, then doubled back towards where he had come in. Jock was there with the pick handle. The dingo turned back and made straight for Bentley. To our surprise, Bentley dropped the axe and jumped into the dam. The water was about eight feet deep in the middle. Then we got another shock – Bentley couldn't swim. Jock called to me, 'He's drowning!' I had no alternative but to jump into the water and pull Bentley out. We both got a ducking, as he grabbed me and I had to dive down under him to make him let go. Finally I got him out. The Boss had joined Jock at the spot where the dingo had got in, so Jock ran to my assistance and helped to drag Bentley up the side of the dam on to the level ground. He vomited from all the water he had swallowed.

The dingo just stood looking at us. When Bentley was safe we helped him to where the Boss was and I said, 'I'll get the rifle and finish that dingo off.' Harry, the Boss, gave a grunt and said, 'Are you scared of it?' This amused Jock and he said to me, 'I bet you're not game to tackle it with a stick.' I picked up the mattock handle that Jock had left near the opening and advanced towards the dingo. He was still standing on the bank of the dam. As I approached him I noticed the bristles on his back were up. This was a sign of fear. He ran around the dam towards the opening. This was funny for a moment as Bentley soon got over his sickness and jumped over the fence. The Boss also scrambled over. Jock grabbed a shovel that happened to be there, and as the dingo approached him, he let out a terrible yell. This frightened the dingo and he ran back towards me. I had followed him around when he had made for the opening.

Now the fun turned into dreadful fear for me. That dingo knew he was cornered, so he sprang straight at me. Lucky for me I had the mattock handle above my head in a striking position. By the time the dingo got close enough for me to strike him, his head – with teeth bared – seemed to be going straight for my throat. Aiming between his ears, I brought the mattock handle down with all my might ... the blow got him where I wanted it to. He collapsed into a heap on the bank of the dam and I gave him two or three more blows to make sure he was finished.

In a few seconds just before the dingo sprang, I think I was the scaredest that I had ever been in my life. The Boss, Jock and Bentley all agreed that they had the scare of their lives too. They were as relieved as I was when the dingo fell. I scalped the dingo as I had done with the others – the scalps were worth one pound each.

We finished our job the next morning at this dam and packed up ready to shift. We had an early lunch and went onto the next dam at a place called Karlgarin. We had to do the same work at this dam as we had done at the last dam only the job was much harder. The catchment was heavily timbered, so we had to do more clearing. However, we finished our work without any further incidents of note, although we still had trouble with dingoes. We always had to be sure that our food, especially the meat, was out of their reach. I think Bentley was more frightened now of dingoes than ever before.

44

KICKING AROUND

We arrived back at the depot at the end of the third week of August. We had to wait until Mr Sublet came to be given our next job. He turned up two days later with bad news – our gang was to be put off as the kind of work we had been doing was finished. We were all paid up and Tom drove us into Wickepin in the buggy.

Jock and I went to Mrs James' boarding-house and booked in while we made up our minds what we would do next. Board and lodgings were one pound a week.

We were offered a job burning and chopping down timber about a mile and a half west of the town for a man named Louis Smith. He was paying fifteen shillings per acre and there were two hundred acres to be done. I wanted Jock to go partners with me to do the job but he wanted to go down south where a timber firm was building a railway and advertising for plate-layers. Jock had done this work before and liked it. The pay was good and the work wasn't hard, but as I didn't know anything about plate-laying, I decided to stay at Wickepin and see what happened. Jock left the following Tuesday by train.

The Sunday before Jock left, I was invited to play in a football game – Australian Rules. Wickepin was playing a team from Narrogin and was short of players. I had learnt how to kick a football but didn't know much about the game. I had watched several games while living with my stepfather in the city – he had been a good footballer in his younger days – so I had some idea, although I hadn't actually played in a match. I agreed to be one of the team. All football was played on Sundays in the country.

I don't think I will ever forget that game of football. Several of the Wickepin players talked to me before the match. One was the captain and he said that he was short of ruckmen, and as I was tall he thought I would be good in that position. I asked him to explain to me some of what I had to do – there were rules on things you could and couldn't do. The captain explained these to me, but he told me so many things it was impossible to remember them all, especially when the game was on.

For a start, every time I got near the ball the umpire would blow his whistle and give one of my opponents a free kick – he would call out 'around the neck', 'over the shoulder', 'push in the back', 'holding the ball', or 'running with the ball'. Believe me, I must have given twenty free kicks away during the first half of that game.

At half-time the captain and the full-forward came to me and explained it all again. During the second half I did much better and got some free kicks, but I felt sure I was the worst player on the ground.

After the game the captain told me that for a chap that had never played before, I had done well, and he would like me to come to training on Tuesdays and Thursdays. They wanted as many players as they could get as there was to be a return match at Narrogin in a fortnight's time. He said, 'We want to beat them as they won easily today.' I told him that if I stayed at Wickepin I would come to training but it all depended on what work was about. I explained about the chopping-down job and said that if I could get a mate to come in partners with me, I would be stopping at Mrs James' boarding-house for a couple of months.

The day after Jock went away, I met a young chap looking for work. His name was Robert Howe, (Bob) and we chummed up. He came and stayed at Mrs James' place and agreed to come into partnership with me on the chopping and burning job. He was a nice chap, twenty years old, tall and wiry like myself and a good worker. He was also a good footballer, as far as country players go, and went with me to training.

Our work was only a little over a mile from the boarding-house, and Mrs James agreed to cut our lunches if we would board with her while we completed the job. So we started work for Mr Smith on the first of September.

The day before we started the job, I borrowed a saddle-horse and rode out to Aunt Alice's place to spend the whole day with Grandma. It was my eighteenth birthday. Grandma was so pleased to see me and we had a wonderful day. Aunt Alice and Uncle Archie and all my cousins made me welcome and wished me a happy birthday. Grandma wanted to know how I had been getting along with my schooling. I told her that, owing to shifting about so much, I had neglected my books but there were many things I could read well enough to be able to follow, and I could write a letter and sign my name very well. Grandma shook her head and said it was a shame that I hadn't had the same chance as the others to go to school. She said I was very bright as a child, and if given a reasonable schooling, she felt sure I could have gone far. As things were, she thought I would always have to do hard work for a living.

The work for Mr Smith was very hard. Chopping scrub and trees down, and cutting logs for burning the large trees down. With a breeze blowing you could burn down a large green tree in a little over a day. We would have as many as twenty trees alight in one day, and while they were burning down we would cut the scrub and small trees down. The job was finished when all the scrub and timber had been felled. For this we were paid fifteen shillings an acre. Working long hours we earned a little over five pounds a week each.

We never worked on Sundays but played football with the Wickepin team when they had a match. Bob was a good player. He played at full-forward and taught me quite a lot about the game. Our return match with Narrogin was a triumph – we won well. Several games were arranged with other teams and we won more than we lost. My game improved and I was mentioned as one of Wickepin's best players several times. I was very proud of this.

We finished our contract with Mr Smith at the end of November. After that Bob got a job in a blacksmith's shop – he had served an apprenticeship as a blacksmith a few years before so he was at home in his new job. I got a job working for a carrier, Jack Adams, at Wickepin. This was only a temporary job but an easy one. I had to drive a horse and lorry delivering goods in and around the town and carting goods from the railway station to the hotel and stores. I also delivered the mail to the Post Office.

I worked at this for two weeks, and then Mr Adams gave me a job wheat-lumping at the Wickepin railway yard. He employed two other men. Our wages were one penny for every bag of wheat that we lumped or one pound each day, which ever was the greater.

It was very hard work – the farmers around Wickepin had had a bumper harvest. The money was good though, and we got extra pay from the farmers for unloading their superphosphate when it came. This saved them paying demurrage as some of them were thirty miles or more away from a station and only came in for their mail once a week. A lot of them wouldn't be putting in their first crop till the next winter but had to get their super then to get the benefit of a railway concession. (The concession applied to the super that had come in the trucks consigned to cart the wheat back to the Port of Fremantle.) We used to get four shillings per ton for unloading it out of the railway trucks. We had to do this in our own time, before the yard opened at eight a.m. or after five o'clock in the evening. When the farmers came for their super they were only too willing to pay us because demurrage could be charged up to thirty shillings a day if the super was not unloaded within thirty-six hours.

This job lasted until the third week in February 1913. We did very well out of it, as, between the three of us, we lumped one hundred and sixty thousand bags of wheat. Most of them we had to handle twice. When there weren't any railway trucks on stand-by, we stacked the bags, and then loaded them later, getting a penny for both times we lumped them.

Although the three of us worked at full speed, I have seen as many as thirty teams waiting to be unloaded. Every bag of wheat had to be weighed, the weight put on a docket and stamped onto the bag. A clerk did this. The farmer would put each bag onto the scales which were on a platform level with the back of the waggons to make the job easy. The platform had two sets of handles on each side and was moved from the back of one waggon to another as they were filled.

45

Solidarity

I finished the lumping job and was wondering where to look for work. Then I noticed quite a lot of men turning up at Wickepin – some staying at the boarding-house and many pitching tents on the reserve – all waiting for something. This puzzled me until I met Jock McKay walking along the main street. He was all smiles and told me that the Government was going to extend the railway line from Wickepin through to Merredin, and that he hoped to get a job on the plate-layers gang. He suggested that I put in for the job with him. He said he was what they called a 'dogger'. His job was driving in spikes to hold the rails firmly against the sleepers. The spikes were called dogs, so hence the name. I said I hadn't ever done work like that and wouldn't have any idea what to do. He said he could teach me in a few minutes and the pay was good – one pound for an eight-hour day. So he talked me into having my name put down for the job.

The Engineer had an office in the railway yard and Jock took me to him. Jock introduced us and told the Engineer that I was a dogger and had worked with him before. That satisfied the Engineer and he asked me my full name and age. Jock said that I was twenty. The Engineer said, 'If you're half as good as Jock at driving dogs, you'll do.' When we were away on our own again I told Jock he shouldn't have fibbed about my age and about me being a good dogger. He replied, 'You will be a good dogger before we start on that job because I'll show you all there is to know. As regards your age, that won't matter. If we had said your proper age he may have been suspicious about your experience.'

For the next two days Jock showed me how to use the special hammer for spike driving. It had a long narrow head so that it could hit the spike without touching the rail.

The first Monday in March a large gang of men were sent out; some to start on the formation work and others to put in the culverts and bridges. Jock and I, and several other men, were told we would be taking the train out of Wickepin the next morning. We had to go to Narrogin, then catch the train to Perth and travel to Spencer's Brook, a railway siding about five miles south-west of Northam. From there we were to catch the train going to the Goldfields and get off at Merredin. There we were to join another gang of men. All these men were expert at plate-laying. (All except me of course.) There were forty-two of us altogether, not counting the Ganger, who was the boss.

We started laying and fixing the rails to the sleepers on the first Thursday in March. The town of Merredin, where we commenced work, was only small. There was a hotel and shops, a boarding-house, a school and a place where we could get a meal at certain times during the day. We had all our meals there – a Mrs Wilson was the proprietor and the food was very good.

We worked for the first two weeks doing shunting lines and points in the railway yard before we started on the new line. Mrs Wilson offered to follow us along with supplies and provide us with three meals a day for twenty-five shillings a week, providing we would all patronise her and she could get some help from the authorities to move her along close to our work. (Mrs Wilson had done this work before. She had a travelling kitchen and a large marquee tent with tables and chairs to seat fifty people.)

We called all the men together and decided to help to shift her along as requested, on Sunday mornings. The Engineer gave her an assurance to keep her supplied with plenty of good water and wood and said that she could use the trolley for supplies whenever she wished. She said she would let her place at Merredin while she was away.

I didn't like our ganger, but the Engineer was a nice understanding man and all the gang liked him very much. This section of the new line had already been formed with culverts and bridges, and temporary rails had been laid.

Our job was to complete the line ready for traffic. This was all strange to me but after a few days I felt quite at home – I had some anxious moments though, and broke the head off some of the spikes. When this happened I had to get a brace and bit to bore another hole, then enter another spike and drive it home. Hitting the spike too hard was what broke the head off. Jock was a good mate. We had to finish the day together, so when a spike or hammer handle broke, we would help each other by slipping over onto the other's rail and driving some spikes. We had to watch to be sure that the Ganger wasn't around.

Everything went fine for the first six weeks. Then one day – I think it was in the third week of April – I was forced into a fist fight. This happened over the breaking of two spikes in succession. The Ganger was standing close by and it made me nervous so that I missed a spike and broke it. Feeling uneasy with him watching me, I missed with the second spike and the Ganger called, 'Clumsy fool.' I picked up the brace to bore another hole and he said, 'What will you do when you run out of room on the sleeper, goat?' I didn't answer him but just went on boring the hole. This seemed to annoy him and he called me a 'clumsy bastard'. I threw the brace down and walked over to within two or three yards of him and said, 'I don't mind what you call me, but don't you put a slur on my mother. You take it back.' He just stood there and stared at me. Then he said, 'I'll see you in hell first. So what are you going to do about it, mug?'

This man was over six feet tall and about fifteen stone. He looked very strong and powerful, and although I hated him at that moment, I must admit that I was afraid of him. I must have shown it because Jock called out to me, 'Don't take any notice of him Bert. He's trying to aggravate you into fighting. He has done it before and the men that have fallen for it have ended up getting a hiding, then the sack. He is too big for you Bert.' The Ganger turned on Jock and said, 'Shut your mouth or I'll shut it for you.'

By now all of the men within a hundred yards had stopped work and were watching to see what was going to happen. The Ganger turned on me again and said, 'Well, what are you going to do? What are you going to make of it?' I said (and I was scared stiff of this giant of a man), 'If you won't withdraw what you said I'm prepared to test you with your king-hitting business. You can't say that about my mother.' He walked into a clear space some ten or fifteen yards away and said, 'We'll settle this here and now.'

All the men close had gathered around, some trying to talk me out of it and saying that he would kill me. Others were saying that the Ganger was a big bully. One of the men around the fifty age mark came to me and said that his name was Mr Strong and that he had been a boxer in his younger days. He asked me if I had had any experience with this sort of thing. I said, 'Only a little with Charlie Burns for two years or so.' He knew Mr Burns well and told me to keep the Ganger off by using a straight left if I could, and to keep him from grabbing me.

So the fight was on. The Ganger came at me like a mad bull and swung a terrific right at my head. I ducked and drove a straight left that hit him flush on the mouth and nose. He increased the force of my hit by rushing in and I put everything I had into that punch. It stopped him and blood started running from his mouth and nose. Without easing up I repeated the punch again and again, and each time a punch landed his head jerked back. Blood started to run off his chin all over the front of his shirt. Now all fear had left me and I was in full command of the fight. I was able to side-step him and hit him at will – he was very groggy. We had only been fighting two or three minutes when a right cross to the chin dropped him into a sitting position. He sat there dazed for a full three minutes. Then I said, 'Come on, get up. I want to finish this.' He held up his hand and said he had had enough.

I told him to withdraw the slur he had cast on my mother or I'd belt him until he did. He said, 'You go get your time and get out of here, you're finished.' I grabbed him and started to pull him to his feet to give him some more and he said, 'I'm sorry about your mother but you're still sacked.' He got a red time ticket out of his pocket, filled it out and handed it to me saying, 'Get going.'

Then something happened that surprised us both. The whole gang came to where we were and demanded their time tickets. When he refused them, they sat down and refused to work under him unless I was reinstated. It was now about eleven o'clock in the forenoon. The Ganger refused their request and got on a trolley and went towards Merredin.

We had a meeting and as they were all firm in their support for me, I offered to pull out as I felt I was the cause of the trouble. They wouldn't have a bit of that. A lot of the men had worked under the Ganger before and there wasn't one that spoke a good word of him. They all seemed pleased that they had a chance to get rid of him. We waited for someone to turn up or something to happen. After awhile Mrs Wilson's dinner gong sounded so we all went and had some lunch. We had just finished when the Engineer and the Ganger turned up. The Ganger had some dressing on his lips and he looked a sight. I was lucky – he hadn't managed to hit me so I didn't have a mark on me.

The Engineer called us all together and said, 'I have heard the Ganger's story about this. Now what is your story?' He was addressing me. Just as I was about to speak, Mr Strong chipped in and said that he had seen and heard everything and would be glad to tell the Engineer the whole story. The Engineer said, 'Are you men satisfied for Mr Strong to be the spokesman on this?' They all agreed and then he turned to me and said, 'What about you?' I replied, 'Mr Strong was close to me when the incident happened. Jock McKay was closer but he is my mate so I think Mr Strong would be the best to explain everything.' Everyone agreed so Mr Strong quietly explained the whole affair as it had happened.

When he finished explaining, the Engineer turned to the Ganger and said, 'That just about finishes you with this gang.' The Ganger protested and claimed that Strong had told lies. He said, 'That bloke there – pointing to me – hit me first without any provocation.' With that several men came forward and said that they were prepared to swear on the Bible that what Mr Strong had said was true. The Engineer said to me, 'Give me that ticket of dismissal you have.' He tore it into pieces and threw them away. Then he said, 'Men, this business is all over. Get back to your work and forget this has happened. There won't be any loss of time and I'll arrange for another Ganger to be with you during the afternoon.

We all went back to work, very happy – we had had a victory. My victory was doubled many times, as I had, that day, made forty-one very staunch friends. The fight was the talking-point of our gang for weeks.

Just before knock off time the new Ganger arrived. Mrs Wilson was pleased that we had got rid of the old one. She didn't like him as he used to make very rude cracks at her and her girls. She had a daughter, about fifteen years old, and she also had a woman helping in the kitchen and a waitress about nineteen. None of them liked him. Our new Ganger was tops, he was very fair in his judgement and we all liked him.

In time I became quite expert at my job as dogger.

The new line passed through some of Western Australia's best wheat growing country. We had reached the place called Bruce Rock by the end of May, and Corrigin in early August. Our gang was then taken to Wickepin.

Arriving at Wickepin, I was asked to go to the Post Office as the Post Master wished to see me urgently. I went there and he had bad news for me – my mother had died suddenly. He showed me a telegram that had come two days earlier. I saw our Ganger, who gave me leave to go to the funeral. A friend at Wickepin drove me to Narrogin where I caught the midnight train to Perth, arriving at eleven thirty the next morning. I caught a taxi and went straight home but was too late. The funeral had been at eleven o'clock.

Although my mother hadn't been a good mother to me, I felt her death very much. Jack and Mollie, her youngest, were still children and also felt the loss of Mother terribly. I stayed at home two more days to help out and then went back to my work on the railways.

At Wickepin we were to finish the new section, working from Wickepin back to Corrigin. We completed our work on this line by the third week in October, 1913. This meant that I had driven nearly every spike on one rail from Merredin to Wickepin, a distance of about one hundred and twenty miles.

46

Prize Fighter

When we got paid off we all boarded a train to Narrogin. We intended going to the Narrogin Agricultural Show. This was on for two days and was one of the biggest agricultural shows outside Perth. We had been starved for entertainment for the past six months so we all went. We just about took up all the accommodation at the Narrogin Railway Coffee Palace and the boarding-houses and hotels.

A lot of men got full, but Jock and most of the others were looking forward to the show. I liked these country shows. They were great fun with the side-shows and ring events – there wasn't a dull moment. Mr Strong, Jock and I kept together and stayed at the Railway Coffee Palace.

The show was grand fun, and as we did the side-shows, we tried our skill at everything until we came to the boxing marquee. It had a platform out front with several boxers challenging all comers. There were light-weights, middle-weights and heavy-weights. The heavy-weight was a large Negro man. The man running the boxing offered five pounds to anyone who could stay in the ring for four two-minute rounds with the Negro. Several challenges were made by men in the crowd so we paid our four shillings to go into the marquee and see the fights. There were to be three fights in all.

The man running the show knew Mr Strong, and after an excited greeting and warm handshake, he asked him to referee the fights and he agreed.

The people filled the marquee – at a guess I would say there were over three hundred. When announcing the names of the boxers, the Manager told the crowd that Bill Strong had agreed to referee the fights. A local boy, Patsy Armstrong, won the first fight on points. In the second match (middle-weight), the local lad was knocked out in the second round. The heavy-weight match went on for the full four rounds and the Negro won on points.

Jock and I waited for Bill Strong and when he joined us we went and had a cup of tea and a sandwich. He told us while we were having our tea, that the Negro was a push over for anyone who could box. He said, 'Why don't you take him on Bert? You would beat him easy with that straight left of yours.' I said, 'No, not me. He's too big for me. He didn't look too good but he may be kidding because that bloke he beat didn't know anything about boxing.' 'That is it,' Bill said. The Negro should have put him down in one or two rounds, but he was puffing and blowing and so badly out of condition I didn't think he would last the four rounds. The other chap didn't have any idea of how to protect himself. I feel sure that the Negro has been drinking a lot of beer. There's an easy fiver for you there Bert, what about it?' Jock joined in and also wanted me to have a go. I didn't like the idea as that Negro (they called him Darkey Brown) was about fifteen stone and I was under twelve stone.

When we finished our tea we walked around the show ground and another big crowd had gathered in front of the marquee. They were having a job to get challengers. Then the Manager called out, 'I will give anyone two pounds for each round that he can stand on his feet against Darkey.'

This was too much for Jock – he called out, 'Righto, here's your man.' He pushed me forward and a roar went up from the crowd. I felt awful, I could have flattened Jock. This was just what I didn't want but it was done – I either had to show cowardice or take a belting. I had to get up on the platform and stand alongside of this big dark man –I must have looked small next to him.

The Manager (whose name I found out was Mick Flynn) got onto the stage and again announced the terms of the contest. He said, 'Five rounds of two minutes, and I will pay him two pounds for every round he stays on his feet, and I will give him ten pounds if he can defeat Darkey within five rounds.' This extra round troubled me – why an extra round? Mr Flynn said that this would be a special contest and it would only cost the people two shillings and sixpence to see it. I didn't like it one little bit but there was no getting out of it, as the marquee was filled in a few minutes.

Bill Strong was asked to referee the fight but he refused, saying he had worked with me and it wouldn't be fair to Darkey. So Mick Flynn announced that he would be referee and he asked me my name: I said, 'Just call me Punch.' (That's what I was called as a kid and what the men on the gang called me after the fight with the Ganger.) He also asked me my weight and looked surprised when I said, 'Eleven stone ten pounds:' I didn't feel very pleased with the groan from the crowd, as Darkey's weight was fifteen stone four pounds. He looked a perfect type for a boxer and wasn't I scared.

Bill Strong came into my corner as they were putting the boxing gloves on me. I had taken my coat and shirt off and also my boots. I preferred to box in my bare feet because my only chance was to be able to move around fast. Bill told me to keep moving away from Darkey and to keep pushing my straight left into his face as he came in. If I could I was to try and land it into his stomach just above the belt. He said he felt sure I could beat him. Now all was set. The time-keeper asked the referee if all was ready. The gong sounded and the fight was on.

Darkey came out of his corner and charged at me, swinging punches in all directions. I dodged and ducked and never had time to think about trying to hit him. I was all over the ring and I felt sure that Darkey would try and end the fight in the first round. He would have done just that if one of his terrible looking swings had landed. We seemed to be fighting a long two minutes before the gong went to end the first round.

As I sat in my corner Bill Strong said, 'You're doing fine. Just keep it up.' 'But I haven't hit him yet,' I said. He said, 'No, but the most important thing is he hasn't hit you yet either.' The gong went to start the second round.

This time Darkey didn't charge at me. He came out very steadily but still looking menacing. I moved away as he tried to land a punch on me. This happened several times, then I noticed he wasn't trying to protect himself – his face or stomach – he seemed bent on landing a punch that would end the fight. I was careful and kept moving sideways or back. Near the end of this round, as Darkey came in after me, I suddenly ducked under a right swing and put everything I had into a left, straight into his stomach. He stopped and doubled up as the gong went.

Bill and Jock were delighted as it was the first punch I had used during the two rounds. The crowd gave me a cheer. I don't know if it was meant as sarcasm or praise but it gave me courage at the commencement of the third round. Darkey was a changed man – he didn't want to mix it with me. He kept in a crouching position with one glove protecting his stomach, so I knew that punch must have hurt him. I started to drive straight lefts to his face, hitting him on the mouth and nose. His nose started to bleed freely and his head went back with a jerk each time my left landed. This sent the crowd wild. There was no doubt now that they were all on my side. This third round was my best. I must have hit Darkey with a dozen good straight lefts. When I went to my corner Bill said, 'Keep it up. You've got him.'

About half way through the fourth round I almost met with disaster. I was intent on landing another stomach punch that I felt sure would end the fight, when a long right hook from Darkey landed flush on my chin and I fell on my side to the floor. I could hear the referee counting four, five, and by the count of seven, I was on my feet again. Darkey came after me and he looked twice as big as usual. He threw punches at me from all directions but I had recovered enough to keep moving away and sideways. Then the tide turned in my favour. Darkey rushed me and I met him with another perfect straight left to the stomach. This doubled him up – in fact, he fell with his gloved hands resting on the floor. At the count of four the gong went.

I went to my corner and Bill said, 'What's up with Darkey?' He hadn't reached his corner and was bent over vomiting onto the ring floor. The referee went over and spoke to him for awhile, then made an announcement declaring me the winner as Darkey was not able to continue. Bill, Jock and most of the crowd went wild.

I got dressed and went to see how Darkey was. He said he was much better but very sore in the stomach. Mr Flynn paid me the ten pounds and asked me if I would like to travel with his show. He said that the show would only last about one more month, and he would like me to be with them. He offered me two pounds a week with all expenses paid, and said, 'If you like, you can book on with me for next spring.' He intended to take a troupe through the eastern states commencing in South Australia in July. He said that if I wanted experience, here was my chance.

So I booked with the show known as 'Mickey Flynn's Boxing Troupe'. We showed at Katanning, Albany, Bunbury and finished in Northam in the third week of November. Darkey left us at Albany. This was hard work but exciting, and I had some wonderful experiences. I had eleven fights during this short period and I won every one of them. Then the troupe broke up until the next spring so I went home to see my stepfather and the others.

47

MARKING TIME

I got a job as a linesman with a surveying firm, Goyder and Davis, surveying land throughout the outer wheat-belt of West Australia. The Head Office was on a farm at Corrigin. There were seven men in the gang and I was employed to do axe-work, cutting a line through the bush and scrub for the chainmen and for the theodolite.

It was a good-paying job – three pounds a week plus food. We worked six eight-hour days and had Sundays off. A cook was employed and we made camp at convenient places and travelled to work in a buggy drawn by two beautiful horses.

We travelled into many districts surveying land for the new settlers. This was a lonely, quiet job but I liked it and the work was much easier than wheat-lumping. We were given a fortnight's holiday for Christmas so I went home and had Christmas at my stepfather's place. After the holidays we all came back to the surveying job. I loved the bush and stayed on with the job until April 1914. We were all put off then as Mr Goyder became ill and had to stop work for several weeks. I returned to Perth.

My stepfather, who was a life member of the Subiaco Football Club, took me to their training ground and introduced me to their captain, secretary and several of the players. He said, 'This is my boy.'

They all welcomed me and invited me to join in the training. At that moment they were practising marking and kicking for goals. Several were guarding the goal-posts while others were trying to kick the ball through from some forty-five to fifty yards distance. They were using drop-kicks and punt-kicks. I was able to do both of these kicks fairly well and I did well at marking (or catching) the ball.

I was now six feet tall and weighed just over thirteen stone. I must have pleased the captain because he invited me to come and train with them again on Thursday evening. I did this and did much better and so I was then invited to try my hand playing in the team. My stepfather said it was most unusual to be put in the team after only two practices.

So I played League Football. The first few games I wasn't very good. I was on the receiving end of many spills and bumps, but I got used to the tricks of the game – and believe me, there were many – and they were not all in the rule book. I started to give as much as I got and sometimes a little more, and was respected. I liked the game very much. I played football until June when I had to leave to rejoin the boxing troupe.

I had kept up skipping and ball-punching and had done a bit of boxing. I used to have a few rounds with any boxer that was training for a match when I happened to be at home. At times I sparred with Alf Morey, Dick Cullen, Mick King and many others from time to time. I loved boxing and was always ready to have a few rounds. Even when at work in the bush, I always had boxing gloves, a punching-ball and a skipping-rope with me. Several of the chaps I worked with used to have a spar with me but I always promised not to hit them too hard. I wanted to practise, so with my workmates I always went easy, but even sparring lightly kept me very fit.

I was looking forward to starting again with the troupe and was thrilled at the chance. I was sorry to have to leave football but boxing had more appeal for me.

48

MICKEY FLYNN'S BOXING TROUPE

We sailed from Fremantle in the last week of June on the *Orontes* (one of the Orient Line ships) for Port Adelaide. In the troupe there were two heavy-weights and two middle-weights, as well as a light and a feather-weight boxer. We had all been schooled by Mr Burns and had known each other as boys – in fact, all except me had been recommended by Mr Burns for the trip. The sea was very rough and I became too seasick to train on the trip.

We arrived at Port Adelaide and got a shock when we found out what was expected of us. We found that there was more hard work involved than boxing. Travelling with the troupe was very tiring – we didn't get enough sleep. In fact the only time we got a real rest was when we were travelling by train from place to place. We were busy most of the time; loading our materials and luggage on horse-drawn lorries to be taken to the place where we would then erect our marquee for the show (mostly this was on a show ground or sports oval or public reserve) and put in the seating. We would reverse the procedure when the show was over. We also had to take our place as a boxer or a challenger at all the towns and places where we showed. Some of us had to mix with the crowd and appear as strangers to the troupe – if there weren't any challengers coming forward, then one of us in the crowd would accept a challenge, using another name. We only took up the challenge to fight our mates of our own weight. This was done as a last resort to get the show started.

It was amazing how the public responded to this. It also gave the local boys the idea that they could hold their own with us because when we fought each other, we always fought for a draw. Our boss offered good money to anyone who could defeat any one of us over four to six rounds.

The charge for seeing a fight was two shillings for adults and one shilling for boys. In large towns we would stage four to six fights each day, and sometimes we would stay a whole week in one town. This was according to the size of the crowds we received. Two to four hundred paying patrons was considered very profitable. We were all paid two pounds a week plus our living and travelling expenses.

We showed at Adelaide and several towns in South Australia; then travelled into Victoria and showed at Ballarat, Maryborough, Castlemaine, Bendigo and Melbourne; then at Sydney and Newcastle in New South Wales.

Despite the hard work, my trip with the troupe was a wonderful experience. I had some twenty-nine fights and was lucky enough to win them all. I had what was called a perfect left straight and most of my opponents were inexperienced and not very fit, and were easy targets. Most of them weren't able to go more than two or three rounds.

Two heavy-weights I fought had a lot of experience – there was one in Melbourne called Merchant. But he couldn't keep out of the way of my left. He was a hard puncher and his left and right hooks had plenty of sting in them, but I had a long reach and could keep him away. Each time he tried to get in close my left stopped him, and the way he moved in made the punch more damaging. His face was badly swollen and one eye was closed so that at the fourth round of our six round bout, he retired.

The other boxer that gave me a tough bout I met in Newcastle – this fight was over six rounds also. He gave his name as Morgan and was the best opponent I met on tour. He was six feet three inches tall, about thirteen stone in weight and had been sparring with champions such as Bill Lang, Dave Smith and Jerry Jerome. He was a lively boxer and I feel sure he hit me with every punch in the book. I had to cover up, duck and dodge all around the ring. Twice in the first and second rounds he hit me so hard that my legs felt like jelly – I felt I had met my Waterloo – but I managed to stay on my feet. When we came out for the third round he must have thought he had me because he rushed straight at me and didn't protect himself. He must have been carried away by the crowd. I put everything I had into a straight left and it landed flush on his chin. He stopped, his head jerked back with the impact and his hands dropped leaving his face unprotected. I drove a right hook to his chin and he took a nose dive to the floor and was counted out. For a few seconds I didn't realise that it was over and I had won. I felt that I had got the worst of it and was very lucky to win.

In August we received the news that Britain was at war with Germany and there was talk that Australia was sending a force of twenty thousand troops. Everybody was talking about the war and Germany's invasion of Belgium. I was now nearly twenty years old.

Mr Flynn asked us all if we intended enlisting and we asked him what he thought about the war. He considered for a few minutes, then told us to please ourselves. He continued by saying, 'Some of you could be ruined for life by going to a war. It is not a picnic. I went through the South African war so I know. Don't any of you go taking any notice of the Government's promises. They will tell you anything to get you in but when you 'do your bit' as they call it, you will soon be forgotten and so will the promises – don't you forget that. Now you must do as you think right. If some of you leave the troupe I will have to stop the tour, so think over what you wish to do and let me know as soon as you can. We have been a very happy troupe and a very successful one. I must say we have done very well – the best and most profitable troupe I have ever had and some of you have a great future in boxing if you take it on professionally.'

The rumour about sending troops became fact: twenty thousand troops were required and the Commonwealth Government was calling for volunteers. This caused a lot of excitement. We all felt that we should go – we were fit, and another thing that appealed to us was that we would be travelling overseas and would be able to see what the other part of the world was like. So we had a meeting and decided that those who felt they should volunteer could do so.

We called Mr Flynn into the meeting and told him of our decision. He was quiet for awhile, then he said, 'Well, what are you going to do? Enlist here, or do you want to go back west to enlist there?' Most of us came from Western Australia and we wanted to enlist in our home state. Mr Flynn was very nice about this (his home state was New South Wales). He told us that those who wished to return to the West would have their fares paid on the first ship to sail from Sydney. He would pay our wages until the day we landed back at Fremantle. He left after ordering us to pack all the troupe gear and our own things, and be ready to move to Sydney.

Mr Flynn intended to store all his gear for the time being and see what happened. With so many young men rushing off to serve their country his immediate future with the boxing show was uncertain. I asked him if he thought of enlisting as he wasn't very old – he was just a little over middle-age and a lot of men of his age were volunteering. He promptly replied, 'Not me. You boys can have this one all to your-selves. I have had all I want of war. I didn't see much of it, but what I did see was enough to satisfy me. It's not pretty. Don't go off thinking that you're in for a bit of fun – it's not like that.'

So three days later – in the second week of September – six of us boarded the P and O line's passenger-ship *Moultan* at Sydney and set off for our home state, Western Australia. The ship called at Melbourne, then sailed straight for Fremantle, arriving near the end of September.

WAR

1914–1915

'You boys didn't sleep, you died.

49

MILITARY TRAINING

I had a few days at home, then went to the military camp that had been set up at Blackboy Hill. This was some fifteen miles east of the city of Perth. A sergeant-major took my name, age and address, pointed to a large tent and told me to wait in there until my name was called. The time was now ten thirty a.m. I was told that some of the chaps waiting had been there for hours the day before. They were growling about the delay. Outside we could hear the loud voices of command putting the men through the necessary military drill. Every half hour or so some names were called out. Volunteers were coming in all the time.

It came midday and my name hadn't been called. A sergeant came and told those of us waiting to follow him. He took us to a large tent where there were long tables with forms to sit on along each side. One of the chaps remarked, 'Looks like they're going to give us a meal.' We were given a mug of tea and some sandwiches, then we were taken back to the waiting-room again.

I waited all that afternoon and was still not called. About four thirty a sergeant came and told us that two of the doctors had been called away so we wouldn't be examined until the next day. We were told that we could go home or stay there for the night. A lot of us who had homes in the metropolitan area decided to go home and come back the next morning. The Sergeant gave us a leave pass until nine o'clock the next morning.

It was after ten o'clock the next day when my name was called. I had to strip off all my clothes and lie down on a form with a rug under me. A doctor came in and examined me from head to toe. He tested my heart and blood pressure, then made me do some exercises and tested my heart again. Finally he said, 'Okay, you're one hundred percent fit. You can get dressed now and report to the Sergeant in there.' (He pointed to a door leading to another tent.)

I was measured around the chest and waist, my weight was taken and then my height. My height caused quite a controversy. The

Sergeant – who did the height measurements for all recruits – seemed to take a long time. He kept on saying, 'I don't believe it.' As I stood in my bare feet on the platform he checked my height several times, then told me to stay put while he got a doctor.

He returned with a doctor who also checked my height and remarked, 'It cannot be.' He told the Sergeant to bring some other people, and mentioned some names. All this confused me – I was wondering what was wrong. While the Sergeant was away the doctor again checked my height and said, 'It just cannot be.' The Sergeant returned with two more doctors who also checked my height. After all this I was informed that I was the only man out of the thousands measured, who was exactly six feet tall. So I had, in their opinion, a height all to myself.

The Sergeant (an Englishman who had been in the army for many years) said that he had taken the height of Englishmen, Indians – many thousands – but never had he seen one who could be claimed to be exactly six feet tall. After giving blood and water samples I was passed fit to be an Australian soldier.

I had my first taste of army stew and I liked it. After lunch, those passed fit – about three hundred of us – had to attend a large tent for a series of lectures. The lectures were given two to three times a week. We were told about health and hygiene and the various kinds of diseases and their symptoms. Several doctors addressed us during the afternoon.

The following days we had to learn army drill. This was the most humorous part of army life. There were dozens of sections of raw recruits, each under a corporal or sergeant shouting orders such as: 'quick march', 'left wheel', 'about turn', 'right turn', 'left turn' and 'halt'. The instructors used to get really mad at the recruits for being so dumb. For instance at the call of 'halt!', some would keep going and some would stop; at the call 'right turn', some would turn left and some would keep straight on.

The instructors didn't allow for a man from the bush not being acquainted with any kind of army drill or discipline, and there were many country men that had been very keen to answer their country's call. All that was required was a little patience. Non-commissioned English instructors wishing to assert their authority in a bullying way were no good to the man who had been used to going his way and go-as-you-please freedom. (Probably this worked under conscription conditions in England but not in Australia.) So it was a common sight at Blackboy Hill the first few days, to see a sergeant or a corporal get a punch on the nose or his nose pulled. Of course, this meant the offender being paraded to the Senior Officer who usually gave him a lecture and another chance. This officer was very understanding and his technique nearly always worked. Some hot-headed men would at times walk out of the camp and not return.

For the next two weeks we got army drill and lectures on how to use a rifle. Then, when we were about used to the drilling and getting to a stage where we didn't make many mistakes, they changed the section style of drilling. The old style we had mastered was for the organisation of men where there were eight companies to a battalion. Now suddenly this was changed into four companies to a battalion and four platoons to a company. The new drilling was called platoon drill and was different altogether, so we had to start all over again.

When we got used to it we found the platoon system was a much easier and quicker way of manoeuvring – it was all in fours. Each platoon consisted of sixty privates with seven non-commissioned officers and three officers. There were four platoons to a company, four companies to a full battalion and four battalions to a full brigade. Our battalion was the Eleventh, and we were attached to the Third Brigade that was made up of the Ninth, Tenth, Eleventh and Twelfth Battalions.

At the end of October our company was shifted to a camp near the Swanbourne Rifle Range to do our musketry training. A man wasn't accepted as a full soldier until he had passed his musketry test, because rifle-shooting was important and there were standards that had to be passed. If a recruit didn't pass first try but showed promise, he would be given another test. If he failed again he was declared unsuitable and discharged. Not many failed as most Australians then were good shots.

We were camped at Swanbourne for about one week. I could shoot very well because of the kangaroo-shooting I had done. The still target was especially easy to me – it was very seldom I had shot at a 'roo that wasn't on the run. The only moving target at the range was a figure on a chain at a distance of four hundred yards. This target kept bobbing up and down every few yards and was much easier to hit than a fast moving, dodging kangaroo.

We were required to hit targets at one hundred yard intervals. I got a possible (highest possible score) at one hundred yards, two hundred yards lying down to shoot, three hundred yards both lying and kneeling and at five, six, seven and eight hundred yards all lying down.

At the end of the fifth day we had finished shooting up to and including the eight hundred yards range. I didn't feel well and after the midday meal, I reported to one of our sergeants. He took me to the doctor, who, after taking my temperature and giving me the once over, ordered me to hospital. He said I had the measles and that I would have to go to hospital in a hurry as my temperature was one hundred and two.

My company had only one more range to shoot to complete our musketry training – the nine hundred yards. I was unable to take part in this but, owing to my scores up to then, I passed with flying colours.

I was taken to the Fremantle Army Barracks where one large room on the second floor had been turned into an infectious diseases hospital. When I arrived there was another soldier there from the Twelfth Battalion, also with the measles. We were at Fremantle for about nine days when another case was brought in. He was supposed to have measles but two days later they found it was scarlet fever, so instead of getting out as we expected, we had to wait until the quarantine period was over. In the meantime we both got scarlet fever, and the outcome of this was that we didn't get out of the Fremantle Army Barracks until after Christmas – in fact it was January 1915 before we got back to Blackboy Hill.

My battalion had left for overseas so I was put into the third reinforcement of the Eleventh Battalion. Before I was discharged from the hospital, Joseph, my eldest brother, came to see me. He was in the Tenth Light Horse Regiment from Western Australia and they were expected to sail before my regiment.

50

THE MIDDLE EAST

We finished our training and were issued with all of our equipment; then in early February 1915, we sailed on the troopship *Itonus*. I learnt that Joseph had sailed five days earlier with the Tenth Light Horse. On our ship were the first and second reinforcements for the Eleventh Battalion, and the reinforcements for the Twelfth Battalion and other units, making a total of approximately seventy-five troops.

We sailed direct to Aden, then through the Red Sea to Suez. We were taken off the *Itonus* and camped in tents for a whole day at Suez, then went to Cairo by train. The sea trip was lovely, but the train journey from Suez to Cairo was the worst I had experienced. There weren't any proper toilets on the train – empty open trucks with about one foot of dry sand in the bottom were put in between the carriages to be used as lavatories. The sides of these sand trucks were only eighteen inches high. The trip took nearly a whole day and we had only one stop, so everyone had to use the sand trucks.

I often wondered what the Egyptian people thought after seeing this sight. Sometimes there would be eight to a dozen men in a stooping postion with their pants down relieving themselves, besides many standing to urinate where anyone could see. Sometimes this was happening while the train was running through a village or town. I was shocked. I was now twenty years old but very modest. My Grandma had taught me to be this way and always to be respectful and honest. The troops were not to blame but the Senior Officer and the Military Authority deserved the most severe reprimand.

When we arrived at Zagazig – the junction where the line branched off to Port Said – our train had to stop for forty minutes so a guard was put on all entrances to the station. My mate and I were placed on guard at the main entrance, with instructions that no soldier was to be let out unless he had written authority from the Australian Commanding Officer, and no civilians were allowed in or out. (While at Suez most of the troops had got beer and whisky and were intoxicated by the time the train left. Some were very drunk.)

The troops who wished to have a meal at Zagazig could do so, as the army had set up a canteen at the station for this purpose. That was the reason for the forty minute stay.

The guard job at the main entrance became quite a problem, as hundreds of Egyptian people wanted to sell goods to the troops – especially booze. They got so cheeky that we had to take drastic action to stop them. If anyone approached the entrance with bottled drink for sale, we had to break the bottles with our bayonets. I alone broke thirty-six bottles that were supposed to contain whisky. The smell of the contents would have almost knocked a man down. I took several bottles and asked one of our officers to try to find out what the contents were. He said that he would have them analysed when we arrived at Cairo. He said, 'From the smell of them, the results of the analysis should be interesting. I'll let you know.'

We finally got on our way to Cairo and during this part of our journey there was some terrible conduct and carrying on. There were drunk soldiers vomiting all over the seats and out of the windows; some were trying to fight, and the language they shouted at each other was terrible. We finally arrived at a station just outside of Cairo and disembarked. A lot of the troops had to be carried off as they were so drunk they couldn't walk.

From here we had to march to a place called Abbassia, some two and a half to three miles from Cairo. All the drunks had to be taken on donkey lorries. We arrived at our camp at about nine o'clock that evening. Tents were already there for us and fourteen of us were to occupy each tent. We settled for the night, in full battledress, and slept on the sand floor of the tents.

The next morning the place was a mess. There didn't seem to be anyone in charge. No officers about, no sergeants – there were a few Corporals but they were at a loss to know what to do. They said that they couldn't do anything unless they received orders from their commanding officers and they didn't know where the officers were. No provision had been made for food. There were several large mess huts with tables and stools but no food.

We waited around until late in the afternoon but there were still no officers. We went in to the town part of Abbassia, looking for somewhere to get a meal. Those of us with money were okay but there were men who had spent their money. The ones who had enough money treated the broke ones. (The drunks had sobered up and some were craving for more liquor and for food. They were in an awful state.)

What a situation – in a strange country with little or no money and no food. The next day we found out that there was an army barracks about half a mile away from our camp. This barracks was the permanent station for some sixty thousand English troops.

We got all our troops together and held a meeting to see what could be done. I suggested that we send three men to see the commanding officer at the English barracks and put our plight to him, to see if he could help us to get food, at least until we contacted some authority of our own. The troops agreed to this and three of us were appointed – a Corporal, a private and myself.

We set off for the barracks and on arriving there, came up against an armed guard at the entrance gate. I explained our mission to the guard and he sent for a sergeant-major. This sergeant-major was about the rudest man I had ever met. He yelled at us to stand at attention when addressing him and not to refer to the Colonel as his 'boss'. He was done up like a prince with all kinds of polished brass buttons on his uniform. His moustache was waxed and stuck out like bullock horns. When I finally got him to listen to our troubles, he snorted and said it was none of their affair, and it wouldn't be any good seeing the Colonel. He suggested that we find some other way and told us to get in touch with the military police. He then told me, when I asked for the Colonel's telephone number, to get the hell out of there before he threw me in the guardhouse and put me on a charge of insolence. I replied, 'All right, you just do that. I'm not scared of you pommy upstarts. That will be one way of getting somewhere or getting someone to see our position is desperate.' I looked around to my mates. One had gone but the Corporal had stuck beside me.

Then all at once the Sergeant-major said, 'You two wait here and I will see what I can do.' He went away and returned about half an hour later. He told us that we could come into the barracks and that the Colonel would see us. He took us along several corridors and up several flights of steps; then, stopping at a door he said, 'The Colonel is in here. Don't forget to salute and be very careful how you speak. Do not use slang.' With that he knocked on the door and a voice called out, 'Come in.'

We had to wait a few minutes and then we were called in. The Sergeant-major told the Colonel who we were and then left. We both saluted. The Colonel returned the salute and told us to take a seat. He then asked, 'Well boys, what is your trouble?' I explained what had happened and about us having no food and no money. He listened, then pushed a button on his desk and an orderly appeared. The Colonel told him to ring Australian Army Headquarters and then put the call through to him. He sat back and asked us what part of Australia we had come from and what the Australian people thought about the war. Then the phone rang. It was now about midday. The Colonel spoke to someone and was put through to the person he wanted. He turned from the mouthpiece and asked us where our camp was, how long we had been there and how many of us there were. When he put the phone back on the hook he told us to go back to our camp and that he felt sure our troubles would be over that afternoon. We both stood up and saluted him and I thanked him. He replied that it was a pleasure and that he was glad to be able to do a service for one of England's dominions.

We left him and as we went out of the gate, one of the guards asked us how we got on. They seemed surprised and said, '"Old wire whiskers" (meaning the Sergeant-major) is always like that. He thinks he knows everything.'

We went straight back to our camp and explained the situation to our troops. They were also surprised at the outcome because the chap that had left us had come back with the story that we looked like getting put into the clink.

So now all we could do was wait and see. Some of the men said that leaving us without officers and food might be a sort of a test, as we were going to war and no doubt there would be times when we would have to do without food and other things for long periods. We talked about many things but the most thought about thing was a good meal.

At about three thirty in the afternoon a car came to our camp carrying three officers: a captain and two lieutenants; and a sergeant-major. They came to where the troops had gathered and said, 'We have come to see what is going on. We believe you haven't any food and your officers have left you. We want to see the two that went to see the English Colonel this morning.' My name was called out and also the Corporal's. We came forward thinking we were in for some trouble. The Corporal was quick to say that it wasn't his idea. He was nervous and was about to say something more when I cut in and told them it was entirely my fault; that I had made the suggestion to the men and moved the resolution at a meeting to send a deputation to see the Colonel. I said to the Captain, 'It was carried unanimously and that is how it all came about, sir.'

The Captain ordered the Corporal and I to follow him. We went to the car and he ordered us into the back with the Sergeant-major. The three officers got into the front seat and one of the lieutenants started the car. Without any further word he drove off.

The Corporal and I didn't have any idea about where we were going or what was going to happen to us. After about a twenty minute drive through thickly populated towns, passing thousands of local people walking and riding donkeys, we crossed a large river and arrived at a big military camp. I was fascinated at the way the driver of our car could drive through these intensely crowded streets.

The car stopped at a large tent and we were ordered to get out and stand at attention. The three officers went into the tent and the Sergeant-major told us to stand at ease. I asked where we were and was told that this was the Mena Camp. There was a large pyramid close by, some hundreds of feet high – it looked huge.

Mena Camp was the main base for the Australian Imperial Forces in Egypt. There were hundreds of Australian soldiers in the area surrounding the tent and they all seemed to be looking at us in wonderment. They no doubt thought we were in some kind of trouble. At last one of the officers emerged from the tent. We came to attention and he ordered us inside. We marched in and were halted. Sitting at a large desk was an Australian Colonel and two officers. We saluted and they returned the salute, then asked us to take a seat at the table. The Colonel said, 'Now, tell me exactly what happened from the time you reached Abbassia up to now.' I looked at the Corporal. He seemed dumb. The Colonel noticed how nervous he was so he said to me, 'You, Private, can tell the story.'

I explained what had happened and noticed that a Corporal was writing down all I said. When I had finished they asked many questions and then finally the Colonel stood up and we came to attention. He said, 'Thank you boys. We will get onto this at once. Sorry you have been treated so badly, but I assure you, you won't be left like this again.'

Without any further delay we went out to the car, and were ordered in. The officer who had driven us to the camp had been instructed to take us back to our unit. I sat in the front with him on the way back and he became very talkative. He told us that the Colonel was a staff officer and a very understanding and fair man; he would start things moving and it wouldn't be long before we were eating a good meal. The Lieutenant pointed out many places to us on our way back – the river was the River Nile – and he showed us the big pyramid near the camp.

We arrived back at Abbassia at about five o'clock in the evening and already there were a lot of Egyptian cooks and assistants busy in and around the mess huts. The men asked a lot of questions about where we had been and what had happened. While this was going on several donkey-carts and cars arrived with supplies, and cooking arrangements were well under way. We had our first meal, and believe it or not, it was fried steak and eggs with plenty of bread and butter and a large mug of good tea.

The next morning our own officers and sergeants came into camp. Our Captain ordered all troops to fall in as soon as the bugle call was sounded. We lined up into our proper formation and a sergeant of each platoon called the roll. When this was completed the Captain addressed us through a microphone. He said, 'I want to apologise about your being left here without food and without command. I feel very sorry because it was partly my fault. Before I left you the night we arrived here, I left an order with a sergeant to be given to an officer, authorising him to supply your general requirements and take care of the camp until I arrived back. The sergeant got drunk and lost the order – he is being dealt with. I had been called away to a conference in Cairo. I will be leaving you again now for a fortnight because my officers and I have to attend a briefing school. While we are away you will be under English officers. They have been doing service in Ceylon and we expect them here tomorrow. I want you to co-operate with them. They will teach you all the latest about trench warfare, how to use a hand-grenade, and extended order attacking.'

51

BEFORE THE STORM

The next day the English officers arrived and took over. A lot of amusing things happened. The officers were hard to understand and very regimental; their high-faluting way of speaking and giving commands was something new to us. We got into a lot of strife laughing at their commands. The punishment they ordered was usually the stopping of evening and weekend leave. I feel sure that they regarded us as inferior to the Englishman.

We proved this untrue – at least on the sporting field – when the British and Australians held a sports meeting. Any soldier could take part in the sports which included running, high jump, hop step and jump, broad jump, boxing, wrestling and many other events. I won the high jump – clearing six feet – and the hop step and jump with a jump of forty-nine feet. I also won the heavy-weight boxing contest on points over four rounds. Our unit was also successful in the one hundred and two hundred yard sprints and one of the hurdle races. The sports were held on the Cairo sports ground.

The English officers left us near the end of February when our own officers returned. From that time we were put on very rough training. Three days each week we had to march right out into the desert with an eighty-pound pack – a full battle kit. We marched ten miles out, had about one hour's rest, then marched back again. This used to make us very tired. We also had to do drill and attend many lectures on diseases of all kinds, and what we must do if captured. This went on for almost a month. We were given leave passes to go into Cairo, especially at weekends, but had to be back in camp by eleven o'clock each evening. I was always glad to get back by about ten o'clock.

Cairo was a dirty city after what I was used to. The Egyptian people were ragged and poorly clothed. Those who could speak English told me that they were paid paid five piastres a day (equivalent to an English shilling), and the living conditions of the poor were terrible. I saw a married couple with several children, eating and sleeping with the house goat, all in one room.

We had to keep a close watch on our clothes and equipment or it would be stolen. I had one of my tunics taken, and as soon as I missed it, I reported it to our Commanding Officer who informed the military police. The next day an Egyptian ('gyppos' the men called them) came to our camp wearing my tunic. It was about four sizes too big for him but he didn't mind. He told the military police that he was an Australian soldier. It didn't seem to occur to him that he would be arrested for stealing.

A lot of lads from our unit used to visit Cairo every chance they got. I would get a mate and go around sightseeing. Cairo wasn't very interesting to me. I was shy where women were concerned and we had been lectured several times about the bad women who had come to Cairo when it was known that the A.I.F. was there. One lecturer told us that it was estimated that there were some thirty thousand women doing a roaring trade as prostitutes, and the authorities were trying to make them submit themselves for examination for venereal disease. Many soldiers had contracted this dreadful disease. The lecturers didn't pull their punches when describing what could happen if you got a dose of venereal disease. So I completely refused to have anything to do with these women.

The Egyptian religion permitted one man to have as many wives as he could afford to keep. On one shilling a day many were battling to keep one wife, but the rich had many. The sheiks had harems. I saw several sheiks, at different times, taking their families for a drive in donkey-carts. Each cart could carry from four to six adults. They used to take these drives on nice sunny days and I have seen as many as twelve donkey-carts travelling along, one behind the other loaded up with the wives and the children of one man.

I often walked along the Nile, looking at bridges that were built to carry all sorts of traffic, and at the hundreds of women and men doing their work along the banks of the river. The women all wore hoods and veils – the married women wore black and the young girls wore white. These people had me fascinated. Some of the things they did seemed strange to me. For example, they never used soap to help get their clothes clean. They just kept dipping them into the river and out again, squeezing and wringing them. Some of the people whacked the sopping garments onto flat rocks.

While I was watching these people one day, a very old Egyptian man spoke to me in good English, and asked what part of Australia I came from. I told him and then he wanted to know all about Australia. He was amazed at its size and prosperity. He told me that he had lived in Egypt all his life and that Egypt was a very poor country. Before British protection his people were in constant danger from raiders who would come from the many surrounding Arab tribes. The raiders were of a different breed, and killing and stealing was their way of life. He said that before the Suez Canal was built they had all lived in dreadful fear.

I explained to the old man that the trip over here as an Australian soldier was an eye-opener to me – the bridges and the pyramids were wonderful. I had climbed to the top of the pyramid near the camp and I was amazed how those heavy stones got all the way to the top. (We could see a pyramid from where we sat on the bank of the Nile.)

He was quiet for a few minutes and I was wondering if I had hurt his feelings. Then he said, 'I can tell you something of the building of the pyramids. My father's fathers lived all their lives in Egypt and in their younger days the raiders were very bad and fighting was by sword or knife. The raiders took food, stock, chickens and valuables and also young attractive women or girls for their convenience, and to work. So the pyramids were built for protection, for storing food and as places for women, girls and children to go. The entrances of the pyramids were made so that they could be easily defended against any raider. A few could hold back an army. There were many more pyramids then but not as large as the ones you see left here now. They were pulled down and the stones were used for building in and around Cairo.

'Now, how did our forefathers get those stones to Egypt and up onto the top of the pyramids? This is what my father told me,' he said, 'you can take it for what it is worth. Many years ago, when the pyramids were being built, in this place and in many surrounding countries there were large lizards. They were dinosaurs. They had four legs and were very big, with a long thick tail, long neck and large body. When standing on the ground the full-size ones were from ten to twelve feet high and weighed about six to eight tons. They were very strong and could carry huge loads strapped onto their backs. They lived on many things – all kinds of vegetables and fruit – and could go long periods without food or water. They were an African animal, very quiet and were easily tamed and trained. My forefathers used them to cart the stones you see in the pyramids. They were carried many miles to the River Nile, put on large barges and floated down to the pyramids. The dinosaurs would crawl up the pyramids with a large stone on their back. They were very intelligent and quiet – much like horses to handle.'

I asked the old man what had happened to these lizard-like animals and he said that his father had told him that they had been the victims of an incurable disease that had affected their young. As the older ones died there were none to take their place and the whole species died out.

I visited Mena Camp near the big pyramid. Two mates and I paid a guide to take us into the pyramid to see the place where the ancient kings were buried. We followed the guide down the steps for what must have been hundreds of feet. It smelt awful – a musty stink – and made me feel sick.

The guide showed us a large candle that was burning near the entrance to the tombs. He explained that it had been burning for over one thousand years and had never been allowed to go out. One of the soldiers who was with me became very interested. He asked the guide (he was a little worse for liquor), 'What about when the candle is burnt down to the end. What do you do?' The guide said, 'We light another before it goes out and stand it alongside, so that when the first is spent the other keeps on burning.' With that, to the surprise of us all, my mate gave a puff and out went the candle. 'There, it is out now,' he said.

The guide went crazy and grabbed him and started to shake him. My other mate struck a match and lit the candle again. I grabbed the guide and made him let go. I said, 'There you are, it is alight again.' He was too upset to listen. He went down onto his knees and prayed to Allah. When he got up he said in English that he would not guide us any longer. He walked away and we followed him up and out of the pyramid. He never bothered to get his guide fee but just walked away, mumbling something in broken English. We were on pins and needles for the next few days, expecting something to happen, but nothing came of the incident.

During the rest of the month of March we went through the same routine of marching and drilling. Then, near the end of March, we got word that the Australian Forces had left Mena Camp and sailed from the Port of Alexandria for an undisclosed destination. The next day we were ordered to move to Mena Camp and this is where we finished our training.

At about eight p.m. on the eighteenth of April, an urgent message came through that men were required for replacements to the battalions. The officer in charge came in and rounded up twelve of us and one corporal, and the officer on duty for the second reinforcements just over from us, also nominated twelve. We were told to be ready for action with full marching dress and to report back to our orderly for further orders in one hour. There wasn't enough time to bring any of the men back from leave. This left sixteen still at camp on guard duty.

We were taken to Cairo in army cars, put on a special train and travelled through the night to Port Alexandria where a ship was waiting for us. We had no idea where we were going. We asked several sailors if they knew our destination but they said they had no idea either and that the Captain was under sealed orders. We were all making guesses but all we knew for sure was that we would be sailing into the submarine-infested Mediterranean Sea.

The ship was a large one and the only distinguishing marks were the numbers painted on both sides of the hull. The name had been painted over in the same colour as the body – a watery grey. We were told by the members of the crew that the ship's name was the *Sussex*.

Although we had been rushed away from camp, the ship didn't seem to be in a hurry to sail and we didn't leave port until late on the nineteenth of April. On board were replacements for the Australian Forces (approximately three hundred and forty), some New Zealanders and two companies of English troops – in all, some nine hundred men.

The crew told us all about the submarine activities and the large number of ships that had been sunk. This didn't make us feel too secure. The day after we sailed we had rescue drill – and every day after that – and we were lectured on submarine attacks. The sea was very rough and the crew said we were less likely to be attacked by submarines in the conditions. So, although I was the worst sailor in the world, this was one time I didn't mind how rough the sea was. And a most peculiar thing about this was I didn't get seasick.

52

GALLIPOLI

After the best part of a week we arrived at a place called Lemnos Island and entered a harbour. At first sight it didn't look much, but as our ship sailed in we were all surprised at the size and beauty of the place. Some of the ships anchored there were enormous – there must have been at least sixty vessels of all sizes and kinds: transport ships, battleships, cruisers and many smaller craft, but there still seemed to be plenty of room for movement. My brigade – the Third – and other troops were already there in their ships.

Some time after we arrived motor launches began to come along side and take off troops. Finally the Corporal who was in charge of us (the twenty-four replacements for the Eleventh Battalion) ordered us to get into full battle dress and fall in, as our turn to be taken to our battalion would be soon. We got ready with our full kit and then climbed down into a motor launch and were taken to one of the transports.

When we had been put aboard, an officer called us to attention, and from a list of names, assigned us in small groups to the various companies of the Eleventh. Seven, including me, had to go to 'D' Company. A sergeant said, 'Follow me men', and took us to the Major in command of our company. The Major told us that he was glad to have us in his command, and that we would be going into action soon. We were then taken to the sections that were in need of replacements. I was attached to No. 4 Platoon 'D' Company.

The men in my section were from different parts of Western Australia. Quite a few came from the seaport of Bunbury, south of Perth. They were all strangers to me and were anxious to know how things and the folks at home were. I told them all I could but it wasn't much more than they already knew, as I had left Australia only about six weeks after they had. Then a sergeant came and called my name, and took me to the top deck where all the replacements had assembled. We had to wait a few minutes, then an officer told us to gather around and lectured us on what was expected of us when we went into action. He told us that he didn't know at that moment when or where that would be but it was likely to be soon. We were then examined by the battalion's medical officer before returning to our units.

While we were waiting in our troopship the main topic of conversation was where we were going and who we would be fighting. We were nervous now that we were so close to going into battle, but glad too that the time had finally come.

It was very calm in the harbour and there was a peaceful kind of feeling, at least to me. Many of the men settled down to write letters but I had written already to the only two people I wrote to – Grandma and Laura.

In the harbour there were French and British ships and several of these had brass bands aboard. While we were there, as if someone had given the signal, all the bands commenced to play 'Sons of the Sea', then followed this with some beautiful waltz tunes. This was a wonderful thrill; it was simply beautiful.

We left the harbour – Mudros Harbour I had found it was called – on the afternoon of the twenty-fourth of April. We were nervous and excited, knowing that we were finally on our way into action. We sailed all afternoon through a calm sea. That night we turned in to sleep in hammocks. I was very tired and despite the excitement, went to sleep.

The next thing I knew, I was being shaken awake by a corporal. The ship was moving slowly, some lights were on, and everyone was busy packing up and getting into battle dress. I noticed that stripes and rank markings had been removed from uniforms. One of the sergeants said, 'It's not far now. All portholes are blacked out and no lights on deck.'

The officers and sergeants were called to report to the Company Commander. Now excitement ran high. A few minutes later they returned and told us that we were to land on the Gallipoli Peninsula in Turkey.

When we were called to our sections our officer gave us a briefing on the proper instructions for landing. We were told that our ship would move as close as possible into shore but would keep out of range of the enemy's shelling. He said, 'They will throw everything they've got at us as soon as they wake up to what we're doing. Now, when the ship stops you will be called to the side and lined up. On the side of the ship is a rope net already in place. A destroyer will come alongside and you will climb over the side and down the rope onto the deck of the destroyer when ordered. When the destroyer has enough men it will pull away and go towards where you are to land. Close to shore you will be met by a small motor boat towing rowing-boats. You will climb into the rowing-boats and the motor boats will take you as close to shore as possible. There will be sailors in the rowing-boats and they will take you into the beach. Now you are to get ashore as best you can and then line up on the beach and await further instructions.'

This was it. We were scared stiff – I know I was – but keyed up and eager to be on our way. We thought we would tear right through the Turks and keep going to Constantinople.

Troops were taken off both sides of the ship onto destroyers. My platoon and other 'D' Company men were on the same destroyer. All went well until we were making the change into rowing-boats.

Suddenly all hell broke loose; heavy shelling and shrapnel fire commenced. The ships that were protecting our troops returned fire. Bullets were thumping into us in the rowing-boat. Men were being hit and killed all around me.

When we were cut loose to make our way to the shore was the worst period. I was terribly frightened. The boat touched bottom some thirty yards from shore so we had to jump out and wade into the beach. The water in some places was up to my shoulders. The Turks had machine-guns sweeping the strip of beach where we landed – there were many dead already when we got there. Bodies of men who had reached the beach ahead of us were lying all along the beach and wounded men were screaming for help. We couldn't stop for them – the Turkish fire was terrible and mowing into us. The order to line up on the beach was forgotten. We all ran for our lives over the strip of beach and got into the scrub and bush. Men were falling all around me. We were stumbling over bodies – running blind.

The sight of the bodies on the beach was shocking. It worried me for days that I couldn't stop to help the men calling out. (This was one of the hardest things of the war for me and I'm sure for many of the others. There were to be other times under fire when we couldn't help those that were hit. I would think for days, 'I should have helped that poor beggar.')

We used our trenching tools to dig mounds of earth and sheltered from the firing until daylight – the Turks never let up. Their machine-guns were sweeping the scrub. The slaughter was terrible.

I am sure that there wouldn't have been one of us left if we had obeyed that damn fool order to line up on the beach.

53

THE FIRST DAYS

When daylight came we were all very confused. There was no set plan to follow so we formed ourselves into a kind of defensive line, keeping as much as possible under cover from shell-fire. The shelling was very severe and machine-gun fire was coming from all directions. Snipers were active too and were picking us off.

By midday we had moved a distance forward by crawling along, and at times, running from covered positions to new shelters. We were moving forward in small groups, sending scouts ahead to find new positions, and then charging them or getting there as best we could. Often it was the men in the ranks with the Corporals and Sergeants making the plans. Many of the officers were dead – the snipers seemed to be picking them off in preference to the lower ranks.

We met a lot of resistance that first day but I found out later that we had missed most of the Turkish counter-attack. The full blast of it was to the south of my group and the casualties there were even more shocking.

By nightfall our small group had moved into a gully which later became known as Shrapnel Gully. This was one of the hottest spots that we had to face. On each side were very high hills and on the hills were the Turks, including many snipers. They had the advantage because they had a clear view of the whole valley. We used our trenching tools to dig mounds of earth to protect us from stray bullets during the night. We kept guard in turns all through the night. Nobody slept much – if at all.

By this time we were short of ammunition and water. (We had strict orders not to drink any water we might find unless it had been tested for poison.) In the morning a group was sent back to the beach to get supplies and to report our progress and position. It seemed to me that we were only about a quarter of a mile from where Headquarters had been set up on the beach.

GALLIPOLI

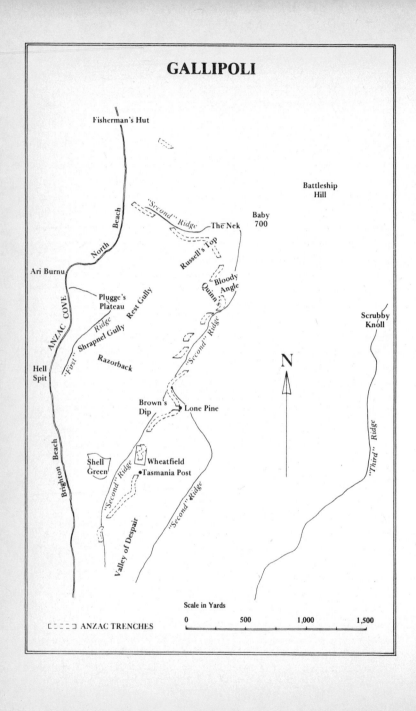

Fisherman's Hut

Battleship
Hill

"Second" Ridge

North Beach

The Nek

Baby
700

Russell's Top

Ari Burnu

Bloody
Angle

Quinn's

Plugge's
Plateau

Rest Gully

ANZAC COVE

"First" Ridge

Shrapnel Gully

"Second" Ridge

Scrubby
Knoll

Razorback

Hell
Spit

N

Brown's
Dip

Lone Pine

"Third" Ridge

Brighton Beach

"Second" Ridge

Shell
Green

Wheatfield

Tasmania Post

"Second" Ridge

Valley of Despair

Scale in Yards

0   500   1,000   1,500

▭▭▭▭ ANZAC TRENCHES

When the men returned they had plenty of supplies and brought with them more troops and a lieutenant and sergeant. They reported that the Engineers were building a jetty so that small boats could come alongside with supplies, reinforcements and so on. The officer told us that our troops had moved inland for some distance and were to the left and right of the main landing spot so that our holding was a sort of half circle in from the beach. We were to try and make contact with troops on both sides of our group and hold that contact. If we were hard pressed we were to dig in and hold our position at all cost.

We were a mixed group of troops from different states – Victorians, South Australians, New South Welshmen, Tasmanians and Western Australians. Most of us were young and in battle for the first time.

Our casualties were heavy. We lost many of our chaps to snipers and found that some of these had been shot from behind. This was puzzling so several of us went back to investigate, and what we found put us wise to one of the Turks' tricks. They were sitting and standing in bushes dressed all in green – their hands, faces, boots, rifles and bayonets were all the same colour as the bushes and scrub. You could walk close to them and not know. We had to find a way to flush these snipers out. What we did was fire several shots into every clump of bush that was big enough to hold a man. Many times after we did this Turks jumped out and surrendered or fell out dead.

All the second day we advanced slowly along the valley. We were joined by other troops and late in the afternoon plans were made to get snipers off the hills. As well as the ones hiding in bushes, we were being continually sniped at from above. These snipers were in fairly secure positions. They were concealed in shallow trenches and would take cover in these whenever the shelling was bad. When the shelling eased off they would bob up and start sniping us again.

What we did to tackle this problem was form into three groups of about ten men. One group's job was to observe the Turks' positions and find out exactly where the shots were coming from by looking for the puffs of smoke that a rifle makes when discharged. To draw the fire they had four dummies made from tunics stuffed with scrub and with Australian hats on the top. They moved these around to make them look like the real thing. When the snipers' fire was fixed the other two groups would move in from the sides and attack the Turks with bayonets. The first group would keep steady fire up at the snipers' position to distract their attention while the other two groups were approaching. This was a very successful method of attack and we managed to clear a lot of snipers off the hills on both sides of Shrapnel

Gully. Those Turks we didn't kill or capture soon got out because they didn't like the bayonet.

It is a terrible thing, a bayonet charge. I was in several in the first few days, and about eleven altogether. You would have to be in a charge to know how bad it is. You are expecting all the time to get hit and then there is the hand-to-hand fighting. The awful look on a man's face after he has been bayoneted will, I am sure, haunt me for the rest of my life; I will never forget that dreadful look. I killed men too with rifle-fire – I was on a machine-gun at one time and must have killed hundreds – but that was nothing like the bayonet.

People often ask me what it is like to be in war, especially hand-to-hand fighting. Well, I can tell you, I was scared stiff. You never knew when a bullet or worse was going to whack into you. A bullet is red hot when it hits you and burns like mad.

Fear can do terrible things to a man. There were a lot of nerve cases that came from Gallipoli, and sometimes a man would pack up under fire. A frightened man is a strange thing – you could grab him and pull him up and say, 'Come on, you're all right. Come on, you can shoot, go on, shoot', and he would turn right around and be all right (if he didn't run like hell). I was so frightened myself one day I didn't know I was injured. Several of us had been sneaking along one of the Turks' narrow trenches to get into a position to charge a bunch of snipers. A machine-gun opened fire but seemed to be firing at random because we were not exposed – there was scrub on both sides of the trench. Suddenly the Corporal yelled, 'Look out! Get down!' They were cutting the scrub off with machine-gun fire. We all ducked down quickly into a crouching position and shuffled along on our haunches to safer ground. When I stood up one of my mates said, 'Hey, what's that!' At that moment I could feel what was wrong. I always carried a knife and fork pushed down into my puttees and when I had squatted down the prongs of the fork had pierced my flesh to the depth of an inch or more. I had been moving along with a fork sticking out of my bottom and hadn't known. I don't think you can be more scared than that.

Despite the fear the men mostly took everything that was thrown at them. I saw some very brave things at Gallipoli. One thing that made a big impression on us was the actions of a man we called 'The Man with a Donkey'. He was a stretcher-bearer, or so we were told, and he used to carry the wounded men down to the clearing station on the beach. (They were then put onto motor boats and taken out to a hospital ship anchored a good way off shore.) This man, Simpson his name was, was exposed to enemy fire constantly all the days I was there, and when I left Shrapnel Gully he was still going strong. I considered, and so did my mates, that he should be given the Victoria Cross.

By nightfall on the third day, we had established a temporary firing-line linking up from the sea and circling half a mile or more inland. Our bridge-head covered about a mile of seashore. For this piece of land the casualties had been shocking.

We now had more officers and non-commissioned officers and our actions became more orderly. The first two days had been a shambles. It seemed that many small groups had gone off after the enemy and been cut off. Those that returned had lost more than half their troops.

We continued moving up to the head of Shrapnel Gully and kept after the Turks on the hills. The Turks kept shelling us all day long. We had wonderful assistance from the British Navy which kept up a continual shelling, mostly shrapnel, mostly forward of our position. They read our signals well – on only a few occasions did we get shelled by our own.

On the fifth day we dug ourselves in, making a temporary firing-line at the southern end of the Gully, where the ground rose sharply forming into a ridge. We were getting sniped at from this ridge and during the day we got continuous shelling. (That is one of the things I remember most clearly about the campaign – all the shelling. It seemed as if you could always hear it and weren't far from it even if your own section wasn't at that time under fire.) We built a sand-bag protection for extra cover.

The graves at Shrapnel Gully mounted. We buried most of our dead in this valley near the sea, and as things became more organised, a wooden cross was placed at the head of each grave and on each cross was printed the soldier's name and regimental number.

Eventually word came along to the effect that each brigade had been allotted a section of the main firing-line. The Third Brigade's section was from a point at the head of a gully (near a place later to be known and remembered as Lone Pine) curving back towards the sea at what was called Brighton Beach. The other brigades were to take up positions in turn to the side of us, making a more or less continuous front. All personnel were to make their way to their designated areas.

At these positions over the next few days, we managed to get what was left of us into our units and build a proper trenchline. From this time on the fighting changed. It was now trench warfare. We were told that we had to hold our present line at all costs.

54

IN THE TRENCHES

Digging a trench with a pick and shovel was hard work. The main trench had to be from seven to eight feet deep and made in a way that it would protect us from shrapnel and rifle-fire. Every few yards a parapet was constructed so that we could get into a high position for keeping an eye on the enemy. Sand-bags were arranged to protect us while we were in the parapets on look-out duty. These bags were built up at least eighteen inches higher than a man standing, and had spaces left between, about five inches wide and six inches high. These holes were used for observation and for sniping through.

The Turks established a trench firing-line in front of ours – in some places they wouldn't have been more than twenty or so yards from our line. We had been told to always be ready for a counter-attack. During the first weeks of May, the Turks made no move in force to drive us out but subjected us to terrific shell-fire.

An invasion that did occur at about this time was body-lice – millions of them – and didn't they give us hell. Some of them were as big as a grain of wheat and they seemed to just come up out of the ground. The nuisance was made worse because we were compelled to wear cholera bands covering our kidneys and the lower parts of our body. These bands were made of a flannel material and had a strong smelling medicinal treatment in them to help combat the cholera disease. The lice didn't mind the smell at all, and used to get under the bands and give us hell until we could get off duty from the firing line. Then we would strip everything off and crack all the lice and eggs between our nails to give ourselves some relief.

The food that we were given wasn't very good. All we had to eat was tinned meat and dry hard biscuits. The meat was very salty and the biscuits were so hard that we had to soak them for a few hours to be able to scrape the outside off. We would eat this and then soak them again. These biscuits were about five inches square with holes through them about an inch apart. Oh, what we would have done for a good meal.

Enemy submarines were operating against our ships in the Mediterranean Sea and the Aegean with some success, so supplies were hard to get through to us. This may have had something to do with the kind of food we were getting.

The isolation in the trenches, and being confined to one area, was hard to take. It wasn't so bad when there was action, but living day in and day out almost underground and being lousy all the time got us down.

Our daily duty was two hours on in the frontline trenches, then two hours in the first line reserves, two hours in a dugout and then back to trench duty again. That was our routine – the only break we got was when it was our turn to go to the beach Headquarters and guard a donkey train of supplies up to our unit. Each company had to send its own guards for its supplies. (The donkey trains were worked by Indians who had been sent to Gallipoli with their donkeys especially for this purpose.)

It was while I was doing guard duty on one of these trips that our section was treated to a change of menu. I managed to secure a fourteen pound tin of butter and a kind of cheese. The cheese was round like a grindstone, and about eighteen inches across and four to five inches thick. Both the cheese and the butter looked very appetizing to me. I hunted around and found a bag to put them in, then slung the bag over one of the donkeys, telling the boss Indian that it was for me.

The supply trains travelled only in darkness because of shelling during the day, so it was next morning before my section divided the food. The butter was beautiful. We were now getting a few loaves of bread – one a week – so we had something to spread on it. After dividing the butter we set about cutting the cheese into fourteen pieces, a piece for each man. When I drove my bayonet through the middle of it, the stink that came out of that cheese would have to be smelled to be believed. I was advised by my mates to throw the cheese into No-Man's Land as they felt sure it would stink the Turks out of their trenches. So, although we were starving for a change of food, we weren't able to touch that cheese. I dug a hole and buried it about three feet underground.

Water was another problem for us in the trenches. We had to carry all our water up from the beach near Headquarters and each section had to carry its own. Each day four men were detailed for water-carrying duty – we all took turns at this. Each man would carry two two-gallon cans which meant that we had no hands for our rifles. It was a common thing for us to be walking along with a can of water in each hand and our rifles slung over our shoulders, and have one can or both punctured by shrapnel. That meant a return trip to the beach to start all over again. That is, if we were lucky enough not to have been hit ourselves. None of us liked water-carrying; it was a very dangerous job.

On about the seventeenth of May we noticed the Turks becoming very active at night. We could hear their carts rattling down the roads, travelling towards the British positions to our right. There also seemed to be Turkish troops massing in and along our front, and during the daytime we could see, by looking through field-glasses and telescopes, quite large numbers of troops moving about. After this we received a message to the effect that a mass attack was expected at any time and every man was required to stand by.

On the evening of the eighteenth of May, the Turks bombarded us heavily for a time. Then in the early hours of the morning, before daylight, the attack came, and every available man was in position. The Turks had to come over a small rise and our trenches were just below this so that when the enemy appeared they showed out clearly to us. They were running but we were able to shoot them down as fast as they appeared. When daylight came there were hundreds of dead and wounded lying in No-Man's Land, some only a few yards in front of our firing-line. The Turks hit our line in places for what seemed like a couple of hours. My section was rushed a couple of times but we stopped them before they reached us – not one Turk got in our trench. Finally the Turks called it a day and word came through to the effect that we had defeated them all along the line.

No-Man's Land was now littered with bodies. Attempts were made to remove these for burial but enemy fire made this impossible. Many of our men were hit trying to bring in the bodies. The weather was very hot during the day and before long the corpses began to rot. The smell from this became almost unbearable, particularly when there was no breeze blowing.

At this time we had a distinguished visitor – a high-ranking British officer. He came along our main frontline trench with several of our Staff Officers and Commanding Officers. He got a whiff of the smell coming from No-Man's Land and asked the Australian officers, 'Why don't you bury the bodies?' Our Commanding Officer explained that the Turks opened fire every time this was attempted and that we had lost men trying. The officer's reply to this shocked all of us who heard him. He said, 'What is a few men?' He was standing only about ten feet from me when he said this and I was disgusted to think that life seemed to mean nothing to this man. We referred to him as 'Lord Kitchener' from then on.

Later the Turks sent an officer in under a white flag – he was blindfolded and on horseback. He was taken back from our lines to Headquarters to see our Command. Later, we received word that an armistice had been arranged for the twenty-fourth of May to enable both sides to bury the dead.

I will never forget the armistice – it was a day of hard, smelly, nauseating work. Those of us assigned to pick up the bodies had to pair up and bring the bodies in on stretchers to where the graves were being dug. First we had to cut the cord of the identification disks and record the details on a sheet of paper we were provided with. Some of the bodies were rotted so much that there were only bones and part of the uniform left. The bodies of men killed on the nineteenth (it had now been five days) were awful. Most of us had to work in short spells as we felt very ill. We found a few of our men who had been killed in the first days of the landing.

This whole operation was a strange experience – here we were, mixing with our enemies, exchanging smiles and cigarettes, when the day before we had been tearing each other to pieces. Apart from the noise of the grave-diggers and the padres reading the burial services, it was mostly silent. There was no shelling, no rifle-fire. Everything seemed so quiet and strange. Away to our left there were high table-topped hills and on these were what looked like thousands of people. Turkish civilians had taken advantage of the cease-fire to come out and watch the burial. Although they were several miles from us they could be clearly seen.

The burial job was over by mid-afternoon and we retired back to our trenches. Then, sometime between four and five o'clock, rifle-fire started again and then the shelling. We were at it once more.

On May twenty-fifth something happened that shocked all who saw it. Quite a few of us were sitting on the edge of our dugouts watching the navy ships shelling the Turkish positions away beyond our frontline. One large ship, the *Triumph*, was sending shells over our position from what seemed about two miles off shore. Suddenly there was a terrible explosion and for a few seconds we wondered what had happened. Then we realised that the *Triumph* had been hit by a torpedo. She started to list to the side and within fifteen minutes was completely upside down with her two propellers out of the water. In another half an hour she had disappeared completely. After the torpedo struck, the guns, both fore and aft, were firing as fast as they could and those gunners must have gone down with their ship. We considered this one of the most gallant acts of bravery that we had seen and we had seen many by this time. Most of the crew jumped overboard, and destroyers and small boats went to their rescue. We were told that about four hundred had lost their lives.

A few days after the armistice we received some trench comfort parcels from home. Everything was very quiet this day, and a sergeant-major and several men with bags of parcels came along our line and threw each of us a parcel. I got a pair of socks in my parcel. Having big feet – I take a ten in boots – I called out to my mates saying that I had a pair of socks that I would be glad to swap for a bigger pair as I didn't think they would fit. Strange as it seems, I was the only person in my section to get socks; the others got all kinds of things such as scarves, balaclavas, vests, notepaper, pencils, envelopes and handkerchiefs. I found a note rolled up in my socks and it read: 'We wish the soldier that gets this parcel the best of luck and health and a safe return home to his loved ones when the war is over.' It was signed, 'Evelyn Gibson, Hon. Secretary, Girl Guides, Bunbury, W.A.' A lot of my mates came from Bunbury so I asked if any of them knew an Evelyn Gibson. They all knew her and said that she was a good-looker and very smart, and that she came from a well-liked and respected family. I told them that she was mine and we all had an argument, in fun, about this girl and we all claimed her.

The socks, when I tried them on, fitted perfectly and they were hand-knitted with wool. That was the only parcel I received while at Gallipoli.

55

Fighting On

Our position in the trenches became a stalemate, a kind of cat-and-mouse affair. We had to work hard digging new trenches. Some of the trenches were tunnelled and we carried the dirt out in small bags, tipping it into the valleys and gullies. The Turks would not know about the tunnelled trenches until they were finished and opened up. After we had carried all the earth out from underground, we would open them at night and put sand-bags in front to form parapets every twenty feet or so. When daylight came the Turks would see that our line had moved closer. They would shell hell out of the new trench for a day or two.

It was during one of these shellings that I received a nasty wound. A piece of shrapnel struck me on the left side of my face, knocking four of my teeth out and loosening several others. It made a cut some three inches long, level with my teeth, then embedded itself in the roof of my mouth and right jaw, loosening some teeth on that side as well.

I had to go to our frontline dressing-station. The doctor there had a look at my face, and after a lot of pulling and working the shrapnel about, he got the piece out. However, my mouth was in a mess so I was sent down to the beach dressing-station near where the first landing took place. There another doctor made an examination, then said he would have to pull out the broken teeth and the very loose ones. 'Or,' he said, 'better still, we will send you over to the hospital ship and they can fix you up.' I asked the doctor not to send me away and suggested that he go ahead and pull the teeth himself as I didn't want to leave my mates – we were very short-handed. In fact, my battalion was only half strength at that time. I said that it hadn't knocked me out and I felt okay, only a little sore.

After speaking to another doctor he agreed to pull the teeth out there. Three big strapping orderlies held me in a sitting position, and without any anaesthetic, the doctor, who was a big strong man, pulled the teeth out. This was very painful while it lasted. The doctor washed my mouth out with some kind of solution and made me lie on a bunk in a dugout for about two hours while the bleeding eased. He then painted my mouth and the wounds with some kind of antiseptic paste and made a cradle out of bandages to hold my face and jaw firmly in place. He said I would only be allowed to have liquid foods until my face healed. I was then allowed back to join my mates.

I looked a fright; the bandage cradle covered nearly all my head. The doctor gave me several tins of condensed sweetened milk and some soft biscuits and ordered me to report back every two days. My face healed quickly and at the end of two weeks I was nearly okay again. They put some kind of strapping around the left side of my face covering the scar and gave me an ointment to put on the scar twice a day. With this treatment I was able to remain at the front and cope with the bully beef and hard dog biscuits again.

It was some time in June when the fourth and fifth reinforcements arrived and my brother Roy was with the fourth. He thought I was in 'A' Company and asked to be drafted there. When he found out that I was with 'D' Company he made an application to be transferred. It was an army regulation that when a transfer of this nature was required the older brother had to make the application. Roy's officer told him that it would take about fourteen days before this could be arranged and the elder brother had to move to the younger.

The routine continued: observing, tunnelling, a little sniping, killing lice, doing water-carrying duty, and guarding the donkey trains carrying food and ammunition up to our position.

On a date I will always remember – the twenty-eighth of June – word came through to our Commanding Officer to the effect that the English were hard-pressed at Cape Helles a few miles right of our position, and we were to make an attack on the Turks in front of our trenches to draw them away.

At some time in the afternoon we got an order to go over the top and attack the Turks. I was in the first lot to go. We had to run down hill as our trenches were on a higher position than the Turks'. Below the hill there was a dry watercourse – it was some distance from our position but only about thirty yards from the Turks' trenches. Some twenty of us reached this watercourse and we were quite safe there from rifle-fire, but the Turks gave us a bad time with shelling. A lot of the boys were killed and many wounded. We waited for the shelling to ease off before we charged the Turks' trenches. Just before we made our move we picked up a signal to retire back as we had achieved our objective –

the Turks had broken off the attack on the English at Cape Helles. We had to get back as best we could and were ordered not to take any unnecessary risks. We decided to stay in the watercourse until after dark as we were sitting ducks in the daylight.

We got back safely to our fire-line after dark (that is our little group), and on arriving back I was told that Roy had been killed. He and his mate had been killed by the same shell.

This was a terrible blow to me. I had lost a lot of my mates and seen a lot of men die, but Roy was my brother. We had been through a lot together and always got along fine. I had been looking forward to having him with me.

I helped to bury Roy and fifteen of our mates who had also been killed on the twenty-eighth. We put them in a grave side by side on the edge of a clearing we called Shell Green. Roy was in pieces when they found him. We put him together as best we could – I can remember carrying a leg – it was terrible. He was to have been transferred to my company the next day.

A few days before Roy was killed, my eldest brother Joseph had arrived. He had enlisted with the Tenth Light Horse and they had gone to Egypt with their horses, but owing to the shortage of men for Gallipoli, the authorities turned them into infantry to help us out. My job was now to find him and tell him the terrible news.

My Commanding Officer gave me permission to visit Joseph. I found out from Headquarters at the beach where he was; his unit had taken up a position away to the left of our bridge-head at a high, hilly spot called the Apex. He was very upset and swore revenge for Roy. He promised to come and see me later.

July was passing and Joseph hadn't turned up – my battalion was ordered out of the trenches for a few days' rest and our position near Lone Pine was held by another battalion. We rested under the protection of a steep cliff in dugouts prepared for the purpose, just above Shell Green where Roy was buried.

While we were resting I got permission to visit Joseph again. I found him without any trouble and asked why he hadn't come to see me. He said that his Commanding Officer had given him permission to visit me but while he was walking up along the valley that leads to Lone Pine, a huge shell had come from nowhere and exploded into the hill on the left, sending tons of earth and rocks tumbling down into the valley. 'That was enough for me,' he said, 'so I came back.' I explained that this often happened. Every day those shells (they were thirteen-inch shells and made a hell of an explosion) came over. They seemed to come from a fort on the narrows some seven or eight miles away and were trying to silence the battery of Australian Artillery that had dug in on top of the hill on the left-hand side of the valley. (This battery was called Browne's Battery, after its Commanding Officer. The Turks had tried all kinds of shelling to put it out of action.)

We weren't safe even while we were resting. Browne's Battery used to fire over our resting place and one day one of their eighteen pounders had a premature burst, killing and wounding twenty-one of our mates.

When we were resting we were allowed to go down to the beach and have a swim, but only near Headquarters. The beach nearest to our position was within range of Turkish snipers and would have been too dangerous. The bay was continually under shell-fire but this didn't worry us because we could hear a shrapnel shell coming and would dive under the water just before it exploded.

We used to go on the swimming trips a section at a time under the command of a sergeant. We enjoyed them very much and were able to get ourselves clean.

One day we got a shock. It had been reported that several men who had gone on one of these trips hadn't returned. Army Headquarters had set up a military police patrol, whose job was to guard the supplies and Headquarters, and also to watch the beaches at night. We heard talk that the Turks had tried to land spies from the sea under the cover of darkness, using small row-boats.

But one day, when our section was swimming near the end of a jetty, a sailor suddenly called a warning to us to get out of the water quickly. I was the furthest away from the end of the jetty and he yelled to me to look around. I looked and spotted something – the head and body of a creature I had never seen before. It had, I thought at a glance, one big eye! It was moving towards me. I gave a terrified yell of, 'Look – get out!!' Being a good, strong swimmer it didn't take me many seconds before I reached the end of the jetty and climbed on. My mates had done the same, and when we were all safe on the jetty I asked the sailor what it was. He said it was what they called an 'old man squid'. He told us that the eye I had seen was really two eyes but that it looked like one. The body was about three feet across and round and it had very long tentacles with suckers all along them. The sailor said that if it got its tentacles around you it would pull you under.

We decided that that was probably what happened to the missing men. That was the last time our section went swimming at Gallipoli.

56

THE BATTLE FOR LEANE'S TRENCH

After a full week's rest we were ordered to relieve a battalion of Tasmanians who were occupying a position named after their own state – Tasmania Post. This was one of the hottest little spots we had been in since the landing. The post was forward of the main trenchline. Here the Turks' trenches came within forty yards of our firing-line. They were at the edge of a cliff which cut away behind into a steep gully called Valley of Despair. The ground between the Turkish trenches and ours was a flat plateau. To the north of both our positions was a field of wheat that had come into head. Our Commanding Officer wanted the Turks' position taken.

Several of the staff heads came to have a look at the lay-out of the area and our Engineers were sent to report on the ways and means of taking the ridge from the Turks. The Tassies had raided it earlier and chased some Turks out but the Turks had come straight back.

We were all set to work digging tunnels from our position towards the Turks' trenches.

The idea was to go under or near the Turkish trenches and explode charges, blowing them up. This kind of trench warfare was practiced by both sides – a lot of men were buried or blown up in trenches and tunnels. Ex-goldminers were used a lot for this kind of work throughout the whole time Australia was at Gallipoli.

The tunnelling had to be done in silence. We carried the earth out in small bags, each bag holding about one hundred pounds of earth. We had to be very careful to conceal the place where the earth was being dumped so the Turks wouldn't know what we were doing.

We worked in teams for two hours on and two hours off around the clock, and by the end of July we were getting close to the Turks' position. The earth was easy to dig. We couldn't use picks or shovels because it would give our position away, so we loosened the earth and clay with a crowbar and pushed it into the bags without making any noise. We weren't allowed to speak and we used candles for lights, and signs or notes to let each other know what we wanted to pass on.

By the end of July we were ready to try and take the Turks' position. About two hundred men were picked to do the job. The attack was to take place after dark. Charges in the completed tunnels were set to go off at a given signal and were expected to blow sections of the Turkish trench up. We were to rush the Turks in groups of fifty when we heard the charges go off.

We were all keyed up. I don't know how the others felt but I know I was very frightened and nervous.

All was in readiness. We were waiting for the first signal – a red glow on a rise behind us. The red glow appeared and most of us in my section were on our way out of our trench. However not all the charges set exploded – the one to where we were heading didn't go off. This was confusing and caused some to hesitate.

I arrived at the Turks' trench with two others – one was a Bunbury man I knew well. As we went over the parapet into the trench two Turks fired at us, killing the man I didn't know. The Bunbury man had his rifle in the on guard position. A bullet struck the rifle and flew away not harming him. I dealt with one Turk and he the other. We seemed to be alone for a few seconds, then suddenly we realised that there were many Turks in the trench. Some came at us but seemed confused. We had only the bayonet for a weapon and believe me, we used it to perfection. Our Turkish counterparts didn't like this and soon made themselves scarce. After fierce fighting our forces were able to capture and secure the entire trench. Apparently the charge below our position never went off, but I heard that one of the others near us did when our troops were in the Turkish trench fighting.

We opened up the tunnels where the charges went off and eventually managed to get the wounded back through for treatment. The Turkish trench was on the edge of a drop, so we pushed the dead Turks over and let them fall down to where their own mates could bury them. We then worked all night reversing the parapets which were facing our line so that they now faced the Turks.

The following morning when daylight came the Turkish Artillery opened up onto this trench and all we could do was lie down flat at the bottom and take it. The sand-bags we had placed in position to protect us were blown down into the trench in places and many of our men were killed or badly wounded. Some were blown to pieces. The tunnels were our only safe way of communication.

The shelling went on all day at intervals but when darkness came it stopped. (Apparently this was because at night our navy could detect the guns' positions by the flash when they went off, and so the Turks didn't want to give themselves away.)

For three nights, as fast as we built the parapets up they would be blown away again next day.

New reinforcements joined us a few days after we had taken the trench, and small groups of them were allowed to come into the position and be schooled in this type of trench warfare. A lot of us old hands who had taken part in the charge hadn't had much sleep and by the sixth day were almost dead on our feet. Our officers said that we should be given a rest and they considered that the reinforcements, with some old hands, could hold the trench. So a number of us went back to our reserve trenches to have a well-earned rest. The change was made after dark and we were so tired we fell asleep as soon as we lay down.

Just before daylight we were awakened with the shocking news that the Turks were back in the trench and were also in the tunnels. They had killed most of the men who had remained there when we left.

By the time we were fully awake we were ordered to charge again. This time the charge would be in broad daylight. I had seen some hot spots during the campaign but this was terrible. The little strip of land that we had to cross was being swept by machine-guns and fire from all angles. Our casualties were heavy; nearly all the men to my left were killed. Somehow we recaptured the trench and sand-bagged up the tunnel, blocking in some Turks. They had hand-grenades and had been using them to keep us out. We had grenades ourselves but we had to use these to stop the Turks from climbing up into the trench again as they had done to retake it earlier.

Our grenades were getting low so a lieutenant ordered me to take a message back to our Commanding Officer, asking for more quickly and telling him about the Turks in the tunnel. He told me he was sending me because I was an old hand at using shell holes for protection. I slipped out of the trench and crawled into a large shell hole. Then I noticed another hole about ten yards away at an angle to the left. I jumped out and ran and fell into it safely. Then about twelve yards ahead to the right I saw another hole and got ready to make a run. Suddenly a large shell went into the ground a few yards beyond this hole and the whole world seemed to explode. I hadn't moved from cover yet – the hole I was in saved my life. The shell was a large one and must have been fired from a fort because it didn't explode for a few seconds after it had hit the ground. The dust, smoke and the earth that showered into the air when it exploded gave me ample cover to run straight into our original firing-line.

I got into our main trench close to where the tunnel started. Our colonel was there and there were several men lying at the bottom, some dead and some badly wounded. I hurried to give the Colonel the message. He was very excited and ordered me to take charge of the tunnel, explaining that the Turks were near the entrance and were throwing grenades.

I summed up the position and told all those near the tunnel entrance to get back and take cover. Two more grenades came out and exploded, but no damage was done. Then I got four men to get a full sand-bag and hold it in an upright position so their whole body would be protected. I then told them what we wanted to do. I ran into the mouth of the tunnel and put my bag on the ground. The next man put his on top of mine, and so on until we had that end safe and blocked, and the grenades couldn't do us any further harm.

A few minutes later, while I was explaining the position of our troops in the recaptured trench to our colonel, a noise came from within the tunnel, then a white rag tied to the end of a bayonet appeared. I said to the Colonel, 'They're surrendering.' With that we moved the sand-bags that we had used to block the tunnel and eight Turks came out, one by one. We took their rifles and felt for concealed weapons, then they were put under a guard. Several men loaded with grenades were sent along the tunnel to our mates in the captured trench. The trench was completely ours again. (It became known as Leane's Trench after the officer who led our attack.)

Now I went through another terrible experience. The Colonel was so delighted to see the tunnel cleared and the Turks captured, that he went into his dugout and came out with a pannikin containing about half a pint of raw rum. He handed it to me saying, 'Here my boy, drink this.' I said, 'Sorry Sir, I don't drink any intoxicating drinks.' (We got a rum ration often and I always gave mine to my mates.) He replied, 'You drink that, it is good for you.' I hesitated. He then said, 'That is an order.' So I explained to the Colonel that I had made a promise to my Grandma not to drink intoxicating liquor. He then apologised to me and said, 'You stick by your promise.'

Now our position was secured, the Colonel put eight of us in charge of the prisoners. We were ordered to take them to Headquarters to be interrogated.

Now a most extraordinary thing happened. We had arranged the guard down to Headquarters so that we had an Australian soldier in the lead (we had to go along the trenches in Indian file), then a Turk, another Aussie, then another Turk, and so on, with a corporal at the rear. After travelling along the trenches towards the Headquarters for about two hundred yards – the Turks were sending shells and shrapnel over as fast as they could – a shrapnel shell suddenly exploded just about us, killing the first, second and third Turk and badly wounding the fourth. Not one of us Aussies was touched. For me, this was one of the miracles of the Gallipoli Campaign.

57

ANOTHER BIRTHDAY

Not long after delivering the prisoners and returning back to my unit, my part in the campaign ended. While I was on look-out duty, a shell lobbed into the parapet of our trench and exploded, killing my mate. Several bags filled with sand were blown on top of me – this hurt me badly inside and crushed my right leg. I had difficulty walking or standing upright, and then, while moving to the tunnel to go through to the doctor, a bullet hit me in the shoulder.

The doctor examined me and ordered me to be taken away. At the dressing-station I was bandaged and sent on to the main clearing-station at Headquarters. From there I was to be put on a hospital ship anchored about one mile off shore.

A motor boat took me and some other wounded men out to a hospital ship but we couldn't go aboard. The ship was full – in fact overcrowded – so we were taken across the bay to Imbros Island and put on a troopship. There were already three hundred sick and wounded on board. One of the crew told us that the ship was the *Ulysses*. All that was on her for identification was a large number.

It was the nineteenth day of August 1915. I had been on Gallipoli only six days short of four months and I want to say now that they were the worst four months of my whole life. I had seen many men die horribly, and had killed many myself, and lived in fear most of the time. And it is terrible to think that it was all for nothing.

We didn't know where we would be going when we left Imbros. The island had a harbour large enough to hold about twelve ships. The entrance had a submarine net across it and a tug would open a section to let a ship in or out, and a torpedo boat was always on patrol.

Everything seemed so quiet in the harbour – no shelling, no rifle-fire. Most of us were cot-cases and were in beds that were bolted to the deck of the ship. We couldn't help thinking of our mates that we had left behind at Gallipoli: I still had my brother Joseph fighting there and Roy was also on my mind – he would never leave like me. We had plenty of time to think and we all thought that the whole Gallipoli Campaign was a mistake and a terrible, unnecessary loss of life. We also worried about what would happen to that loyal brace of men that we had been forced to leave behind. When we were fighting we used to envy mates that were sent away sick or wounded, but now all that we felt was sadness and sorrow, and that we should be back with them.

I think that it would be true to say that all the men who were at Gallipoli wanted to stay with their comrades. It wasn't that anyone wanted to be a hero, it was just that we were very close after four months together under such terrible conditions. A sort of love and trust in one another developed in the trenches. It made us all very loyal to each other.

That evening we had our first real meal for just about four months and were given clean beds and clean clothes. We were bathed and it felt wonderful to be really clean again. These were simple things but they were marvellous to us.

All the wounded and very ill were put into beds up on the first deck and we had lovely nurses to look after us. I didn't know where the nurses came from but they were there. The not-so-ill, or those sent away because their nerves had given out on them, were put in hammocks down in the lower decks below the water-line. This nerve sickness was very bad. The men who suffered from it couldn't help it. They were unable to sleep properly and from day to day they got worse. I have seen men doze off into a light sleep and suddenly jump up shouting, 'Here they come! Quick! Thousands of them. We're doomed!' We had to grab them and hold them down until a doctor or medical orderly could come and give them a needle to quieten them. The doctors wouldn't allow men with nerve sickness to stay at the Front because they would be upsetting to the others, especially those who were inclined that way themselves.

The first night on the ship we didn't want any sleeping drugs; we were so tired that most of us were sound asleep before dark. When we awoke next morning we found that the ship was anchored in Mudros Harbour at Lemnos Island. One of the men asked a nurse what had happened and she said, 'You boys didn't asleep, you died.' She then told us that our ship had left Imbros Harbour at about eleven o'clock the night before and sailed during the darkest part of the night because of the submarine menace.

The harbour was full of ships of all sorts and sizes waiting to sneak out and hoping to dodge the submarines. Small torpedo boats kept a continuous patrol around the outside of the submarine nets across the mouth of the harbour. An officer on the *Ulysses* told us that we may have to wait several days before we got the all clear to sail to Egypt.

On the morning of the twenty-fifth we awakened to find that we were well out to sea and one of the orderlies told us that we were going to Egypt. We seemed to be alone, we were unable to see any other ships. The Mediterranean Sea was beautiful – a lovely deep blue and as calm as a lake. Looking at this beautiful sea it was hard to believe that there were great dangers lurking under the surface.

A few days later, in the afternoon, our attention was directed to a ship that was travelling the opposite way to us, probably to Lemnos Island. An officer said that he thought it was a troopship loaded with men and that it looked like the *Royal George*. We were all watching when, to our surprise and horror, there was a loud explosion. The troopship was almost cut in half from the force of a blast that hit it in the centre. It lifted the ship, bulging the centre part upward, and when the ship settled down again it started to sink, going down with both ends lifting high out of the water. After about fifteen minutes the ship seemed to fold up and it disappeared completely.

We expected our ship to go to the aid of the men who had jumped or had been thrown overboard by the explosion. To our surprise the *Ulysses* turned away with all engines at full steam ahead; it fairly shuddered with the vibration of the engines. One of the sailors explained that if we had stayed to rescue the men we would have also been torpedoed and sunk. He said that the submarine that had torpedoed the ship was no doubt after us now. This put us all on edge as, if we were hit, most of us would be doomed.

The *Ulysses* had a small naval gun mounted at the stern and a gun crew, which gave us some comfort. The sailor explained that the gun had a range of approximately four miles, so the submarine would have to keep out of range during daylight. We were safe until after dark. Under the cover of darkness the submarine could surface and travel as fast or faster than us. Our ship was using a zig-zag course and would have to keep this up until after dark.

All night the *Ulysses* travelled flat out with all lights out. We put life belts on (all who could get them on). Those who were too ill to be put in the belts had their beds unbolted from the deck and airtight drums attached to them. Straps were placed around the beds and patients to hold them together. That night is something I am sure none of us who experienced it will ever forget.

The danger was not only the submarine chasing us; there was the possibility of another one being contacted to wait in our path. In that event we would be absolute sitting ducks. Nobody slept that night. We were too frightened and we felt so helpless. I hated the trenches but at least there you had a chance. One thing that was in our favour was that it was a very dark night.

When daylight came we were still intact and there was no sign of submarines. Later that morning we were met by a French battleship, two cruisers and four destroyers. They steamed past our ship and we were told that they were after the submarine. This gave us a wonderful feeling. Later that afternoon one of the destroyers came back and escorted us on the rest of our journey to Egypt. For the first time in many months we were safe.

We arrived at the Port of Alexandria just before noon on the twenty-ninth of August. We were taken off the *Ulysses*, put onto a hospital train and taken through to the No. 1 Australian General Hospital at Heliopolis, a suburb of Cairo. From there we were sent to different hospitals. With many others, I was sent to a converted sports arena called Luna Park where they looked after us very well. I had my twenty-first birthday there but didn't tell anyone. It wasn't a time for celebrations.

After about four weeks of treatment a lot of us were sent to a convalescent home a few miles outside of Cairo.

I received word while at the convalescent home that my brother Joseph had been killed at Gallipoli. I was told that he had been bayoneted while on guard duty at an outpost. He was with another Australian soldier when the Turks crept up in the dark of night and jumped them. The soldier with Joseph ran away and left him and he had tried to defend the outpost on his own. He was found later with seven bayonet wounds in him. I was very upset by the news. I wasn't as close to him as I had been to Roy but he was my brother. That was two of my brothers dead on Gallipoli. Joseph's Commanding Officer wrote a nice letter to our sister, Laura, telling her all about his end.

During my third week at the convalescent home I went before the medical board. After being given a lengthy examination and answering a lot of questions, I was told that my wounds had healed but the board wasn't satisfied with my condition. I was still suffering faintness and internal pain, and vomiting blood – the cause of this had the doctors baffled. They recommended that I be sent away from Egypt to England or Australia for six months of further treatment and observation. They asked me to choose and I chose Australia.

A week later I was sent by train with many others to Port Suez. After a few days we were put on a troopship fitted out for the occasion and set sail for home.

ANOTHER LIFE

1915–1976

AFTER OUR MARRIAGE MY LIFE BECAME SOMETHING WHICH
WAS MUCH MORE THAN JUST ME.

58

EVELYN GIBSON

We arrived at Fremantle near the end of November 1915, after a very rough trip. I was very ill and still vomiting blood and getting those nasty fainting feelings; the doctor on the ship had kept me in bed. I felt as if there was something amiss deep down inside. I had had this feeling ever since I was wounded. The hospitals in Egypt had given me all sorts of treatment and medicines, including hot and cold packs and massages – these remedies gave me severe pain so they stopped them.

On arriving at Fremantle, about one hundred of us were taken straight to the No. 8 Australian Military Hospital at Fremantle. From there I got twenty-four hours leave and was allowed to go home to my stepfather's place in West Perth. My relations and friends were all pleased to see me home again.

When I reported back to hospital the next morning I was ordered to bed and there I remained until Christmas time. Many doctors and specialists examined me but none of them were sure what was wrong – my wounds had all healed. I was put through all sorts of tests. One I will never forget – a plaster about six inches square was placed over my heart. It had a drawing effect and caused a blister to form the full size of the plaster, and when the blister had drawn the fluid out about half to three quarters of an inch, the nursing sister would put a kidney shaped bowl underneath and tap it. About half a pint of fluid would run out into the bowl – it was the colour of muddy water. The sore that was left was dressed and bandaged until it healed properly, and then they would put another plaster on and I had to go through the same routine again. The doctor said that this was drawing fluid from around the heart. He suspected that the shell bursts had affected my heart badly and that this was what was making me feel faint and giddy so often.

Late in January, after weeks of this treatment, they stopped it and I felt much better. I was allowed to get up and could walk around the hospital a bit. My right leg, which was severely crushed in the blast, never really recovered and walking was difficult. Then I was allowed out on daily leave on the condition that I didn't do anything that would excite me. I had to move slowly and keep away from crowds and report every morning to the head sister any faintness, giddiness or trouble, such as pain and headaches.

One day while on leave, I went to Perth with another soldier from the hospital (these daily leaves were from eleven a.m. to eleven p.m.). We were walking down Barrack Street in a northerly direction when we saw two girls coming towards us. We were in uniform and had our battalion colours showing on the arm near the shoulder. To our surprise the girls stopped us and one of them said, 'Please excuse us, you're returned men from the Eleventh Battalion aren't you?' We replied that we were. Then one of the girls said, 'We are from Bunbury.' Addressing me she said, 'You resemble a boy we knew who enlisted from Bunbury.' I replied that I was with a lot of boys from Bunbury at Gallipoli and I mentioned several. Both girls knew the names that I mentioned. I then asked the girl who had spoken to me her name. Now. What a shock I got. She said, 'My name is Evelyn Gibson.' Straight away my mind went back to the trenches at Gallipoli, and a pair of socks that I had received along with a note wishing the soldier who received it the best of luck and a safe return home to his loved ones, signed 'Evelyn Gibson, Hon. Secretary, Girl Guides, Bunbury, W.A.'

Although I had never had any real schooling, I knew what the word providence meant and that here it was now. Evelyn was the most beautiful girl I had ever seen. I felt as if I had known her all my life. I was really overwhelmed but I managed to suggest that the four of us go and have a cup of tea and a sandwich and talk about the boys from Bunbury. The girls agreed. They wouldn't go to a show with us later because they had to be in at the lodge they were staying at by nine o'clock, so we took them home. After that Evelyn and I often met, and when I had to stay in hospital she used to visit me as often as she could.

Evelyn and her friend would travel up to Perth on the Friday night Bunbury 'Rattler' and then return again on the same train on Saturday night. They would come and visit us in hospital. And that was how Evelyn and I started our courtship. Later she got a job as a live-in house-keeper in Mounts Bay Road and we were able to see much more of one another.

I was confined to bed often during the next sixteen weeks or more. Then I went before a medical board and was told that I was unfit for further military service and that I would be discharged and put on a war pension. I was advised that I would have to be very careful as the board couldn't guarantee that I would live more than two years. They said that they could be wrong so I shouldn't smoke or drink intoxicating liquor. This gave me a shock as I had proposed marriage to Evelyn and she had accepted me. I had seen her parents and they had given their consent. I felt very sad as I couldn't expect a girl to marry me under such a cloud. I decided to let Evelyn make the decision. That night I told her and she said that she wanted to go on with the marriage; she didn't believe the board's decision. 'Anyway,' she said, 'they are not sure, so we will continue our engagement.'

I didn't know what war pension I would receive or how long I had to wait for it to come through. My health had improved and the faintness was much less, so I started to answer advertisements to try to get a light job after leaving hospital. My military pay was to be continued until my pension started. I received a letter from the military to the effect that I could enter the hospital at Fremantle at any time, free of charge, should my condition worsen.

When I left hospital I went to live at my stepfather's place. My brother Eric was still living there and working for our stepfather in his plumbing business. He later took over the business. He had tried to enlist when the war broke out but was rejected as unfit for military service.

I found out that my other brother Vernon had been into a lot of trouble with the navy. He was a gun-layer on the H.M.A.S. *Sydney* and was involved in the sinking of the *Emden*. He fell out with the captain over that. He felt that the *Sydney* could have stood off out of range and sunk the *Emden* without a shot hitting her in return. My brother reported the captain because he reckoned that by steaming in too close he had caused the death of the twenty-one men who were killed in that battle. Apparently there was a hell of a row about it in the navy and eventually Vernon was taken off the *Sydney* and put on the *Australia*.

Grandma was still up at Wickepin with Uncle Archie and Aunt Alice. I would have liked to have gone to visit her but my health, and needing to find a job so that Evelyn and I could marry, made that impossible. Although I wrote to her and let her know how I was, it wasn't the same.

The only other person I kept in touch with was my sister Laura, who had been left behind in Victoria when the rest of us came west. She had by this time married, and was farming an orchard property with her husband.

One morning in June 1916, while I was living at my stepfather's, I noticed an advertisement saying that a large ironmongery firm in Perth wanted a young man for their ironmongery department – preference given to a returned soldier. I answered the advertisement and was told to call at the firm's office at ten o'clock the next morning. I did this and on arriving, I found that there were twelve waiting to be interviewed, two of whom were returned soldiers. We were taken into a large room and told that our names would be called.

After the first lot of interviews, the two returned soldiers and I were left. Then my name was called again. This time it looked like I had been chosen for the job. The man doing the interviewing was the owner and manager. He asked me a lot of questions about myself and what I knew about ironmongery, and I explained that my stepfather had an ironmongery shop in Hay Street, West Perth, and that I had had quite a bit of experience with all plumbing requisites before I enlisted in the A.I.F. He looked up and said, 'You're our man. Now I want to ask you a few personal questions. Do you get a war pension?' I said, 'I do.' He asked me how much. I replied that I hadn't been notified yet and asked him why he wanted to know. He said that they would have to know to be able to fix my wages. I asked, 'What has the war pension got to do with my pay?' He replied, 'Well, you don't expect to receive a war pension plus full wages do you?' This made me see red. I said, 'What in the hell are you coming at? Are you trying to get cheap labour? If you are, try it on some other mug. What did you do about enlisting and doing your bit or are you one of those cold-footed bastards that stayed home to take advantage of the enlisted man's wife or girlfriend for your own filthy lust!' With that he called an assistant and told him to call the police.

I walked out and slammed the door and told the other returned men not to go in there, that he was only looking for cheap labour. That was my first experience of finding a light job. Some thanks after all the promises given to us, and this firm had a large placard displayed outside saying: *Your country is in danger. Enlist now.* After this episode I was expecting to be confronted by a policeman at any time to answer for what I had said to the firm's owner, but nothing happened.

It upset me to find people who were just out to take advantage of you, especially when it was something like this. After I came back from the war that was the only time that I came across that sort of exploitation, but apparently it went on quite a bit.

There were also a few times when I ran into larrikins who would jeer and sling off at me for going to the war, but I soon sorted them out. I would clout them quick and lively – they would all show a fight until then, but a good straight left would fix them.

Generally though, people were marvellous – trying to get down the street sometimes was impossible. People would stop me to talk, to find out what had happened and what it was really like. They probably had someone who was away in it, or who had been killed, and wanted to know. I was worried sometimes that the police would be after me for blocking the footpath.

People at home were all a hundred percent behind the war. They were all sad about what was going on at Gallipoli, but the feeling was to send more troops to help. They'd have sent everyone they could get hold of to help. Some men who didn't go got a rough time, but we never said anything to them because we thought that they had some brains. I would have stayed behind if I had known.

One day, about a week later, I was in some tea-rooms with another returned soldier and told him about my experience with the iron-monger. He said that I wasn't the only one who has been treated that way and told me about two others who had had the same thing happen. Then his girlfriend Thelma, who was a waitress in the rooms, came and sat with us. She had just knocked off work for the day. My mate told me that her father was a Member of Parliament in Western Australia and may be able to help me. He explained my case to Thelma and she volunteered to speak to her father that night. When I called the next day she told me that her father wanted to see me at eight o'clock that night at his home in Mount Lawley.

When I arrived I was met by Thelma and invited into the sitting-room, where I met her father, Mr Sid Munsie, and Mrs Munsie. They were very nice people and asked me all about my experiences; I felt happy to tell them and then we got onto my problem of finding light employment. I explained that my education was limited as I had never been to school. After a few minutes Mr Munsie asked if I thought I could learn to be a conductor on the Perth trams. The job was light – mostly figuring and counting and changing money. I said that I was good with figures and understood money, so he gave me a letter of introduction to the Superintendent of the Perth Tramways, explaining my war injuries and how urgent it was for me to have light work.

59

WORK AND MARRIAGE

The following day I went to the Tramways Office at the car barn in East Perth, and handed the letter to the boy at the counter. After a few minutes I was shown into the Superintendent's Office. He was a big dark man with protruding eyes and a serious look. He looked at me and said, 'So, you are a returned soldier. You are the first to apply for a job here. Do you think you could stand the noise and the vibration of the trams, and the public?' I replied that I would like to try it for awhile and that it was a job that I thought I could do. He asked me all about my life before I had volunteered for service, and then asked if I drank intoxicating liquor. I replied that I didn't. He said that I didn't look like the type for the Tramways, but he would try me out if I could pass the doctor's examination. He gave me a letter to a doctor and told me to see the staff clerk in the other office who would make an appointment for me. It would cost me five shillings for the examination and as soon as I got the results – the doctor would give me a sealed envelope – I was to bring it to him.

My appointment with the doctor was for the following morning at ten o'clock. I arrived at the Tramways Office just before noon with the doctor's report, and the Superintendent, Mr Shillington, saw me straight away. He looked at the report and remarked that my eye sight and hearing were good and that the report was okay. He said, 'The job is over all sorts of hours, day-shift and night-shift, and as people are depending on us to get to work and back again we must not let them down. That means you must not be late for work.' He then told me to report to the traffic clerk who would explain to me what I had to do.

The traffic clerk was a nice chap and he explained that I would have to work as a student conductor for the first two weeks on half pay. I would be with an experienced conductor who would teach me the whole job. The clerk took me to the storeman who fitted me with a cap and bag. It was a Friday and I would start the following Monday morning at six o'clock.

I was still getting fainting bouts but they weren't as bad as I had been having. The doctor had told me to be careful. He said that if I wasn't a returned soldier he would have had to fail me but they could not reject a returned man on war injuries. He said, 'As long as a returned man thinks that he can do the job we must give him a chance.'

The following Monday morning I arrived at the car barn before six o'clock and was introduced to Conductor Benbow who was to teach me the job. He showed me what to do, explaining all about collecting fares and issuing tickets, and about the difference between sections and transfers from one line to another. In fact, that day he told me so many things that by the time we had finished I didn't know one thing from the other.

I had to walk to work in the mornings – it was two miles from my stepfather's place to the car barn – so at the end of the first week I took board and lodgings at a boarding-house in Adelaide Terrace, only half a mile from work.

How I got through that first week I will never know, but I did get through and by the second week everything was coming along fine. I had to see the staff clerk who asked me lots of questions about different fares, prices and so on. Then to my surprise he said that I was doing fine and had learnt the job as well as any they had had.

So in June 1916, I qualified as a Tramways conductor. (I will never forget the difference in the attitude of the Tramways staff – who were all out to help and understand and do all they could do for me – and the man at the ironmongery store who wanted to use me.)

My war injuries were worrying me quite a lot but I managed to keep going, and after a few weeks Evelyn and I decided to go ahead with our marriage plans. We fixed the day for August twenty-first at Saint David's Church, South Bunbury, at eleven o'clock in the morning.

The wedding went off without a hitch and we had the breakfast at Evelyn's parents' place. It was a small, quiet affair; the war was still on and two of my brothers had been killed – there were so many sad and worried people at that time. After the breakfast we left by train for the city and the small house we had rented in East Perth. Our honeymoon was quiet – I took only one week off work and we had the time together at home. Then it was back to work for me as a tram conductor.

Three weeks later we had a lucky break. An employer of the Tramways, who was going wheat and sheep farming, offered to sell us his small four-roomed house in Victoria Park at very easy terms. The price was four hundred and fifty pounds – no deposit – to be paid off at a pound a week free of interest. The house was built of timber and iron and was on a two acre block. This was considered a bargain so we gladly accepted.

We settled into our new home and I was very happy. I was still feeling my war injuries and lost quite a lot of time off work, but Superintendent Shillington was very considerate and understanding. The vibration of the trams was starting to upset me and my doctor advised me to find another job. As before, my education was against me getting light work.

A friend told me about a job as the assistant caretaker of a large office building in Perth called Saint George's House. My friend gave me a letter of introduction to the manager of the firm that owned the building and I got the job. I left the Tramways with the Superintendent's blessings and started the new job in the last week of April 1917. This work suited me better – it was light, mostly cleaning, and as I was my own boss I could take my time.

The Repatriation Department, formed by the Commonwealth Government to care for returned soldiers, was offering free education to those who were injured and unable to do heavy work. I applied for this, as I was badly in need of schooling. I was accepted and started night-school at Fletcher's Business College in Perth. I took English, arithmetic, book-keeping and writing, attending three nights a week from seven to nine. This fitted in nicely with my caretaker's job. I went ahead fine – I was anxious to learn and did especially well in arithmetic.

By the first week in September 1918, I had passed in arithmetic and book-keeping, and, as my pay was very poor as an assistant caretaker, I resigned to get a better paid job. After trying many places unsuccessfully for about a week, I thought I had probably done the wrong thing and was very disappointed. Then by quite a stroke of luck I met the Superintendent of the Tramways, and he seemed anxious to know how I was getting along. When I told him that I was out of work and explained why, he told me that there was a job as a conductor for me if I wanted it.

Then he said that he would give me a permit to learn to be a motorman (driver). I would have to learn in my spare time but it would only take about a month if I tried hard. As a motorman I would be away from a lot of the vibration because I would be able to sit down while driving the larger bogie-trams. I accepted the job and started on Monday morning.

Superintendent Shillington gave me the permit that week and three weeks later I was given a test drive by one of the traffic inspectors. I passed with top marks and a Motorman's Certificate was issued to me in November, entitling me to be rostered permanently as a motorman. This was much better than being a conductor. It was true that the vibration wasn't as bad, and I didn't get so tired. I liked driving the trams.

60

A Strike

Two days before Christmas 1918 (the war had just ended), the Tramway Union held a meeting of all its members to receive a report about wages and working conditions. The Union hadn't been able to get consideration for better wages and conditions from the Government. After a long meeting lasting into the early hours of the morning, the Union carried a unanimous resolution to go on strike until the Government, who were our bosses, gave improved wages and working conditions. The strike started that day, the twenty-fourth of December 1918.

This was a shock to the people of Perth as the trams were then the only means of public transport.

The Union was asking for one shilling per day rise in pay and for shorter hours. At that time we were getting only nine shillings and sixpence per day for the first twelve months, and then ten shillings and sevenpence per day thereafter. A big percentage of our shifts were spread over twelve hours and the Department could work us ninety-six hours a fortnight without having to pay overtime. If we worked a Sunday we got time and a half.

The strike was well organised. We kept a picket on the car barn around the clock and nobody was allowed to enter or leave, not even the bosses. I was in charge of one shift of eight hours. I had twenty men with me to make sure that the Department couldn't train 'scabs' to do our work; we also had to protect the trams and car barn against damage. The Union at this time was about four hundred and fifty strong.

This strike caused a lot of inconvenience to the travelling public of Perth and suburbs, but when our pay and working conditions were published in the newspapers, the people were soon on our side.

The Government of the day was opposed to the worker in every way. It was called a National Party Government, the worst kind of Government a worker had to put up with. They were, in my view, complete dictators and there was nothing democratic about them.

The public wrote letters to the Press that were readily published – hundreds of them – and very few were against us. Demonstrations were held and the Union marched through the streets of Perth to Parliament House, but all to no avail. Hundreds of donations were sent to the Union and we took up collections on the streets. All the hotels gave us a weekly donation throughout the strike. We held concerts on the Esplanade and in concert halls. The result of this was that the Union had sufficient weekly income to pay strike pay; single men got one pound a week, married men without children got one pound ten shillings, and couples with children got five shillings extra per child.

The unionists were real true blues – loyal and sticking together. To start the strike pay off, some of the members who had their own homes paid for, got further mortgages to get the fund underway. Our President at the time, Mr Tom Bycroft, was the first to do so.

After the strike had lasted eight weeks, the Government cracked and offered us two shillings a day increase to go back to work, and agreed to set up an independent tribunal to hear our case and award what wages and conditions were considered fair after both sides had put their case. The Union agreed to this.

The Chairman of the tribunal was a Mr Canning and the award brought down was referred to later as the Canning Award. This award increased our wages from ten shillings and sevenpence per day to sixteen shillings and fivepence per day, to be made retrospective from the day we commenced work after the strike. It also stipulated numerous improvements to our working conditions and ruled that the Department was to employ extra crews at night. As a result of the Canning Award, the Tramway's strike was considered to be the most successful strike held in Western Australia up to that point of time.

61

ON THE TRAMS

Our first baby was born during the strike – on the third of February 1919 – and it was a son. We called him Albert Barnett (Barney). My wife and I were very happy.

The new conditions made my job much better and more pleasant. I liked being a motorman and my nerves had improved a lot.

I also began to get involved a little in the Union organization at this time. Everyone who was in the Tramways had to be a member of the Union and once you had your ticket you could attend meetings and so forth. I had my ideas about the way things should be done and started getting involved in the meetings and giving my views.

When you get active among men, and start talking about one thing and another, they begin to encourage you to get more involved. I was eventually appointed by my fellows to the Union Committee and I enjoyed this work a lot. I was able to get on well with everybody and felt that I contributed something to the Union. It also gave me another interest and helped to make the job with the Tramways more interesting and worthwhile.

Working for the Tramways all kinds of experiences happened, some very humorous and some very serious. The public could be quite unpredictable. Some days they were very tolerant and other days they were full of complaints, but generally they were a fine lot.

Once I had a narrow escape from tragedy – I very nearly put a tram into the Swan River. Some trams had to run to the Barrack Street Jetty for the convenience of the people living in South Perth who had to cross the river by ferry. I was driving a small tram down to the jetty and as we neared it I went to put the brake on. The chain taking the pressure to apply the brakes snapped with a jerk. This unbalanced me and before I could apply the reverse brake, the tram had crashed into a steel post at the end of the line. (The post had been put there to hold the overhead power lines). It bent into almost a half-circle but stopped the tram from going into the river. Luckily I had the window directly in front of the driver's position open – otherwise I would have been badly cut by glass. As it happened I was thrown through the open window, striking my head on the steel post and knocking myself out for about ten minutes. Other than this I was all right and only badly shocked.

I often wonder what would have happened if that steel post hadn't been there. I think the tram would have gone into the river for sure, and that would have been the end of me.

Many funny things happened too. For example, when I was going into Subiaco once with a loaded tram, a very good looking young girl got on carrying a lot of parcels. There weren't any seats left so she contented herself to stand, holding the parcels as best she could. An old man sitting on a seat next to where she was standing, apologised to her for not being able to give her his seat. He said that he was too old to stand up. She said, 'Oh, that's all right. I don't mind standing.' He then offered to hold the parcels for her but she refused, saying that the parcels were important and that she would rather not let anyone else handle them.

The tram was travelling fast and swayed from side to side on the uneven track. With the stopping and starting the young lady began to get leg weary and the old man could see this so he said, 'I'm too old to stand up Miss and you won't let me hold your parcels for you. What about sitting on my lap? There is nothing wrong with that.' She exclaimed, 'Oh thank you. I'll do that.' So she sat gently on the old man's knee and the tram stopped and started and rocked its way along for the next few streets.

Suddenly the old man tapped her on the shoulder and said, 'Excuse me Miss, please get off my knee.' She responded and the old man struggled to his feet and said, 'You take the seat lady, I'm not as old as I thought I was.'

I liked the amusing little daily incidents like this, and the job went along quite well.

Western Australia had an outbreak of a very severe kind of flu in 1920. It was called bubonic influenza and it killed dozens of people. I got it, but only in a mild form and we were quarantined for three weeks. I was away from work for a month and it was many months before I felt well again.

On January twenty-eighth 1921, our second baby came along. It was a lovely little girl we named Olive. My wife and I were very happy. Evelyn loved babies and she was a very capable person. She made all their little woollies and clothes and dressed them so beautifully. I used to feel very proud of them and we went out as often as my job would permit.

We had a terrible experience in June of that year. I was feeling very ill and the doctor announced that I had diphtheria. They sent me by ambulance to the Infectious Diseases Hospital and my wife and children were again quarantined, this time for fourteen days. I was in hospital for three weeks and after that I didn't seem to recover properly, so I arranged for an appointment with the Repatriation Department. The doctor gave me a thorough examination and told me that I would have to leave the Tramways. He warned me that if I didn't anything could happen to me. He advised me to get out of the city and into the country.

When I told my wife the bad news she sat silent for quite a while. We puzzled our brains as what to do for the best. She reminded me that it was nearly five years ago that the same doctor and six others had given me only two years to live. I carried on working with the Tramways until we decided what to do. Then all of a sudden it came to me one day while I was at work. The Government was settling returned soldiers on the land and as I had a lot of know-how about wheat and sheep farming, I thought I stood a good chance of being selected. When I went home and explained the idea to my wife she thought it was the answer to our problem. I had been losing weight and also a lot in wages because of sickness. On a farm I would be my own boss.

62

SOLDIER SETTLER

I went to the Soldier's Settlement Board and made an application for a wheat and sheep farm, explaining my background. They put me before the Selection Board. I came through fine and then had to select a property. (The procedure was to find a property for sale, and if it suited, make an offer for it, subject to the Board's approval.) I submitted several that the Board said were outside the price that they were prepared to pay.

Then one day I got a letter from the manager of the Agricultural Bank, Perth, to the effect that he would like me to come and see him – he made a day and time in his letter. This man also sat on the Soldier's Settlement Board. So I called to see him at the appointed time. His name was Mr Heuby and he was a very nice, understanding man, and he asked me to take over a farm in the Narrogin District. It was situated twenty-six miles east of Narrogin and ten miles from Wickepin.

This farm had been purchased some two years before by two returned soldiers. They failed to agree on the running of the farm and one of them left the place to the other, who didn't know much about farming.

I got time off and went and had a good look at it. The property consisted of approximately twelve hundred acres, a nice house, several horses and a number of badly neglected farming implements, but there was six hundred acres of cleared land which had been partly fenced. On this land there was an abundance of grass for sheep. This took my eye, as I could see a grand chance of doing well by grazing sheep. My wife was in agreement so we accepted the offer of this property.

Mr Heuby was pleased when I told him and gave me an assurance that he would see that I got a fair deal from the Board. We made arrangements and a date for us to take it over. I use the word 'us' as my wife was to come in as half share partner. We were the first couple to be registered as man and wife under the Soldier's Settlement Scheme. The property was valued at this time at three thousand pounds and the limit on finance allowed by the Board for one soldier was two thousand pounds, so the Act was altered to allow the wife of a returned soldier to come in as a partner, and the allowed amount was then four thousand pounds.

So we sold our home in Victoria Park and I gave notice and finished working on the trams. We packed our furniture and effects, and a carrier carted them to the Perth railway yards and loaded them into a wagon.

There was a railway line with a siding only three miles from our new home. The siding was called Nomans Lake*; the railway line ran from Narrogin to Merredin through this district and there were two passenger trains each week.

We arrived on our farm late in July 1922, too late to put any kind of crop in. My wife, who didn't know anything about wheat and sheep farming, was amazed at the size of the place. After we settled into the house (it had only been built two years), which was four-roomed, weather-board lined with dressed jarrah board, and a roof of iron, we spent a whole week having a good look over our farm and planning what we would do.

Finally we decided to fence as much of the cleared land as was possible and purchase some sheep to graze on it as soon as we could. So we purchased wire and wire netting, and while waiting for this to arrive, we both worked hard putting up the fence posts to hold the wire. My wife worked as hard as I did. By the end of August we had two hundred acres fenced and ready.

There was a soldier settler about seven miles away from our place. Apparently he was not able to make a success of this wheat and sheep farming and the Board was holding a sale of his sheep at his property. As we were wanting sheep I attended the sale. The sheep that were offered for sale were just what we wanted, merino breed with very high quality wool. I purchased two hundred ewes with lambs at foot and one hundred hoggets (that is, year old sheep), which were mixed sexes. The following day, with the help of our neighbour we drove them to our place. Most of the lambs were six weeks old when I bought them, and their growth when their mothers found the delicious feed at our place was amazing; in fact, we sold the lambs in early October and the price they fetched covered the cost we paid for the ewes with the lambs at foot. This was a very encouraging start.

We did our own shearing. I had learnt to shear with blades before I had gone to war. A wool classer called at our place while I was doing

*For the Location of Nomans Lake see the map on page 184.

the shearing. He was out trying to buy wool privately. There was a lot of wool sold privately before the Wool Board was established. He gave my wife a lesson in wool-classing, and although we never sold him any of our wool, he went to a lot of trouble making my wife understand how to class the wool and how to skirt a fleece. (Skirting involves removing the correct amount of stained and straggly pieces from the fleece.) My wife was very proud when she learnt to do this and was a wonderful help to me. I suffered hell with my war disability while doing the shearing, but stuck to it all the same. We sent our wool – seven bales, each weighing about three hundred pounds – to market. My wife got the surprise of her life when the wool was sold, because the price it brought was the highest obtained for the district that year.

Now that the shearing was over and the wool sold, we continued fencing in more land, and by March 1923 we had six hundred and eighty acres fenced in, which included all the cleared land on the property. We put in subdivisions – making three paddocks; one of two hundred acres, one of one hundred and sixty acres, and one of three hundred and twenty acres. We were employing a man to help with our heavy work and by April we were ready to put in our first crop.

We had six working horses and a six-furrow, stump-jump plough. I had to do a lot of repair work on the plough and replace many worn parts before we could use it.

We purchased three merino rams to go with our ewes early in this year and the lambs commenced to arrive late in July. We also had to do quite a lot of repair work to the shed and stable, make a better place for shearing and build sheep-yards. All this took us through to shearing time again.

We made quite a lot of money dealing in the buying and selling of sheep. Many farmers became over-stocked and this caused a shortage of feed for their animals, with the result that their sheep became unfit for market. As we had plenty of feed we purchased the sheep that were in poor condition, then after they had picked up in condition and were ready for market, we sold them at a reasonable profit. One lot of two hundred wethers that I had purchased for twenty-five shillings a head – they were very skinny and we kept them on good feed for six weeks – I sold to a butcher for two pounds and sixteen shillings each, not a bad deal for six weeks. We also built some pig-sties and purchased some young pigs.

63

GOOD AND BAD

Although I had sent her letters I had still not seen Grandma since before I had gone off to the war. By the time I had joined the Soldier Settlement Scheme and moved to our farm, Grandma had left Wickepin. Uncle Archie and Aunt Alice McCall had left their farm to their sons and had moved to a small property in Bruce Rock, which was a town approximately one hundred miles north-east of Wickepin. Grandma had gone with them.

It was impossible for me to go and visit her because of the great distance involved. We were also far too busy establishing our farm. Whenever I went to Perth it was by train and this did not go through Bruce Rock. The nearest it went to Bruce Rock was York which was about ninety miles to the west.

I was sad that I was not able to visit this fine old lady who had been so important in my life up to when I came back from Gallipoli and married Evelyn.

Summer was now approaching again. The weather was getting very hot and I started to cut the hay and harvest the barley, oats and wheat. The barley and oats were a beautiful crop and the wheat was fair. We finished the harvesting and hay-carting near the end of January 1924 and we were still able to afford to employ a man.

My wife had presented me with another baby boy – George – on July seventh the previous year and was due for a holiday. So I sent her off with the three children to her parents' place in Bunbury in the first week of February.

The hired man and I then set about doing some more clearing for wheat growing. Land for the best wheat was the new land.

Burning season commenced on the fifteenth of February each year and closed on the fifteenth of November each year. This had to be strictly adhered to on account of bush fires, and the Australian bush was very flammable during the summer months.

The man and I commenced clearing an unfenced block some three quarters of a mile from our house. With my wife away we had to cook our own meals and look after ourselves. We were both very fond of stew of any kind, so we always drove in a horse and cart to the place where we had to work and then returned home for our midday meal. Then, while we waited for the kettle to boil, one of us would prepare some onions and potatoes and put them into a saucepan to cook while we had our lunch. Then we would leave the fire in the stove, close the fire-box doors and leave the saucepan, pushed to one side, to simmer. When we came home at night we would open a tin of cold meat, cut it up and put it in with the potatoes and onions to cook for a few minutes – then we had a well-cooked stew for our evening dinner.

After our midday meal on one of the hottest days we had had for late February, we left the fire in the stove as usual, with the saucepan put to one side to simmer. We closed the fire-box doors as we had done for the last two weeks and then drove off to work.

We had been working for about one and a half hours when the hired man looked up and noticed thick smoke reaching to the sky – it was coming from, we thought, a scrub plain behind the house. We couldn't see properly in that direction on account of a small hill which was between where we were working and the house. We both jumped into the cart and drove off to investigate – and what a shock we got. The house was on fire. It was burning fiercely, so fiercely that we couldn't get within a chain of it. The grass all around it was also alight. We had to grab a bush each and beat the grass-fire out, and by the time we had done that, everything – the house and everything in it – was destroyed.

I was left with only the old felt hat that I was wearing, a flannel shirt, a pair of working trousers, and a pair of socks and boots – that was all. Most of Evelyn's clothing – she had taken her best clothes with her – the children's clothing and the pram were destroyed.

This was a terrible blow for us – we only had a small insurance policy for fire, and that covered some of our furniture. The house, which had been built about three years before, only had a two hundred pound fire policy on it. We had to do all our work over again.

We had some poultry sheds close to the house, together with incubators and chick-brooders, and these were all lost in the fire. The man working for us also lost everything, his best suit and rugs, everything. I had to go some three miles to a store to get some bedding and food to carry on with until we could build a humpy to live in temporarily.

The fire was probably started when a can of phosphorous rabbit poison I kept on a shelf above the stove exploded. I kept it there so that it would be out of reach of the children. The heat from the fire and from the roof above on that particularly hot day would have been enough to cause the can to explode.

After a few weeks we employed a carpenter who built us another house; a four-roomed, jarrah weatherboard house with an iron roof and a brick chimney, all of new materials. It had verandahs back and front and we could only afford to line the main bedroom and loungeroom properly – the rest of the house was lined with hessian. There was no bathroom and an old galvanised wash-tub was carried into the kitchen so that Evelyn could carry out the Saturday evening bath and hair- washing ritual. The water was heated in kerosene tins on the stove. Evelyn also did the family wash in this tub – with wash-board and home-made soap.

We never lost any stock; we managed to keep the fire from spreading into the paddocks. Building and refurnishing took all our money so we were back to where we had started.

That year we managed to put in three hundred acres of wheat and fifty acres of oats for hay. My health was a little better, the country life was good for me. I was able to work long hours as long as I didn't overdo the lifting. The average man could lift a bag of super or wheat but I used to handle only a four-gallon tin at a time. This took me longer but saved me over-straining myself. Evelyn always helped a lot with the physical farm work and this made it easier for me.

The sheep were our mainstay, in fact they kept us in food and helped us to buy extras for the new house.

Our 1924-25 harvest was good. We got fifteen bushels per acre average from our wheat, and about sixty tons of hay from the fifty acres of oats. Wheat prices were good. However, the price of wool fell to two shillings per pound, which was down sixpence per pound on the previous two shearings.

By 1926 we were starting to get on our feet again.

In the 1927 seeding period we put five hundred acres in and it turned out to be a bad year for wheat. We got a lot of rain in March and April. One storm in March rained over four inches in about three hours. We had two one-thousand-yard dams on the property. One was there when we took over the property and the other we put down ourselves. The March storm put soil, straw, leaves and rubbish into both dams to such an extent that they were three parts full. Our neighbours were in the same plight, so we all joined in and gave each other a helping hand to clean the dams out again, so as to be sure of enough water for the stock through next summer.

After the March storm we got several inches in April, and then no more until well near the end of June, and then the winter rains came and we got too much and most of the wheat became water-logged. Then the hot weather followed, making the ground dry and hard, so the crop was retarded and never recovered – it was a failure. The wool prices fell further, making it a really bad year.

We did, however, have our good times – and there were always plenty of these to make everything worthwhile.

The annual Wickepin Agricultural Show was always a highlight in our lives. The children who were old enough to exhibit used to enter all sorts of things – farm produce, sewing, cooking, flowers, and so on. If they won any prizes, which were always announced towards the end of the day, they would line up to collect the prize money and then rush off to spend it before it was time to go home.

Evelyn used to be sewing for weeks before the show so that the children would all have new outfits for the occasion. They always looked grand. (We had five children by 1927 – Joseph was born in that year and Barbara was born in 1925.)

Another highlight was the monthly trip into town on Saturday morning for the provisions. Whenever possible the whole family would go in on these trips. It was about ten miles and we'd all dress up for the occasion and drive in in the open cart. If the weather was wet all the children were dressed in black reversible raincoats and matching sou'-wester hats. They used to look like a group of little old witches sitting in the cart behind me.

A funny thing happened one time when Barney took Evelyn in for the stores. I was too busy on this day to afford the time and so we decided that Barney was old enough to take charge.

In the mid-afternoon they still hadn't come back and heavy storm clouds began to build up rapidly. It got darker and darker and they still weren't home and I was getting very worried. I was wondering whether to set out on foot to look for them.

The storm broke and darkness fell, there was thunder, lightning and heavy rain, and I was worried stiff pacing up and down the verandah. (The verandah was completely closed in with chicken-wire to keep the poultry out and the small children in.) I couldn't think what had happened to them and was blaming myself for not going in with them.

Suddenly, through the heavy rain and thunder, I heard a 'coo-ee' coming from down the track. (It was a signal that Evelyn and I used to contact each other at a distance.) I was so relieved that I took off in that direction, forgetting where I was, and went straight through the chicken-wire. I fell, tangled in a mess on the ground. Everyone always thought it was very funny.

Our evenings were also very pleasant. We'd all sit around and play cards and other games and listen to gramophone records. One day while I was in Wickepin I bought a battery operated wireless. The children were delighted by it. We particularly looked forward to sitting down of an evening and listening to a serial about farm life called *Dad and Dave*.

As the children got older I also used to enjoy gathering them in front of the fire in winter and reading stories to them. One of the favourites was *Lasseter's Last Ride* by Ion Idriess.

I also built a tennis court at the side of the house – it was only gravel, but we all enjoyed it. I made the net out of binder-twine and fashioned the racquets from pieces of timber. The only problem was that Evelyn always had plenty of cut and grazed elbows to patch up.

One event that is very vivid from this time was when a snake crawled under the house one day when I was away working. Olive decided that she would try to coax it out with a bowl of milk. She put the milk just out from the edge of the verandah and stood on the verandah above it with a garden hoe. While she was standing there waiting the cat came along and drank the milk. After locking it indoors and replacing the milk, she took up her position again and waited. She waited half the day and then just before dark the snake came out and she chopped it up with the hoe. When I came home she was very excited and told me all about it. She said, 'It was a long wait but it was really worth it.'

Our children were wonderful and were always a great joy to Evelyn and I. We were very proud of them.

64

Depression

The 1928–29 year was also a bad year. We got too much rain and the paddocks were water-logged before the end of May. We were only able to put a crop in on the higher ground – all our flat land was too boggy to carry the horses or the machinery. But we managed to carry on and hope for the best. Wool prices declined further.

The following year was the best harvest that we had. Over five hundred acres of wheat were put in, and we had eight thousand bags of wheat for sale in 1930. We were advised to put the wheat in storage. The advice came from the Agricultural Department through their Inspectors, and also from the bank managers. The price of wheat had fallen to below five shillings per bushel. The advice to store our wheat was because they were sure that the price would rise to well over five shillings in a month or two, so we took this advice and stored our wheat.

The firms who stored our wheat advanced us three shillings and sixpence per bushel so we could carry on. The storage was free and we were at liberty to sell at any time we wished. All we had to do was to send a telegram authorising the sale if the price went up to a level that suited us. But now the disaster came. Wheat never recovered, in fact the price fell to a level below the advance we had received. And as it fell further we had to make up the difference between the advance and the lower price, whatever it happened to be. Finally we actually sold our eight thousand bushel bags of wheat for the sum of one shilling and seven pence per bushel.

That wasn't the worst – our wool clip for the 1931 year returned us threepence halfpenny per pound. And we owned some of the finest merino sheep in the district. Our position was becoming hopeless. Wheat growing was a failure because of over-production and no export markets. The Government would not help.

Now to top all that was the rabbit-plague – they came in thousands. They not only destroyed our crops, they also took acid grass and stock food out of our paddocks to such an extent that the sheep and cattle, or any beasts that chewed a cud, were unable to get sufficient acid food to make the stomach work to digest the food. So these animals lay down and died in horrible agony. We tried all kinds of treatment to no avail. We paid veterinary doctors but still our sheep and cattle died. The veterinarians called this thing toxic paralysis. We lost all our cows, seven of them within one week of becoming sick, and eight hundred sheep within four months in spite of our hand-feeding oats and hay to them daily.

My health broke down and I had to go to hospital for one month in 1932. I was very ill, my left arm was useless and there was a bad swelling under the shoulder blade. After fourteen different X-rays they were not able to find what was wrong with it. I couldn't raise my left arm any higher than my shoulder so the doctors decided to do an exploratory operation. The operation found a piece of a bullet that must have chipped off the bullet that had gone into the fork of my collarbone and down into my body. A fibrous tumor had formed around it making my left arm useless. The operation that was supposed to take about twenty minutes lasted about two and a half hours.

When I returned home we were just about down and out. There wasn't any assistance coming from the Government to the farmers. Things were so bad that the city people who were out of work – there were thousands of them – had to be paid enough by the Government to just buy their food. The farmers were told that the Government would pay them ten shillings per week for every man they could keep on their farm. However, we had a full job trying to keep ourselves, so we couldn't keep an extra mouth on the Government's ten shillings a week.

We did have one very pleasing thing happen at this time. The state of Western Australia had a baby competition. The state was divided into districts for this purpose. Our baby at the time was our youngest daughter, Matilda Shirley, who was about four months old at the time of the judging. Several places were clubbed together to make a district. Our daughter was entered in the Great Southern District, which included Wickepin. There were twenty-six districts. Our daughter won the first prize for our District and was selected to go to the final judging. The winner of this final judging would be declared Western Australian Champion. Our baby came fourth and the judges told my wife she was placed fourth because she had a small birthmark on her arm, otherwise she was the most perfect baby in Western Australia. This was one of the proudest days of our lives.

In the middle of the year I received shattering news. Grandma had died at Bruce Rock a few days before – on July first 1932. She was a hundred years old. Her funeral was on the third and I missed it.

Grandma was a wonderful woman and had looked after me and my brothers, Roy and Eric, like we were her own children. She was the closest to a mother that I had ever had. If it wasn't for her I would have been completely on my own for all those years before I came home from Gallipoli and married Evelyn. She was a strong, capable and warm-hearted woman, always ready to help. Grandma Carr was respected and admired by everyone who knew her. Many of the people born in the Wickepin District have her to thank for their birth. She was always on call as a midwife.

I was very upset that I hadn't been able to see her from the time I went to the war. I always wanted to but it was never possible. We did exchange letters but that was not the same. Although it is expected, the death of someone like Grandma is always a tragedy when it happens.

Things continued to get worse. I made a special trip to the city late in 1932 to see the Minister for Agriculture and the manager of the Soldiers Settlement Scheme, and also the manager of the Agricultural Bank. I pointed out to them the hopelessness of trying to carry on unless we were supplied with enough rabbit-netting to put around our property to control the rabbit menace. But all to no avail. There were hundreds of soldier settlers leaving their properties and shifting to the city, or large country towns, as they were starved out. Many of the farmers had been on their farms for over twenty years.

Things were becoming so bad that the machinery people who sold farming equipment to the farmers on terms were repossessing the machinery without court orders, and a lot of the settlers who didn't understand the law let them do this.

When it was too late to save the many hundreds of farmers who had already left their farms, the Government passed a bill placing a moratorium on all debts to try and keep those that were still there from leaving. We had a National Government at the time which changed its name to Liberal, but it never helped the farmers to buy their few stores to live on, or in any other way. All farmers were broke.

One day, at about this time, a chap representing the Agricultural Bank came to see me to try to get a promise of payment on money owing to them. I was out harvesting at the time.

On a previous visit the same man had been shown a dress that Olive had made herself out of an old disused tent. She was very fond of sewing and Evelyn couldn't afford to let her practice on good material so she gave her the old tent. Olive was very proud of the dress she had made and liked to wear it about.

On this particular day when I was harvesting, she turned up, appropriately dressed in her dress, with my morning tea while I was talking to the man from the bank. He seemed suitably impressed and went quiet on his demands for money. I talked on through morning tea about the hard time we were having of things, and how no one would help us at all. It was something that made me very angry and I let him know.

After morning tea I decided that the harvester needed a slight adjustment so I went around to the tool box to get a spanner. When I came back to where the man was, he took one look at me with the spanner in my hand and took to his heels across the paddock. He obviously thought I was going to strike him. Olive and I thought it was a great joke – we never saw the poor man again.

However, the general worry and anxiety were too much for me by this time and so my doctor sent me to hospital in Perth. While in hospital I decided to pack up and leave our farm. We had six children now and I couldn't keep them all on the farm. So when I was discharged from the hospital I made enquiries about finding employment in or near the city – I was prepared to do anything. A patient who was in the hospital (he had a business north of Perth) offered me a job as a truck driver carting lime from his lime-kilns to the city, a distance of twenty-six miles. I accepted this, explaining that it would take me about two weeks to fix up and arrange the shifting. He agreed and set a date for me to start.

I returned to the farm and we got busy with the job of shifting. My wife was delighted and said that if we had stayed on the farm we would have faced starvation. We were packed up and ready to leave the farm within ten days. We sent our furniture and personal belongings by rail in a sealed furniture truck and a neighbour drove us to Perth in his car.

65

RETURN TO THE CITY

On arriving back in the city we rented a house in a suburb north of Perth. It was February sixteenth 1934. My work was twenty-six miles north of Perth at Wanneroo and I had to camp there as there weren't any houses at the job. In fact the nearest house was seven miles away. So I had to leave my wife and family and camp at my work until we could erect a humpy near the lime-kilns. Our boss helped us to do this. Then we were all together again. The only trouble now was that there was no school nearby for our children so Evelyn commenced to teach them herself with the help of the correspondence people.

Our eldest son, Barney, had left school just before we left the farm and he got a job at the kilns with me. Our humpy was too small for us all so he had to live in a tent outside.

My work was very hard with long hours, and my pay was four pounds per week. I had to load seven tons of lime onto a truck three times a day, then drive it to the railway yard in the city and load it onto a railway truck to be consigned to purchasers in the Goldfields. The lime was ninety-eight percent pure and if it got onto my skin it would burn and large blisters would come up. The dust from it was very damaging to my hair – in fact, after a few weeks the hair fell off all over my body and head. I went quite bald. I stuck to this job for five months before becoming ill, and was again ordered to hospital.

I was there for six weeks and was advised by my repatriation doctor to leave the job. So we shifted back to the city. Barney also left the kilns and managed to get a job in a market garden. He loved that kind of work and got along well with the boss – in fact he was liked by everyone who got to know him.

There were thousands of men out of work and I was unable to find a job for quite a while. It was terrible. People were very upset about not being able to find work. They cursed Australia and the state it was in. Returned soldiers particularly were upset that things weren't better for them. They didn't fight a war for this. If anything they should have cursed the Government. It was shocking – the McLarty Government – they didn't do much to help anyone. There were little groups of people, political groups, who attacked the Government but most of the people didn't direct their anger and hostility in any constructive way towards doing something about the situation.

I was better off than most because I was getting a pension – a pound a week – for my war injury. At least it was something. A lot didn't have a shilling. They had to go around to try and cadge food and money just to stop their families from starving. It was terrible, so many people not having enough to eat.

Finally I got a job with the Perth Roads Board with a surveyor, as his assistant. This was an easy job but it only lasted for three months before it ran out.

It was now the middle of November 1934. Before the job finished with the surveyor, I got a half day off and went to see my old boss Mr Shillington, the Superintendent of the Perth Tramways. After explaining to him my plight of having to find light work owing to my war disabilities, he said that the Department was thinking of putting on a few men in a week or two. He asked me my address and promised to let me know when they wanted men – he also said he would try his best to get me back. He said that if I got back I would be breaking a record so far as the Tramways were concerned, as it would be the first time someone had been employed for the third time.

So the day I finished with the surveyor I got a message from the Superintendent to the effect that some men were to be employed the next day, and be sure to be at the office before nine o'clock.

The next morning I arrived at the Tramways office at eight forty-five and what a shock I got. There were over one hundred men waiting to be interviewed – they were all lined up from the office door, along the passage, then out into the street. Each one joined the line at the back as he arrived, some having been there since before eight o'clock.

The Superintendent arrived just before nine o'clock and on the dot of nine he started to interview the candidates for the job. It was after ten before my turn came. As I went through his office door he called to me in a really loud voice, 'Shut that door.' I did this and he said to me, 'Where in the hell have you been?' I told him that I arrived well before nine o'clock and I had had to wait my turn, 'There must have been close to a hundred here when I arrived.' He said, 'Yes, yes I know things are bad but never mind, I think that they will improve. I like you, are you still a non-drinker?' I replied yes, and that I always would be.

Then to my surprise he said, 'Here' (handing me a piece of paper), 'that is a note to the traffic clerk – you can start straight away. Now go out the back way, we only want two more.' So out of one hundred and twenty-seven applicants there were only three employed.

Mr Shillington had a heart of gold. In fact he was the most understanding man and the best boss I had ever had, and this fact was well known to at least ninety-five percent of his employees. The clerk gave me an order to get a cap from the uniform storeman and to put in the rest of the day travelling all over the Tramway system, especially over the new lines that had been put down since I left in 1921. He told me to have a good look over these lines because I would be booked on a run the next day as a motorman. I was a motorman before I left some twelve or thirteen years before. While I was travelling over the new tramways, some of the motormen let me drive to get my hand in before I started next day. After the first few minutes it became quiet natural to me.

When I told my wife the good news she was delighted. We had rented a small house about five miles from the city and I had a push-cycle to travel to work and back again. The work on the trams as a motorman was a clean and permanent job.

Early in 1935 I applied for a position as a trolley-bus driver and was accepted. I had to attend a school twice weekly in my own time to learn about trolley-buses and their workings. Then I had to have a written test, and after passing that test I had several driving tests and I finally got my licence to drive trolley-buses. This was much easier than driving trams as it was done in a sitting position and this suited me better on account of my war disabilities. And I also got more money.

Just before taking on trolley-bus driving Evelyn and I purchased a four-roomed house and four acres of land in Tuart Hill, a suburb north of Perth, on very easy terms – one hundred pounds down, then one pound per week, free of interest, and the total purchase price was five hundred pounds. This place was six miles away from the depot so I was still able to ride my push-cycle to work.

We settled into our new home. It was only four-roomed, but by enclosing the front verandah we managed to find enough sleeping space for the eight of us. We were able to grow our own vegetables and the man that we bought the property from had quite a quantity of fowls which were sold to us with the property, so we had our own eggs. This helped us quite a lot as my wages averaged four pounds per week and our budget was very tight. My wife managed quite well and I often wondered how, but I always got plenty to eat and the children were all well looked after and content. Evelyn was wonderful – she knew all the things required for making good palatable meals, and what she knew about making children's clothes was something you would have to see to believe.

Barney was still working for the market gardener in Wanneroo. He had settled in well and was not living at home now. He had grown into a very fine specimen, very tall, over six feet.

All our children were helpful and good. Our third son, Joseph, was an extraordinary boy. We used to give those that were old enough to go to the pictures on Saturday nights, a shilling each. That was sixpence to pay their way in to the pictures and threepence to buy an icecream at the interval. Many times Joseph would bring the threepence change home and give it back to his mother.

One thing that we all used to get a lot of fun out of was playing cricket. We used to play in the side-road next to the house – there wasn't a lot of traffic about in those days – and all the neighbouring children would join in. I would pick two sides and we would have a real game of cricket. We used to look forward to this as it was a family affair – with Evelyn, our children, the neighbouring children and I all joining in the excitement.

My job was very interesting, quite a mixed experience. The shifts were not all trolley-bus driving – some of the shifts were half on the trams and half on the trolleys. The trolley-bus was the best kind of public transport of all I think. Very fast, no noise, no smell, no pollution, ideal for large densely-populated cities and they were beautiful to ride in. I was in much better health now and enjoyed life.

We were always a little short of money. My pay was now averaging five pounds a week, sometimes a little more, and out of this five pounds came one pound for the payment on the house, Roads Board rates and insurance, and then there were the usual school books, clothes, boots and many small expenses. My wife was truly a genius when it came to making money stretch to cover all our needs. We were a close knit family, each member helping the other. To help us with finance our second son George and our third son Joseph, who we all called Joe, used to go caddying at a golf-course about a mile away from our place and they always used to bring home a few shillings. This happened at weekends and on holidays when the golf matches were on. Evelyn taught the girls to sew their own dresses and so most of our clothes were home-made. This was quite a saving for us.

On returning to the Tramways I became involved again with the Union and its general running. I got back onto the Committee and spent a lot of my spare time on Union business, and by 1937 I had become the Vice-President of the Tramways Union. I enjoyed this work very much. There was always something going on. We had a long battle with the Government of the day to improve the general working conditions – it was a hard fight, but we slowly wore them down.

The biggest problem I had was with trouble-makers and agitators within the Union. There was always an element who wanted to be causing trouble and who would stir the men up, complaining about everything and always wanting to strike first and talk later. I always believed that if there was a problem that it was better to talk things out – I was always good at this, both with the men within the Union and the Government representatives. I was able to get on well with everyone, even those I disagreed with. I was forever talking to them. If you just kept talking you could slowly win them around. I was able to get a lot done this way and things were improved. I even got things improved by the Liberals, and got on well with them, although I had no time at all for them – they'd fight the working man all the way.

It was difficult work, and there were always problems, but it was something I enjoyed.

Early in 1939 we got the shock of our lives. Our youngest child, Shirley, was now seven years old, and one day Evelyn quietly informed me that she was going to have another baby, and sure enough, it arrived on September twenty-first – a son, Eric – and what a time Evelyn had bringing him into the world. We nearly lost her. I haven't ever seen so much suffering and pain, as the doctor wouldn't help her. He didn't believe in giving anything to ease the pain. He insisted that she should go through the thing in agony. What a doctor! After that confinement and after Evelyn had recovered from the ordeal I took no time in getting rid of that quack, that so-called doctor. Our son, luckily, was fine – he was a lovely child.

I must tell a secret that Evelyn and I had during the last month of her pregnancy. Several times I heard the baby crying, quite loudly at times. I told the doctor and he said that it could happen.

66

Another War

A few days before Eric was born World War Two broke out – our eldest son Barney was twenty now – and our worries commenced again. At first the Federal Government called for volunteers for the three armed services. Our son volunteered and joined the Second Fourth Machine Battalion, Western Australia. He was training for several months, and then his unit finally sailed to Singapore and Malaya. They, with other units, were sent to try and stop the Japanese who were moving down through Asia to capture Singapore.

I tried to join up again but was rejected, so I attended an air-raid wardens' school and got an air warden's certificate. I was appointed as an air-raid warden in charge of the Tramways Depot. I was also a St John Ambulance man. I had many years of service as an ambulance attendant and for long periods used to voluntarily assist once a fortnight with casualties at the Perth Public Hospital. I received much knowledge in the handling and care for the injured. I also attended a Home Nursing class and obtained a Home Nurse's Certificate.

Our second son George also volunteered and went into training. After their initial training there was some considerable delay before his unit went overseas. George, a wild boy, ever in a hurry, couldn't stand it and so he stowed away with a couple of mates on a troopship taking another unit to Britain. When they were discovered they were brought back, punished, and eventually sailed with their own unit to New Guinea.

It was difficult to see our boys go off, knowing what they would be going through. I said to my wife when the war broke out, 'What do you think?' and she said, 'Well, I suppose they will want to go.' I went to the first war with my brothers without a second thought so I knew that they would want to do what they felt like. I said to Evelyn that whatever they wanted to do they should do. 'If they want to go they should go, if they don't, that's fine, but it is up to them.' We agreed on that.

They all came to me and said, 'Dad, what would you do?' and I said, 'Well, when I was your age I was stuck into it – that's what I thought then and so that's what I did. You should do what you think.' I didn't try to stop them at all. I didn't put anything in their way. I'd told them all about the war many, many times – I had explained the whole business, so they knew, as much as they could, what to expect.

When they did go I felt very sad, and so did Evelyn. But we knew that they had to do what they wanted. And it was terrible while they were away – we would always be looking for every bit of news we could get. We would ask people we knew that had boys away if they had heard anything. We would read all the papers. Anything that might give us an idea of what might be happening. Every morning the paper would have lists of dead, missing and wounded, and that was always the first part of the paper we would read. It was a terrible time for us.

It was during the years of the Second World War that my wife went through a change of life. It was a very bad time for her. When Singapore fell Barney was reported missing and we didn't hear anything of him until just before the war ended – nearly four years. It was a terrible strain, with Barney missing and George in New Guinea. Then just before the war ended Joseph had joined up. All this added up to my wife having what they called a slight stroke. One side of her face fell and the feelings on the other side of her body weren't functioning properly.

I don't know how we got through the four years that Barney was missing. We used to be hungry for news – if we overheard anyone saying anything which sounded interesting we'd listen in and ask them questions. We would have given anything just to find out something.

Evelyn was beside herself with worry. I felt bad but I had expected it. I knew casualties would happen because I had seen so many at Gallipoli. I knew that they would be lucky if they got through it. I used to tell her, 'Look, what's going to happen will happen – it happened to me – just when you least expect it.' I told her that we could receive news any day and I think that helped her. We knew then, from the start, that the chances were that something would happen and one of them might be killed.

Evelyn would sit down at the kitchen table to write to Barney while he was missing and tears would run down her face onto the paper while she was writing – not knowing if the letter would ever reach him. It was a very trying time for the whole family.

We were all involved in the war. We spent our time helping to raise money for the Comforts Fund to send things to the men in the battle areas. Dances were held and popular girl competitions organized to raise money. Barbara joined the Land Army which was made up of girls who were willing to go and work on the farms in place of the men who had enlisted. She went to a dairy farm in Capel in the south-west of the state. She met her husband there and married in January 1945 and went to live in Bunbury. Olive had already married in January 1943 and had left home. During the last years of the war only Shirley and Eric were at home. It was a lonely, sad time.

Then on May twenty-third 1945, whilst I was at work, I received word that Barney had been killed on February fifteenth 1942 during the fall of Singapore to the Japanese. He was driving a truck when it was bombed in an air attack. It received a direct hit, killing Barney and four others. He was twenty-three.

Although I had expected this news I was devastated. I didn't know what to do. It was Evelyn's birthday that same day and I had organized a small surprise party for her and bought a present. I also arranged for a birthday call to be made on the radio – something to brighten her day and lift a bit of the sadness. I decided, after a lot of thought, that it would be best not to tell her and go through with the party. I thought it best for her to have the little bit of happiness because once she knew about Barney it would be a long time before she would be able to be happy again.

It was very hard carrying on and keeping it to myself and late that night after the party I told her. It was the worst time of our life. She collapsed, it was too much for her. It was terrible, and I didn't give my beautiful wife and life's mate much hope of getting over this shock. But she did.

Our youngest child, Eric, was now nearly six years old. He was such a bright, lovely little boy and his lovely, cheerful little ways and winning smiles helped his mother to recover. Evelyn treated all the children alike – she thought that the sun shone through them.

On August fifteenth 1945 the war ended. We were overjoyed and relieved. George and Joseph came through all right. Evelyn was on top of the world when the boys came home.

By 1946 all the Australians who had managed to live through the war and the prison camps were home. Although they had tasted victory and were very proud, their thoughts seemed sad. They were all down in the dumps, especially those who had had the misfortune of being a prisoner-of-war. They had had a very raw deal from their enemy, the Japanese. They were starved and badly treated.

People do terrible things in wars, in the name of their country and beliefs. It is something that I find very sad and frightening.

313

My experience in the First World War and now the Second World War changed my outlook on things. It is hard to believe that there is a God. I feel that the Bible is a book that was written by man, not for the good of man but for the purpose of preying on a person's conscience, and to confuse him. Anyone who has taken part in a fierce bayonet charge (and I have), and who has managed to retain his proper senses, must doubt the truth of the Bible and the powers of God, if one exists. And considering the many hundreds of different religions that there are in this world of ours, and the fact that many religions have caused terrible wars and hatreds throughout the world, and the many religions that have hoarded terrific wealth and property while people inside and outside of the religion are starving, it is difficult to remain a believer. No sir, there is no God, it is only a myth.

67

POULTRY AND PIGS

In 1947 we managed to set up a small poultry farm on our property at Tuart Hill. Joe had a great liking for poultry so we set him up with four hundred hens. The poultry houses were on the property when we bought it in 1934. Our second eldest son, George, had returned from war and was working for a monumental firm and he was getting good money. This upset Joe, on account of the small amount he was getting out of the poultry, and as George's boss wanted more youths to train for their business, they offered Joe a job. We then had to decide what to do about the poultry farm.

I had three months long service leave due to me from the Tramways and, having gained some knowledge by reading and learning about poultry and egg production, and working out the profit we had made from four hundred fowls, I found that if we had two thousand head of poultry we could make a better living than me working for the Tramways. When I explained to the Superintendent the position I was placed in, he advised me to apply for three months leave without pay to see if the poultry worked out all right and if it didn't, he said that I would come back to my job. He also said that he would grant me the leave if I applied, so I did, and leave was granted. So we became poultry farmers in the later part of 1946.

By this time I had been President of the Tramways Union for about five years and had been Vice-President for several years before that, so I also applied for leave of absence from the Union for three months and this was also approved. At this time I had also been, over the previous two years or more, a member of the Perth Roads Board, representing what was known as the Osborne Park Ward.

We built the poultry farm up into a very good business and our profits were more than twice the wages that I would be receiving from the Tramways. Things were settling down from after the war, people were returning to the city and home building was booming. Because of this we were told that the poultry farm would have to be shifted further out of the city, so we bought forty acres of virgin land about ten miles north of the city in what was known as the Wanneroo District. Here we built poultry sheds and a bush humpy to live in. Then we sold our home in Tuart Hill and shifted to the Wanneroo property and went into the poultry business in real earnest. We built our flock up to two thousand hens.

We also built a four-roomed house by ourselves, with jarrah timber and asbestos outer walls and plasterboard linings and ceilings, and a roof of iron. I couldn't get builders owing to the boom in the building of homes. I had never built a real house but had worked as a builder's labourer for a time and had some idea as to how it was done. Having worked out what timber, iron, nails, bolts etc. would be needed, I bought the materials and set to work. With looking after the poultry and doing the odd jobs, it took me nine months to complete that house. I was so proud when I finished and so was Evelyn. I also put in a bathroom, laundry with dry-wells and a toilet. Everything we did ourselves. We pioneered what is known as Warwick Road, Wanneroo.

Evelyn and I worked very hard to make a good living out of the place. My wife would don a pair of bib and brace overalls and help with all the work of raising chickens. It seemed that there were always eggs to clean and pack. I had a truck and every second day would load the eggs up and take them into the market in Perth. I also had a little egg round on the side. I would go around to houses in the area selling the eggs direct at a discount. It was hard work, but we made a good living, and best of all Evelyn and I were working together and for ourselves.

The only problem we had was with foxes. They were trouble, always finding a way to get into the fowl sheds. We lost a lot of fowls through foxes. The fox would get in and run around and around under the perches and the old fowl would be looking down and get so giddy from watching, down she would fall. It was amazing. I never saw anything like it.

In 1949, having previously resigned from the Perth Roads Board when we moved to Wanneroo, I was elected to represent the South Ward of the Wanneroo Roads Board. I spent a lot of time working to get the roads and other services in the district improved, and in most cases, established.

At the end of 1949, in November, George married, and then in August of the following year our youngest daughter, Shirley, left home. She married a chap named Bill Cockman, a descendant of a well-known Wanneroo pioneering family. Now Eric was the only one left at home.

Late in 1950 a man called at our place and wanted to buy our property. As everything was going along fine we told him we didn't want to sell. He went away and came back three days later, almost begging for us to sell. He had a poultry farm in the city and had to move out further. He got so persistent that I said to my wife, 'Suppose we put a price on the place well above its worth and demand cash, that will scare him off.' At the time our youngest son Eric had to travel over thirty miles to school each day by bus, sixteen miles each way. This was our only drawback at Wanneroo. The little lad came home each school day done in. So we decided that we would sell at a price that would put us in a good financial position.

A day or so later the man came back. He was just as eager as ever and I offered him the place at a price well beyond its value. When I told him he whistled and said, 'Oh, that is too much – and you want cash.' With that he got in his old motor truck and went away. We hoped he wouldn't come back as we loved the place.

We had previously sold ten acres to two returned soldiers from the Second World War. We didn't make anything out of the sale as we sold it to them at the same price that it cost us. We had also sold ten acres to our son-in-law at cost. This left us with twenty acres. All the improvements and buildings were on this twenty acres. The land we had sold had no improvements on it.

Then the man who so badly wanted to buy the property came back again. This time he offered us a price some four hundred pounds below the price we had put on the place, but we stood firm, and after thinking it over for awhile he said, 'Okay, I'll buy it.' That was the end of us at Wanneroo. Well, almost. In later years a street was named after us – Facey Street – and there is also a 'Barney Street' in Wanneroo, named after our eldest son who was killed in the war.

While we were waiting for the settlement of the sale we had to look for another place for us to live, and after looking at many places we purchased a property at Gosnells. This was twelve miles south of Perth and an old property that had an old house on it – falling down. The owner was using the property to run cattle and pigs, and it consisted of thirty-six acres nearly all cleared and fenced – about fifteen acres were pig-proof.

We got this property very cheap and I considered it would make an ideal place for pig raising. After we purchased the place we found out that it had a bad name and were told that the previous owner had not been able to rear any young stock at all. This was very upsetting, but I had first hand knowledge of pig raising so we took no notice of people's talk and went right ahead. (When I mention the word 'we', I mean Evelyn and I – we were partners in everything from the day of our wedding.)

I went over to see a man who was the manager of a large stock firm in Perth. He was also a veterinary surgeon and a top man in his field. He became very interested in our attempt to challenge the ability of this property and its capacity to rear good pigs. He came and had a look at the place and gave me some good advice. One of the troubles had been that the pigs would only live for six to nine days – they would thrive for that time, then go off their food (mother's milk) – then they got very thin and died. My friend the vet gave me a serum to inject into the sows a week before the little ones were born. This worked wonders with the pigs – I had purchased fourteen sows and two boars. I was congratulated by several stock firms on the way we brought the pigs along and by stock inspectors who had seen my pigs. We used to rear the little ones to prime baconers, then send them to market where we got top market price for them.

One of the secrets of our success with the recovering of this property for raising pigs, cattle and sheep, was the advice given to us to top-dress the whole place with concentrates. We were advised to put on a mixture of copper, zinc and superphosphate. We did this and the recovery was remarkable. The first rains after we spread the concentrates brought about a complete revival to such an extent that I bought fifty sheep with lambs at foot to keep the grass down. The sheep improved after six weeks to such a condition that we sent them to market and got a hundred percent profit.

The old house on the property was so run down that we had to build another one. After the success of the Wanneroo house we had no trouble doing this. First of all we built just two rooms, with a toilet and laundry and then later we gradually added further rooms onto it. One of the main attractions of the place was a beautiful row of pine trees down the side of it. We put in some fruit trees and Evelyn, as usual, established a good vegetable garden.

The only downfall was the very strong east winds. These were very hot and dry and came in summer. They blew straight down over the Darling Scarp from the inland. They were so strong that people were always losing the rooves from their houses and sheds if they weren't secure. Anything loose left lying about was just carried away. You'd wake up in the morning and it would be just gone. Of course, holding soil was a big problem.

The first year, without realizing, we ploughed the paddock in front of the house and woke next morning to find about three feet of soil around the front door and all over the verandah. Evelyn nearly went crazy for awhile with all the sand everywhere until we could get grass growing again on the ploughed land.

The wind was so strong, in fact, that it would blow all the sand away from under the pig fences and all the pigs would get out. And it is a terrible job to get pigs in again. They have no herd instinct at all so they won't stay together, and they also have no idea about being chased and going where you want them to go. They're the most frustrating of animals.

In July 1951 our son Joseph married and he and his wife bought a property in Gosnells and started a small mixed farm. We were happy to have him living nearby.

We stayed on our property for three years and made quite a good living. Then late in 1953 a man came along and offered to buy the place for more than twice as much as it had cost us, so again we sold out. My health had been failing badly and my doctor had sent me to Hollywood Hospital for a month. He also advised me to stop trying to do heavy work, and retire.

So when I came home from hospital and we received an offer for the farm we decided to sell out.

68

Grinding To A Halt

I have never ever felt like I was tied down to any one place or any one job. I have always felt that I could sell out or walk off at any time. It didn't matter. I never ever worried about trying something different or having a go at something. I have always believed that if you want to do something you usually can.

I always liked finding a run-down property, buying it, and then building it up until it was a first class place. Even when I had a place that was running well I would always be on the lookout for something else. If I saw a badly kept place, I would investigate it. It was something I enjoyed. I liked the challenge of building up a place from nothing and making a success where another fellow had failed. And once I had a place running well I was always looking for new ways to improve it – something else I could be doing.

But I was always ready to take a risk and try something new. If it worked out, well good, if not I would just try something else.

So once again we shifted. We purchased a small property in the hills about twenty-five miles from Perth in an easterly direction at a place called Mount Helena, in the Mundaring District. We bought a few fowls and a few breeding pigs. The place consisted of six acres with about eighty fruit trees. I felt that I could manage the work.

We had only been at this place for about three months when the people around the district found out that I had been a member of Local Government in Perth, Wanneroo and Gosnells, and many asked me to stand as a candidate for the Roads Board at the next election to be held in April 1953. I tried to get out of it on account of my health but they wouldn't take no for an answer. A group of ratepayers wanted someone with new ideas and a progressive attitude and they insisted that I was the man for the job. So after talking things over with my wife I agreed to stand. When the nominations were called for candidates for the election I put my name and won the election easily, and so I became a member of the fourth Roads Board in a space of approximately twenty years.

I found my job as a council member (I represented what was known as the Chidlow Ward) a very busy one and it took up a lot of my time. But it was the kind of work that I thrived on. I enjoyed public office and helping and advising people.

One of the biggest problems with Roads Boards in the outer areas of Perth at that time was that the Board members, by and large, had little knowledge of the Roads Board District Act which outlined, among other things, means by which Boards could raise revenue.

Most Board members did not know about borrowing money for capital works. They relied on rates for all revenue. As areas became more and more built-up this became a problem – more and more capital works were required, so either the rates went higher and higher to meet these needs, or more often the capital works were neglected. Having been on the Perth Roads Board first I had learnt all about these things and was able to introduce them to the other Boards on which I served. It was often a battle to begin with to convince them that they were better off raising a loan than raising rates every time they wanted to carry out works, but in the end they saw the truth of it. As soon as this happened a lot of public improvements were begun.

Twelve months after I was elected to the Mundaring Roads Board I was elected to the position of Chairman. I was also appointed a Justice of the Peace. I was very thrilled and proud.

Early in 1958 I became very ill – my war injuries were taking the life out of me and I was having more than the usual number of blackouts. Then one day I had a nasty heart attack at a Roads Board meeting. A doctor was called in and he took me to his surgery at Mundaring and gave me a booster injection and made me lie down for awhile. He strongly advised me to resign from the Board and give work away.

I was now sixty-four years old and my war pension was not very much, so I appealed for an increase. About six months before this I twice appealed for an increase but was turned down. So, when I appealed for the third time, two neutral doctors had to examine me as well as my local doctor. After a lengthy wait, I was notified that I had to appear before this review board of doctors to have my appeal examined. I was thoroughly examined by the doctors, who had studied my war history, the hospital files and previous doctors' reports. One of the doctors asked me when my spleen had been ruptured. I hadn't known that it was ruptured. He then told the other two doctors to examine a spot up under my ribs. They did this, it was very painful, and all agreed that my spleen was ruptured. The only explanation I could give them for the rupture was that I had been blown up by a shell at Gallipoli and buried by sand-bags.

I was told to take things very carefully and not to do any work. They said that if I wasn't a teetotaller I would have died long ago. I was glad that I had always kept my promise to Grandma and that I was strong enough to resist the encouragement of others. They would always say, 'Come on, be a man', but I'd say, 'No thanks, I'd rather be a larrikin.'

A week after the examination I received a letter from the Repatriation Department telling me that my pension was to be increased, and that I would get six months back pay. This was good news. It changed my life – I could now live on my pension and not have to worry about having to keep poultry and pigs to make my livelihood.

Our last child, Eric, left home at this time to join the Regular Army. After all the years we were now on our own. Evelyn, however, was not in the best of health either. She had had her gall bladder out and had suffered several heart attacks. So we sold our poultry and pigs and now felt the benefit of not having to look after them. My working life had ended.

Two years later we sold the property and bought a house in Midland, a suburb east of Perth and at the foot of the Darling Scarp, where we were closer to a doctor and a hospital. We realized that we would have to look after ourselves – health was now a big worry for both of us.

In November 1960 our youngest son, Eric, was married – so now all our children, except Barney of course, had gone on to other lives, and to families of their own.

Then in 1967 we were up-rooted by the Government's Main Roads Committee when they wanted to remove our house for a proposed new road. They paid us a good price and we moved to a house closer to the centre of Midland – close to a doctor and chemist.

The following year my wife became very ill and she was sent to hospital several times, for weeks at a time. I engaged several different doctors but she never got much better. She seemed to get worse as the years went by and she had several blackouts. Then, on the eighth of July 1976, she became unconscious and stayed in that state until the third of August 1976. She died at seven o'clock at night in my arms. We had been married for fifty-nine years, eleven months and twelve days. So on this day the loveliest and most beautiful woman left me.

Evelyn had changed my life. I have had two lives, miles apart. Before we married I was on my own. It was a lonely, solitary life – Evelyn changed that. After our marriage my life became something which was much more than just me.

I now wish to end this story. On the thirty-first of August 1977, I will be eighty-three years old – another birthday. The loss of my lovely girl, my wife, has been a terrible shock to me.

I have lived a very good life, it has been very rich and full. I have been very fortunate and I am thrilled by it when I look back.

A. B. Facey, 1981, aged eighty-seven

Afterword

by Jan Carter

Albert Facey is Australia's pilgrim. He wrote about his life as if it were a journey. Along his route, crossroads offered crucial choices – in some cases his very survival was at stake – and the tracks he followed led to learning, pain, and enrichment. Finally all routes, rough and smooth, were brought together in his old age in a powerful outburst of creative activity – the book that integrated the experiences of his 'fortunate life'.

In his early life, Albert Facey travelled alone, although his isolation was reduced, if only temporarily, by unexpected acts of tenderness and kindness from strangers met on the way more frequently than from his kith and kin. His guiding star became hope. There was always tomorrow and the promise of a fresh start. His hope came from facing and surmounting adversity and became a practical belief in the wholeness of most men, despite the evil encountered in some.

Albert Facey's life was a literal journey too. From childhood to old age he was moving on constantly. Parochial as his journeys were (most took place in Western Australia) they were always adventures. Whether he travelled on foot, on horseback, or by cart, train, boat, or tram, it was the travel as much as the arrival which intrigued him.

'This is the true joy in life . . . being thoroughly worn out before you are thrown on the scrap heap . . . being a force of Nature instead of a feverish selfish little clod of ailments and grievances, complaining that the world will not devote itself to making you happy.' This might have applied to Facey, but George Bernard Shaw was commenting on a much earlier writer, John Bunyan, whose odyssey, *The Pilgrim's Progress*, is regarded as an epic journey in English literature.

Every culture needs a pilgrim. John Bunyan was to Puritan seventeenth-century England what Albert Facey is to secular twentieth-century Australia. Like John Bunyan, Albert Facey was uneducated.

Writing a book from a background of poverty and illiteracy is not easy, yet both stories recreate gripping adventures, peopled by lively characters whose ordinary speech is vibrant and recognizable. Facey, like Bunyan, had to work hard to support himself and a family. Neither man had time to write books; both wrote only when periods of enforced idleness gave respite from the practicalities of earning a living (Facey retired; Bunyan was imprisoned). If there were similarities in their background, there were also parallels in their writings. Both drew from everyday experiences in developing characters; both wrote as they spoke. Both argued for the importance of courage and persistence in meeting disappointment, treachery, inexperience and isolation. Both were firmly opposed to the establishment. And if Facey did not share Bunyan's literal religious vision, both believed in a Providence that brought a traveller of integrity through hazard and despair.

Facey has given flesh to many central myths of Australian culture. There are stories of Albert as the abandoned child and as a young boy lost in the bush, as the mate of itinerant bush workers, as the young Australian male 'blooded' at Gallipoli, as 'the Sentimental Bloke' in the love story between Albert and Evelyn, and as the family man, battling against the depression of the thirties. He takes all these ideas and makes them real and believable. Yet it was not Albert Facey's evident personal qualities as an unaffected, courageous man, or even his traumatic experiences, which fired him to give our myths such appealing written life. His qualities are literary as well as human. He has the artistry of a true story-teller, an ear for the rhythms of natural speech; he observes and explains.

The styles of both Bunyan and Facey came from an oral tradition. Bunyan was, by all accounts, a colourful and lively preacher. Facey, too, developed and shaped his stories throughout his life by telling them to an audience. His style was born of an era uninfluenced by electronic media, when story-telling was still a principal form of leisure. He was known as a story-teller to his family and friends; his work as union official and local government member gave him opportunities to express himself and to convince others. The confidential intimacy – the feeling that Albert Facey addresses each reader personally and directly – is related to this, for from early childhood, Albert had yarned. 'So I told them all that had happened to me,' he said as he recalled how, as an eight-year-old, he was found one night by a Scottish family, after he had escaped his captors at Cave Rock. Or, when he arrived at Geraldton, after the cattle drive in the Nor'West, he went immediately to see the proprietress of the Coffee Palace. 'I said I had to tell her all about the trip,' he wrote. 'She invited me to come to dinner one evening and have the talk of our lives.'

Facey's family knew these tales well before they read the book. The stories were told and retold as family history for six decades or more. Then after retirement Albert was restless and time weighed on his hands. His active mind needed more challenge than his vegetable garden offered. Evelyn suggested that he write down his stories for a book. So he set up at one end of the kitchen table and wrote, whilst Evelyn made jam or peeled potatoes, and encouraged.

Albert Facey, like Bunyan, never anticipated the success that would follow the publication of his life story. In cramming his stories into school exercise books, Albert's aim was to ask a publisher to print and bind enough books to enable him to present copies to members of his family. His efforts to get his book published were far from confident and when, in 1979 at eighty-five, he heard that his autobiography had been accepted for publication, he wrote to the Fremantle Arts Centre Press: 'Sir, I am thrilled to know that my book will be published ... I can't thank you and your connections enough ... I feel that you have a job ahead of you and that you won't let me down. Thanking you and wishing you well and the best of luck.'

By this time, Albert's sight was failing and his war injuries from the Gallipoli campaign six decades before were bothering him. 'I would love to come to see you at Fremantle,' he wrote, 'but that is impossible. I have a job to walk and my eyesight is failing badly: I have a job to see forty yards now.' Evelyn's illness and death had profoundly saddened him. Most of what he wanted to say had been written, but in the absence of Evelyn's care, he felt that his manuscript had deficiencies; he knew that his punctuation and spelling, against conventional standards, were very shaky. The gulf between being the family story-teller and the author of a book was a large one.

Apart from Evelyn's encouragement, Albert had worked alone. The rest of his family, with the familiarity that breeds complacence, knew the stories so well as not to see the importance of a book. Books and writing were not, in any case, part of the Facey family tradition. Albert was not 'discovered' by established writers, nor sought out by publishers. The manuscript sat untended in a cupboard for a couple of years, until a neighbour typed it for a fee of $300 from Albert's pension savings. Then the Fremantle Arts Centre Press were asked to help by printing and binding twenty copies or so of the story for the family.

When the editors reviewed Albert Facey's writing, they realized its importance and devoted a lot of time to preparing the text for publication.

To make the book a manageable size, some material from the end of his life was omitted, while spelling and punctuation were, at last, amended. Albert was at this stage in poor health, so he was unable (as most writers would have done) to amplify or refine his text. However, he did comment by tape recorder and these verbal extensions were inserted into the manuscript. During a taping session, the title for the book emerged as Albert reflected on his 'fortunate life'. But the language of the book, the chronology of events, and the style remain Facey's own.

In its first year of publication, 1981, Albert's book, a life written down for his family, sold 8000 copies. The book was awarded prestigious prizes and Facey was nominated as 'Australian of the Year'. Albert Facey, the unschooled, octogenarian kitchen-table writer, became a famous figure. In the last nine months of his life there were receptions, dinners and press conferences, telegrams from Premiers and letters from the literati. Hundreds of people – children, teenagers, old people, immigrants, trade unionists, members of religious communities – wrote to Albert. But Albert's declining health signalled the end of his short, surprise career as best-selling author. He was able to attend the launching of his book in a wheelchair and was aware of his success, although his family considers that he never appreciated its scale. By 1985, three years after his death, about 250 000 Australians would have bought his book and probably many more had read it.

The way in which Facey the writer touched the lives of his readers is reflected in the mail he received. Children commiserated with Albert's unloved childhood; young people felt that they now understood the social changes between the generations. One wrote: 'I find that stories like your own, told to me by my own elders are unbelievable and often I do not accept them as being true, but now after reading your story I have begun to understand that life in the beginning of this century was totally different than it is today, that the traditional roles of the child in the family is different, let alone an adult in society. I cannot believe after all you had been through that you could still call it a fortunate life. Most of the older people I know are always bitter about their past and present lives, including my own father, but you seem quite content in the way your "destiny" has unfolded. Your destiny has been an inspiration to me and has helped in my understanding of the past and how fortunate I really am. I only hope that I can gain as much out of life as you did.'

Facey hardly had a childhood, as we think of childhood today. His lack of schooling, hard work under conditions of slavery, his harsh treatment and the lack of attention to his emotional needs, would be viewed today as marks of a grossly deficient upbringing. Facey's protrait of childhood is a social history of changes in the status of children this century. Many young readers found grounds for sympathy: 'Mr Facey,' wrote Simon, aged seven, and Celia, aged six, 'this is a bit late to wish you a happy birthday. We wanted to send you a card as you did not get any when you were a child.'

For those between youth and old age, *A Fortunate Life* provided the opportunity of a review. 'Your book inspired me to take a look at life from a different angle and to see what are the most important things. Thank you for passing on some of your courage, enthusiasm and inspiration', wrote one. Another said: 'I have learned more about the everyday Australian from reading your book than from all the other history books and historical novels I have read.'

Some of Facey's readers felt they had got to know him well enough to write about their personal feelings. Nearly all found his book a challenge, although the announcement of Albert's anti-religious views took some by surprise. 'Sadness filled my heart on reading that you believe there is no God,' wrote a reader from New South Wales. 'To blame God for allowing trouble and strife to occur on this earth is misplaced. Sir, the blame for those things rests squarely upon man . . . If man was obedient to God's command to love one another there would be no war and trouble on earth, only love and peace. But thank you for enriching the life of each person you have met.'

It is not altogether surprising that Australia's bush Pilgrim should oppose conventional religious institutions: many bush men had done so before him. Yet contrary evidence suggests that Facey was a religious man. He had a keen sense of what he called 'Providence', and his daughter, Barbara, recalls that he felt himself to be in communication with Evelyn after her death. 'I'm off to have a talk to my darling', he would say as he left the house to walk to the cemetery to sit and meditate by Evelyn's grave. *A Fortunate Life* is also a touching love story of a devotion and romance that lasted sixty years. 'To Mum, to my life-long Love and Wife', wrote Albert, in shaky hand on his sixtieth wedding anniversary. His marriage, a rare blend of close companionship and sympathy, healed the wounds from the hurts and pains of his childhood.

No one can predict decay in old age; it is lucky that Facey completed his writing before he was overcome by illness. Old people view his book as a personal communication and wrote to him with their life story in exchange. 'I first saw the light of day in June 1900, so am almost on a par with you,' wrote one woman, nearly blind, at age eighty-two. In a spidery scrawl, she declared 'I have had the extreme pleasure of reading the book written of your life. I was able to enjoy so many experiences, fears, terrors, anxieties, lonelinesses, a love of trees and birds that was especially delightful. The dingoes, yes. They are so frightening. I could go on and on.' Facey was able to express, on behalf of a generation, an experience of people and practices now gone forever.

If Albert Facey's childhood was remarkable, so was his old age. His writing during the last decade of his life could be seen to be part of a normal process in old age: what the sociologists now call 'the life review' – a desire to set the record straight and to integrate the strands of the past and give them a personal meaning. But Facey's life review went far beyond the usual: his career as a writer commenced in advanced old age, at a time of life thought by our society to be past everything. That old people may have latent creative gifts is not considered: the aged are classified generally as being fit only for the community rocking chair. But Facey marshalled one of the precious attributes of old age – long memory – and turned it to the more difficult task of recreating it in writing. It was not only that Facey had a fortunate life, but that he set it down. Without his own creative energy at the end of his time, we would not have known about him, as he had no biographer and no oral historian had sought him out. Many old people have stories to tell: comparatively few ever write them down; others tell them to writers or historians who make records on their behalf. But Albert Facey, alone, wrote his stories down himself.

Eventually, Albert Facey's productivity was brought to an end by failing sight and a broken hip. Barbara, his daughter, had come to Perth to look after him, but she became ill herself and, against her wishes, Albert Facey was admitted to a private nursing home. He seemed ready to die – his work was over and his energy and drive much diminished. It was ironic that the battler who had fought since the age of seven to maintain his autonomy should have had his independence negated at the end. Albert Facey, the confronter of birth and life, was enveloped, at death, by the nursing home, one of the more doubtful institutions of the twentieth century, developed to cushion and disguise the natural processes of death. So a life which began with extraordinary self-reliance ended with an ordinary degree of dependence. He died in February 1982, nine months after his book was published.

What has Albert Facey left us? There is his description of childhood and adult-child relations at the beginning of this century which indicate how great the changes in childhood have been. There is his personal account of the dehumanizing and brutal effects of war (the one defeat he felt morally unable to accept). There is his documentation of the types and processes of work including some vanishing occupations. There are all these things and more, but in the end, Albert Facey's autobiography must be classified as political history, for he contributes to the neglected history of this country. Born on the underside, Facey never joined, or aspired to join, the establishment whose history has been recorded. Facey's story is a social counterpoint to the well-established economic and political themes of Australian history. From Facey, we now know what it was like to be poor and young at the gold rushes, thus balancing the previous accounts of the rich and powerful. We now know what it was like to be an itinerant worker, as an antidote to the histories of established land-owners. We understand the predicaments of a first-world-war private, thereby amplifying the accounts of generals. He describes being a husband and father with mouths to feed in the depression, a neglected perspective compared to that of political decision-makers and academic historians. Now Facey's personal achievement in reconstructing his life belongs to all of us.

Albert Facey has provided for ordinary people an understanding of their past which has challenged their view of the present and realigned their aims for the future. In this respect, his journey was most fortunate for all of us.

Weary: The Life of Sir Edward Dunlop   Sue Ebury

Sir Ernest Edward Dunlop, or 'Weary' as thousands called him, became a hero to many Australians. A brilliant student and sportsman, he qualifed as a pharmacist and surgeon, winning gold medals and scholarships, and played rugby for Australia before going to England to complete his FRCS. When World War II broke out, he volunteered immediately, joining the 2nd AIF in the Middle East. He served in Palestine, Greece, Crete, Tobruk and Egypt before sailing to Java with his medical unit in 1942.

Weary elected to be captured with his hospital, spending more than three years as a prisoner-of-war in Java and on the notorious Burma-Thailand 'Death Railway'. His care for men under his command and his defiance of his captors in the face of brutality, starvation and death, made him a legend in his lifetime.

Sir Edward died in July 1993, much honoured and greatly loved, before this biography, written with his total co-operation could be published. Meticu-lously researched, it gives a rare view of a reticent man who lived by old-fash-ioned values, yet retained a wild streak which gave fire to his character and lifted him above his fellows.

Over My Tracks   Evelyn Crawford

'The past is not for livin' in – but it sure makes for real good thinkin.'

Evelyn Crawford tells the life of an Aboriginal family: as it was in the 1930s – as it is now. Reading her story is like sitting down for a yarn with an old friend.

The red sandhills 'back of Bourke' are the setting for a life rich in experience and achievement. Camps and meeting places, bush schools and pubs, and the colourful parade of characters with whom she played, learned and worked, spring vividly to life.

Evelyn's unshakeable belief that prejudice grows from ignorance led her to an active role in education. Since 1975 she has worked in the school community to bring better understanding and wider opportunities for Aboriginal students. Her warmth, humour and wisdom have enriched many lives.

Here is a woman to remember.

More, Please   Barry Humphries

The details of Barry Humphries' life are still amongst the best kept secrets of our time. Recent volumes devoted to his work and career shed very little, if any, light on this most private and circumspect of artistes. Hitherto, he has deliberately furnished his hardworking biographers with blatant mystifications and whimsical fictions.

In consequence the revelations and confessions contained in this book will astonish his growing international public with their novelty and in no way echo the amiable, but wildly inaccurate, narratives of his recent memorialists. Here, at last, and in his own lapidary prose, is his account of his life up to the present

More, Please was his first utterance and they are the two words that will inevitably spring to the lips of all those who read this book.